TIM'S WAR

My little book, *this* little book, shall be my cupboard and also my friend, to whom I can communicate, though perhaps very crudely, just a few of life's impressions as they appear to me; and then no matter what happens to my companion (this book) we have at least spent many hours of pleasant and absorbing interest together, and I also have the knowledge that the thoughts are not lost. Perhaps even a stranger may take up this book, and though I cannot hope he will approve of me from a grammatical point of view, yet if he will overlook that weakness then I may hope he will glean a few crumbs from my musings.

Timothy Goddard Elliott, chapter 16

At last I have come to know the man who was my Father. I realize now he was a man of many parts, and I never knew the part that his diaries reveal.

Ann Veronica Gregory (née Elliott)

Ever since Ann and I, as teenagers, saw Jean Renoir's film of *All Quiet on the Western Front* (and found it so horrifying we had to leave well before the end) I have been haunted by visions of those Trenches; but after reading what my father-in-law managed to write day-by-day while serving on that same Western Front I find I must adjust all my preconceptions.

Robin Edward Gregory

Burlington-Hub Press
3 Burlington Court
Eastbourne
East Sussex
BN21 4AU

3burlington@post.com

Loaghtan Books
17 Onslow Avenue
Sutton
Surrey
SM2 7ED

info@loaghtanbooks.com
www.loaghtanbooks.com

in
association
with

Published by: Burlington-Hub Press

Typesetting and origination by: Loaghtan Books

First published: 19 July 2013

Printed and bound by: Lavenham Press

Copyright © Robin Gregory, 2013

ISBN: 978 1 908060 07 5

Erratum (by the author)

There is an unintended distortion of Tim's story on Day One of the Battle of the Somme. This will, of course, be corrected in any later edition; but meanwhile I have decided that all future purchasers should receive a four-page essay which explains the error and corrects the information. [The truth makes it even more incredible that Tim survived.] Furthermore, for a limited period, I shall personally offer copies for sale at a huge discount, namely £4.50 (instead of £14.95), plus £3 post and packing. A cheque for £7.50 payable to Robin Gregory should be sent to 3 Burlington Court, Eastbourne, BN21 4AU.

Front cover: Tim relaxes on a gun carriage. Photograph inscribed in ink in his own hand 'T.G. Elliott, Chipilly, On the Somme, France, 1916'.

Rear cover: Tim and Alma on their wedding day. Photograph inscribed in ink in his own hand '31st Dec. 1920, St Barnabus Leicester. The Elliotts, Alma and Tim'.

CONTENTS

Appendices

ILLUSTRATIONS

A PRELIMINARY EDITORIAL NOTE

As Chapter One will explain, this is really Tim Elliott's book. I see it as my main editorial task simply to ensure that he gets the best possible presentation, without my altering or unduly refining his story. Incvitably I have felt it necessary to exercise judgment about how much should appear under the title *Tim's Wars*. If I am accused of too heavy an editorial hand, I say in my defence merely that my intentions have always been

    1 to focus a reader's attention on Tim's part in what we call
    The Great War of 1914-1918, then
    2 to show how that war changed him, and finally
    3 to illuminate his experience of the inter-war years and of *World War Two*.

I have concluded that everything Tim entered in his 1914-1918 diaries (from the moment he landed in France as a soldier, until the Armistice) should appear, unaltered, no matter how trivial. What his entries convey is the **totality** of his army life during that period: boredom is, as it were, as important as excitement! As far as I can trace, his diaries may be unique in that he never missed recording a single day, and this seems to have been achieved by no other unpromoted soldier. In an almost telegraphic form (no doubt necessary because he had little time while at the front to elaborate) he tries to set down a description of how his time was occupied, whether he was fighting, resting, socializing or suffering. His concern for the details of place and time add to the value of his record in that the reader may trace his footsteps and imagine his fear, amusement, boredom and anger, although he made only infrequent reference to his mental state. His wartime diaries tell us essentially what Timothy Goddard Elliott *did* and *had done to him*. Years later, when he found opportunities to set down his recollections and new experiences in greater detail, the effect that four years serving in the army on the Western Front had had upon him begins to appear in his writing, and for that reason I have surveyed his diary-keeping (quoting where relevant) during the inter-war years, continuing this survey to see how he reacted to the arrival of another war in 1939-40.

More fully to understand his record one needs to have some idea of what the young man who joined-up was like. I have therefore

Timothy Goddard Elliott as a young recruit in 1914

felt free to present a chapter drawn from his diaries *before* his military service. These go some way towards demonstrating his pre-war nature and qualities. His wartime entries can thus be set against at least *some* knowledge of what sort of person he was when he enlisted.

Historians will, I hope, be tolerant of any serious errors I have made. I am a psychologist by training rather than a historian, and am therefore more interested in inferring Tim's psychological state than in taking time describing the historical importance of every aspect of each attack and counter-attack.. Having said that, however, I have felt impelled to make some study of the moves and counter-moves of the armies, and may therefore have trodden on ground where I lack education as a historian. I shall welcome correction if I have made any serious errors that need attention.

My conclusion is that these very diaries have the capacity to *change* conventional views of the unpromoted soldier's life in the trenches and off duty. While first and foremost I wish to offer an opportunity to enter Tim's life, I also hope that the conventional view of the meaningless and uncomprehending existence of the ordinary soldier may be belatedly changed by his narrative.

Robin Gregory, Sussex, 2013

ACKNOWLEDGMENTS

Many people have encouraged and assisted me in the preparation of this book. My thanks are due to many of Tim Elliott's family, not least my wife (his daughter Ann) who has read everything, commented, and generally set me thinking along new lines. Of the younger generation I am especially grateful to Dr Graham Elliott, who lives in Delft; to his brother Nigel, who lives in Jersey, to their sister Phillipa who lives in Kingston on Thames, and to Professor Jon Steed who lives in Durham. They have dug out old photos, and offered their considerable expertise in computer wizardry. Their encouragement has been a great boon.

This electronic (sometimes demonic) way of writing and transmitting a manuscript or picture can be frustrating, and I have sought help wherever it could be had. My neighbour and good friend John Case helped me choose my laptop, and whenever it seemed to be taking me over he readily tamed it and showed me what to do next. When he and his lovely French wife were in France there were many others to whom I turned, notably Anton Kazimierski (whose 1939-45 war included enforced residence in the coldest of Soviet camps), Brian Braby, Chris Harris and Philip Anson. Thanks to them my next book should prove far less daunting. If they were unavailable my own brother John (to whom we owe many a successful railway signalling system) was able to diagnose over the phone. And his speed around the internet saved me wasting hours approaching so-called 'publishers' who were interested in nothing beyond one's cash.

Several writers were most generous in sharing their thoughts with me, in some cases even giving permission for me to refer to their published work. That fine actor Cameron Stewart was one, Mike Lucas another. Anne Dearle gave freely of her time to relate her experiences of publishing, as did Michael Harris (author of a novel about life on a cruise ship), Jan Boyes, and Annette Keen (who wrote *The Generation Club*).

Ian Marshall and Rosy Osmaston, who are both 'in' publishing, were also full of useful suggestions. Mike Shields (with whom I share passions for poetry and singers) read one chapter and then came up with what I may call 'the Jarrow view' of life in the trenches, which acted as a counter-balance to my own 'south-of-London' standpoint. [Some of his insights appear herein, by his kind permission.]

Many good friends have made comments that have helped and supported me. [Their names must suffice, or there will be no room for Tim Elliott to tell *his* story.] So grateful thanks to Brian Allan, Bill Allison, Doug Allison (whose father, William, wrote *The Monocled Mutineer*), Tom and Tuta Benning, Anthony Bowden (who was himself a professional army officer), Sandi and Ian Boyland, Marion and John Boyle, Alan Chun (a distant relative of Tim), Dr David and Lindsay Cooke, David Dearle (historian and classicist who straightened some of my dubious historical allusions), Edward Dickinson, Len Donaldson (New Zealand diplomat), Roy Donaldson (his brother, actor and director), Major George Douglas (to whom we owe many a fine display of army pageantry), Helen Elliott, Clifford and Barbara Fisher (he a hero of the Burma campaign, she former Chair of the Yehudi Menuhin School Governors), Stephen Groves, Julian (Nick) Gwinn (another army career, and incidentally my own cousin), Sue Hearson, George and Maureen Henty, Keith Hindell (formerly BBC Correspondent at the United Nations), John Horsnell (who 'ran' the Isle of Wight for years), Ken Hyde (who managed to survive flying from aircraft carriers in WW2), David Inge, Anne Johnson, Elizabeth Muir Lewis, Frances Line (former Controller of BBC Radio Two), Jim Lloyd, Julia Marshall, Tim Marshall, Anthony Merrett, Chris Metcalfe, Roger Motton, Paul Oxborrow, Anna Piper, Ken Richards, Ieuan Roberts, Chris and Tricia Sneath, Robert Spooner, Edward Thomas, Bill Thompson, Noel Thompson, David Tye, Enid Wayman (historian), Geoffrey Wicken (who gave me *Death's Men*, which was written by one of his schoolmasters), Margaret Wicken (widow of perhaps my closest friend, who was in the R.A.F with me from 1952-55), and Oliver Wicken. Peter Taylor of the Imperial War Museum was also very helpful.

And, finally, my thanks go to Sara and George (of Loaghtan Books). I bless the day when Anne Dearle drew my attention to their strangely-named publishing house because they have been everything anyone could wish for in a publisher. They give unstintingly of their time to ensure that my efforts are presented in a workable fashion, and they have taught me to make the transition from old-style publishing (galley-proofs and even hot lead in my Hub Publications days) to the present electronic magic. I could not have found myself in better hands.

Robin Gregory, Sussex, 2013

CHAPTER ONE

FOUND IN THE LOFT

The continuing interest in the 1914-1918 War, as indicated by the production of novels, films and television reconstructions, has no doubt fuelled the publication of a number of first-hand accounts of life in the trenches. We already had, of course, Robert Graves's autobiographical *Goodbye to All That*, published in 1929: a profound and scholarly work recollected in a sort of perverse tranquillity. (Though it should be said that historians have since questioned the accuracy of some of his recollections.) In addition, Richard Aldington's novel *Death of a Hero* was begun immediately after the Armistice, in his billet: a small Belgian cottage. It's a splendid evocation of a generation at war; but it was not published until 1929, by which time the passing of the years had rendered its immediacy less vital.

Of the few early attempts to present the view of the 'other ranks', one of the best is Frank Richards's *Old Soldiers Never Die* (1933), but the reader is soon aware that the passage of time has blunted (or possibly censored) the writer's memories. In contrast, a book that is a historian's considered assessment of all aspects of soldiering from 1914 to 1918 is *Death's Men: Soldiers of the Great War*, by Denis Winter (Allen Lane, 1978 and Penguin, 1979). It focuses explicitly on the 'Other Ranks', drawing on diary extracts, letters home, and so on, while still finding space for a close look at the training of officers. It presents in very readable form the writer's own conclusions about (for example) the manner in which British recruits were **bullied** into obedience to orders, to such an extent that they were poorly equipped to make intelligent independent decisions on the battlefield; and a contrast is drawn with the French training which produced an esprit de corps that better suited warfare as it really was on the Western Front.

More recently Oxford's Bodleian Library published *A Month at the Front: The Diary of an Unknown Soldier* (2006) which purports to be a contemporary account of the initial assault in the third Battle of Ypres; but the language used suggests that it was written well away from the horrors of the Front:

I had a chap next to me whom I shall describe as a fool, for fool he was for certain. That very evening ......this deadly machine-gun began to play on them.

The fact is that although there now exists a number of detailed accounts of the day-to-day life of the common foot-soldier few if any are derived from diaries kept daily while actually at or near the front. Writer, editor and poet Mike Shields comments that most 'common foot-soldiers' of 1914 to 18 were incapable of writing a diary, not being in any full sense of the word literate. He takes the view that History is written by a small section of the victors: an academic, literary, intellectual and often self-promoting elite who corner the market not only in the records but also in their interpretation. When this very selective 'history', he says, is taken up by the poet, the playwright or the journalist, the interpretation flies even further from reality. Books, radio and television then quote this doubly-selective account, and conclude that the 'common soldier' saw himself as a victim of the capitalists who drove him and his comrades like cattle into war mainly to provide profit for the arms trade, whereas in reality the typical surviving lads from farmyard or shipyard in Shields's area of north-east England regarded their time in France as the greatest adventure of their lives. They had seen foreign parts, met 'mamselles' who looked, smelled and acted very differently from their straight-laced wives, and enjoyed the opportunity to handle real weaponry.

Despite (or perhaps because of) the persuasive argument put forward above, we must perforce try to make sense of what little 'on-the-spot' written evidence has come down to us. A superbly written attempt to bring together several chosen recollections is Lyn Macdonald's *Somme* (1983), and since then (especially with the advent of electronic publishing) there have been quite a number of attempts to collate various writings which draw on diaries kept, usually for a relatively short period of time, within the war zones. But few if any rest on the sure foundation of hand-written diaries that were demonstrably put on paper each and every day from 1914 to 1918.

Imagine the excitement, therefore, of an amateur historian who discovers that he has inherited from a close relative not a mere series of Great War 'recollections', but precise day-by-day diaries written 'as it happened'. This remarkable series of documents was left to my wife and me when her mother died. It seems they lay almost forgotten in the roof area of her suburban home at Tilehurst, near Reading, and despite the attack of damp and cold they survived in readable form.

These diaries, written during the years of the Great War in a small but legible hand, are not the considerations of an officer pondering strategy. Nor, as stereotyping might lead one to expect, are they the gibberings of a terrified youngster. Their importance, as I see it, is that they really do have the capacity to change our view of the mental life which was possible, even in those appalling circumstances, for the unpromoted Rifleman. They demonstrate a remarkably sophisticated understanding of what was actually going on. We realize that the writer had an interest in the geography of the area being fought over, and a concern for the feelings of the local population. He reveals an extraordinary sense of duty, and real insight into the strategy behind the troop movements. His willingness (probably illegal) to name names and to identify locations, even when under fire, is astonishing; and his resilience, not to say courage, appears, to our enfeebled minds, utterly amazing.

The writer of these diaries, though a typical representative of the hardy working-class, had literary aspirations. It is intriguing to compare him with the likes of Robert Graves who, despite a relatively privileged upbringing, had little experience of the London theatre before enlistment. By contrast, Timothy Elliott was recording in diaries written before his enlistment his many visits to the theatre and even his own thespian activities.

Both Graves and Elliott were born in 1895. Tim's birthday was January 11th. Both were nineteen when the Great War began. By then, Tim had not only seen many plays and musicals, but had written and produced local dramatic presentations around the area of Merton where he lived. Perhaps because he was not tall, he seems often to have played female characters: Lydia Languish in Sheridan's *The Rivals*, for instance, at the Merton Masonic Hall in January 1911, when he was just sixteen. In the same month he wrote, produced and acted in a farce *Mr Tristy's Love Affair*. By 1912 his accurately written account of Merton Church Choir's outing to 'The Great White City' was published in the Wimbledon Borough News. In 1913 he played Ebenezer Scrooge in *A Christmas Carol* under the direction of Mr Marshall Steel, Professor of Elocution. The local paper described his performance as 'masterly'.

So Tim was no ordinary soldier. Or was he? The trench life (and the rigorous earlier training) that he came to describe was certainly typical and would have been recognized by any fellow soldier of his day. By the time he found himself in France he clearly knew he could write. He must have realized that there was to be no opportunity for long dissertations on the surrounding scenery, nor any chance to do more than record briefly the life (and death) around him. Is it fanciful to believe that he was consciously recording all the facts with a view to writing something of a more extended nature when (and if) he returned home?

One fine account of life in the trenches is to be found in *A Very Unimportant Officer* (Hodder and Stoughton, 2008), which is subtitled *My Grandfather's Great War* in recognition of the involvement of actor Cameron Stewart in the preparation of the manuscript. This impressive document certainly utilises Captain Alexander Stewart's diary entries from 1915 to 1917, and furthermore contains his recollections made some ten years after the conclusion of hostilities. My suspicion is that Tim Elliott intended after demobilisation to prepare something similar to those recollections but then became too involved with his new life to do so. What the Stewart book provides is a valuable alternative view: the Officer as compared to the Rifleman. Alexander Stewart, however, omitted many days, possibly because they were to him unremarkable at the time. In addition the Elliott diaries cover a far longer period of time. Tim enlisted in London on November 9th 1914; Alexander joined the Glasgow School for Officers on July 1st 1915. Tim reached France on June 7th 1915; Alexander arrived at Le Havre on March 22nd 1916. Tim was in trenches just south of Ypres on June 11th 1915; Alexander was in trenches near Béthune on March 27th 1916. In addition, Alexander was wounded on Sep 28th 1917 (a couple of months after being awarded the Military Cross) and on October 2nd 1917 left hospital for repatriation, after which he did not cross the Channel again. His training and subsequent front-line service thus occupied some two years three months, whereas Tim's occupied somewhat more than four years, in which time he recorded a precise daily account of the training regime as well as of life at the front. Both accounts are important documents, and it is instructive to compare and contrast; but Tim's, while lacking the subsequent recollections, is a remarkable story told 'as it happened'. To examine the precise times at which one activity became another is to realize the enormous demands made upon young soldiers in that ghastly war.

While collecting, transcribing and commenting on Tim's diaries, I have been most grateful to a number of publications which have provided some insight into other attempts at documenting individual and collective accounts of the 'War to End Wars'. I have mentioned a few above, but two others have stuck in my mind in a way that suggests they had something special to say.

First, an extremely controversial account of soldiering in the Great War is Ronald Skirth's *The Reluctant Tommy*. On publication, Skirth's account caused something of a furore, especially relating to his stated decision at a critical point in his service to avoid killing anyone, friend or foe. Saga Magazine described it as 'an extraordinary, raging memoir', which indeed it was. However, after a time there were several questions asked about its authenticity, and the Imperial War Museum seems to have become very doubtful about the alleged sources. It is not my place to attempt any conclusion about the writer's, the editor's and the publisher's intentions and assumptions, but as a psychologist I know full well that attempts to recollect details after many years can lead to a sort of 'constructive logicality' whereby a coherent story gets woven round the memories. The book is, though, a great 'read'; and insofar as it is factual (and much of it undoubtedly **is**) it raises vital issues of conscience.

Second is the recent (2012) *The Journey's End Battalion* by Michael Lucas (published by Pen and Sword). Taking as his starting-point R.C.Sheriff's play *Journey's End*, the author produces a scholarly and well-documented account of the Ninth East Surrey's role.

(Sheriff was with the Ninth Battalion of the East Surrey Regiment.) This book really brings what is perhaps the greatest of English Great War stage-dramas into focus as never before. Coincidentally Michael Lucas now lives in Birchington, Kent, which played a significant part in Tim Elliott's life just before, and during the early part of, the 1939-45 War.

———————————————

It seems appropriate to set down here some description of how my father-in-law's diaries took so long to come into my possession. For many years, older relatives of my wife (Tim's younger daughter) had hinted that he had somehow managed to record his daily impressions 'even of life in the trenches'. This did not seem improbable to me because, in later years, I knew him to be an inveterate diary-keeper. He always showed a deep interest in the minutiae of life, and was especially concerned to locate places on maps, to check the spellings of place-names, and so on. Whenever the four of us (Tim, his wife Alma, Ann, and I at the wheel of the car) went on holiday together he would spend part of each evening studying the routes we had travelled, and would then retire to his room to record his impressions. (Ann appears to have inherited these traits.) It seemed, therefore, distinctly possible that he had managed to note down some impressions of army life.

When he died in 1967 I had hopes that I should be able to see these notes, if in fact they existed. But they were not forthcoming. Nearly a quarter-century was to pass before they made their remarkable appearance and I was able to appreciate the importance of the treasure-trove they comprised.

Tim was seven years older than his wife, Alma; and after his sudden death of a heart-attack she stayed on at the family home in Tilehurst, near Reading. Not until 1988, when their older daughter (Joan) moved to Bexhill, did Alma decide that she could no longer cope with the house and garden, and moved to a rest-home in Cooden, near Bexhill. Tim's only son, Royce, took upon himself the task of clearing the house for sale. He sold the standard items of furniture, and recovered from the loft a disorderly pile of small and large notebooks (which turned out to be diaries), photographs and cuttings from newspapers. These Alma handed over to me, giving carte-blanche to make of them what I could.

———————————————

I first set about arranging the diaries (which in all covered fifty years) in some sort of order. The chronology proved more difficult than might be imagined, for Tim's reluctance to waste money became legendary in the family, and in consequence (especially under the exigencies of war) he had frequently used a diary intended for one year to serve for another. Presumably there were occasions when he received more than one diary in a particular year, so he simply made the extra diary serve for a year in which he had received no diary at all. He then altered just sufficient dates to keep himself on track, which fact suggests that he may indeed have had ideas about writing something more substantial at a later date. As an additional complication, some of the diaries (especially those used in war) were extremely small, while others (from later, more peaceful days) were in fact large exercise books which were pressed into service rather than his purchasing the real thing. When writing in a tiny diary in the front line he wrote in a teeny hand, perhaps as a means of concealment, perhaps simply because he had no opportunity to spread himself on a page. 1916 presents a striking example. Charles Letts's

Self-opening Diary (whatever that means!) measures two inches by three. Each double-page covers six (not seven) days. The entries are mostly written in ink using a very fine pen (where did he get the ink? where renew the nib? Did he have a fountain-pen?); but occasionally he has had resort to pencil, which has faded badly. When he wished to record more than could be accommodated in the appropriate space, he inscribed the excess on a page reserved (say) for addresses, with only the feeblest of cross-referencing.

In their totality, the diaries cover the period 1911 until his death, with a gap of a couple of years in the 1930s which is unexplained. Several facts soon spring from his pages. Most notable is the fact that his command of English was such that he could organise his material to accommodate the difficulties he faced. Quite why he alone in his family had acquired this literary skill is hard to discern. Most of his relatives when he was young were engaged in horticulture, and there is no evidence of similar attainment in them. When serving in the trenches, where time and space were necessarily short, he uses an easily understood telegraphic style, whereas on an occasion when he had been made the victim of a three-card trickster during a train journey he writes with the extended eloquence of a nineteenth century novelist.

It is clear, too, that he had a remarkable concern for accuracy and truth not only with regard to the precise details of time and place but also with regard to his own responses to the events with which he was associated. He recorded with surprising candour his feelings about plays and musical performances which he saw (there were many), about his girl-friends (they were legion), and about his colleagues and superiors, whether they were officers in the trenches, fellow riflemen, French soldiery, German prisoners, nurses and doctors, civilians caught up in the war, or others back in Blighty failing to understand the war's significance.

It is fortunate that by the time the Great War started Tim was already an habitual diary-keeper. Had it been otherwise I do not see how he could have disciplined himself to record the daily happenings of which his was a small but typical part. It remains a mystery to me how he found opportunity to make some record during virtually every single day of his war service. Even when he was crouching in a shell-hole expecting to become at any minute another casualty, he managed to make some written reference to the day's happenings, and he would occasionally add a brief reference to his feelings or to his expectations for the future, such as it was. The picture which emerges is of an individual of enormous courage and moral fibre. Not until the war was over did he permit himself the liberty of writing three short essays examining aspects of life at the front. These essays are in a more consciously literary style (Were they perhaps intended for publication?), and they will appear here as they were written; but while fighting continued it was sufficient that things had to be done, and he did them. Seldom is there complaint about the higher echelons of command, and (at least until the last days of the war) little evidence of hatred for the enemy. It was a war, and that was that.

(In later diaries it is fascinating to read comments about oneself and one's doings, or to see what he has to say about the eminent and wealthy with whom his later medical career brought him into contact. His comments upon royalty when he lived in Kensington Palace, or upon men of letters or business, reveal a depth of understanding no doubt fashioned during trench life. But all that is another story, perhaps the subject of another book. For the present we shall concentrate on the years 1914 to 18, then follow through the effect of *that* war on him until the time when, around 1940, the *Second* war proceeded to ruin his life once again.)

Tim's survival, both physical and mental, seems from our more comfortable standpoint a minor miracle. The tale which emerges from his diaries is horrific. Conditions in the trenches were unspeakable, and the deaths he daily contemplated horrible in the extreme. To him, a literate London lad from a settled family, life in the trenches probably seemed far more taxing than to (say) a miner from one of the most unpleasant environments in civilian employment. Mike Shields reminded me that an older relative of his was required to hew coal in an 18-inch seam three miles out under the North Sea, chin-deep in filthy water, fully aware that the roof could come crashing down, gas could seep from crevices or explosions rip him and the seam apart. In the worst of the trenches conditions were not dissimilar, and furthermore a wily enemy was actively trying to arrange your early demise. Perhaps for Tim the very act of writing his diaries acted as some sort of talisman, retaining his sanity when he might otherwise have snapped. We shall never know. On one occasion after I had got to know him (some forty years after his war) he spoke about an incident where he and an officer had agreed to go left and right in order to improve the chances of a vital message arriving at its destination. As they separated, a shell removed the officer's head: one example of what Tim called his own 'luck' in surviving. Interestingly this incident does not appear in the diaries. Did he perhaps find it too horrible to record? Was he perhaps indulging in some unconscious censorship in order not to distress a future reader? Perhaps he was confident that he would be able to recall the occasion should he ever enlarge on his entries at some future, more leisurely, date, and therefore needed no reminding in the form of a diary-entry. What is unquestionably clear is that his written record is the more telling for its lack of sensationalism.

Several questions are posed not only by the existence of all these many diaries, but also by their long disappearance. For whom was he writing? Not, I suspect, purely for himself: indeed, he occasionally addresses an imaginary reader with some such phrase as 'I shall write more about this when I can find time to do so'. And certainly not for his immediate family, because the members of that family later come under his journalistic scrutiny and do not always appear in a flattering light. I am forced to the conclusion that, although he did not perhaps always appreciate the fact when he was putting pen to paper, he was working for posterity. On one occasion, indeed, his writings hint that he did harbour such hopes. He tried sincerely to tell it as it was, and if this involved revealing not only his life as a soldier but also his relationships with girls, then posterity will judge him more honest than most, I suspect.

Another puzzle is why he was never promoted. Did he have the chance and declined it, or was he never picked out as 'officer material'? I think it likely that in those years of squalor, mud and death many soldiers like him were passed over for no other reason than that they were not spotted and did not think to put themselves forward. Although his family back in Merton was never destitute, it was of that mass of near-London folk who at that time took social stratification as somehow God-given. Officers, they assumed, came from other areas and other schools. (If this seems fanciful it is perhaps relevant to reflect that there are still some who regard the ennoblement of an ancestor as somehow qualifying one to legislate.) Whatever the truth of Tim's continuation as an unpromoted soldier, he probably owed his life to that very fact: young officers were the most likely of all personnel to be killed. Certainly there is evidence in his diaries that he was respected by men and officers alike: indeed the easy relationships which he appears to have enjoyed with commissioned ranks come as something of a surprise. He was occasionally given responsibility far beyond his rank: responsibility which, sometimes in the most trying circumstances, he tried to live up to. And is it fanciful to suggest that his relatively short stature may have made him look unlike an officer, besides acting as a reduced target for German snipers?

Throughout, in collating and editing, I have been struck by the pattern which emerges. In common with accepted wisdom I had previously assumed that, to those who took part in that most terrible of all wars, life was a shapeless period of Hell from enlistment to either eventual survival or death. This view, Tim demonstrates, is wrong. Though some with hindsight have concluded that Haig and his kind mindlessly continued to send men to almost certain death long after he should have called a halt, Tim makes it clear that it did not seem so at the time. He perceived a PLAN, not only during each battle, but for campaigns as a whole. If Tim was typical (which we cannot know, in the absence of other accounts to contradict or support), the men understood this Plan and, to some extent, accepted its implications and went along with the tactical details. Furthermore, if we make the common assumption that no thought was given to the men's welfare by their superiors, then Tim disabuses us as he describes what seem genuine attempts to arrange some acceptable form of recreation during periods of rest. We read of concert parties and football matches behind the lines, and a remarkable freedom to explore the countryside. The reader may, like me, be amazed that he could be concerned about the result of a football match within the sound of shellfire, but concerned he certainly was. Even when one was committed to an attack, it appears that one was confident that back-up relief would arrive; and it usually did arrive, even if it cost dearly to bring it.

Despite the evidence which Tim's diaries present of some understanding that there was plan and pattern in the daily round, self-evidently he could have no picture of the shape the entire conflict would take. Even today, nearly a century later, historians find difficulty balancing a description of day-to-day life against the broad picture which unfolded over four years of bloody struggle. As an attempt to set Tim's observations against what we now know of the war as a whole, I have felt it necessary to provide the reader who, like me, is not a professional historian with a short survey of the background, specifically of the battles which Tim describes from his personal viewpoint. This brief information (given in an Appendix) should not be regarded as a full history of the Great War, which was being fought on many fronts. Turkey and Austria were allied with Germany. Italy and Russia were aligned with Britain and France (and later the United States). A lot was going on! But today, to British eyes, the war is usually equated with the Western Front, with the battles of the Somme, with Ypres, with Armentières, and most particularly with the images, terrifying even in contemplation, of thousands of men climbing from a muddy trench to hurl their aching bodies against barbed wire, there to be slaughtered in tens of thousands by machine-gun, shrapnel, bomb, shell and gas. So this Western Front will provide the focus of our attention.

Remarkably, Tim recorded the name of almost every town and village he visited. Even a route-march led him to note down the places through which the column passed. In attempting to identify the names he gives I have allowed myself to make an occasional change of spelling where it seems likely that he made a rare error. My guess is that as he passed through village this-or-that he tried to memorize the name with a view to recording it later, on arrival at a resting-place. The surprise is that his memory was as sure as it was. On the assumption that some readers will find his comments so evocative that they may wish to visit some of the places he mentions, I have occasionally added some brief aid to location, such as 'East of Arras', usually in parenthesis, but no essential change of emphasis has been made.

For readers who have not previously studied the period I should add that the distances are prodigious. It is commonly assumed, quite wrongly, that the trenches occupied just a few miles of Flanders. (Possibly war films have inadvertently conveyed that impression.) In reality, they stretched for hundreds of miles. Much of the countryside of France has never fully recovered from the battering it received as the greatest armies in history set about obliterating each other from the Channel coast to the Swiss border. Some villages simply vanished; others have been so totally rebuilt that it is impossible to discern their former shape. The fact is that to travel at leisure today over the acres where men died in numbers never before equalled in war is an experience both terrible and beautiful. Simple sketch-maps may be useful starting-points, but detailed Michelin maps of each area are indispensable. A trip to France in connection with the 1914-1918 conflict could provide an opportunity to visit the superb Historial de la Grande Guerre (Historical Museum of the Great War) at Péronne, a town that features in Tim's diaries. There the origins and the consequences of the War are brought to life: the viewpoints of France, Germany and Britain are vividly evoked through the museum's valuable collection of artefacts. The Historial's setting in a now delightful small town is most attractive, and there is a welcoming refreshment room. Within easy reach, and run by the Historial, is the Thiepval Visitor Centre which presents the history of the Battles of the Somme. In 1932 a fine memorial was inaugurated at Thiepval commemorating some 70,000 'missing' British and South African troops. Tim could so easily have been one of them.

CHAPTER TWO

TIM'S DIARIES BEFORE HIS ENLISTMENT

Tim's diary-keeping began well before he joined the Army. The better to know the sort of person he was, one needs to look at the entries he had made during his formative years before 1914. Not only did he make records of his activities, but he also retained documents that were important to him at the time, some of which reveal a serious young lad determined not to waste his life. In 1909, for example, when he was about fourteen-and-a-half, he retained the copy of a letter sent from B.Enys King to E.R.Grote, Esq., of the Foster Arc Lamp and Engineering Company, Dorset Road, Merton Park, dated October 15th. Although this copy letter bears no sender's address, Mr King had presumably received an application from Tim to work in London, and took the trouble to recommend him to someone he knew in the electrical business nearer to Tim's home:

Re. Timothy Elliott, Mostyn Dale, Merton Park

Referring to my telephone conversation, the above lad is the eldest son of one of the late John Innes's gardeners, now working on the estate. If I got him work up here his fare to town would swallow up his wages. He is most willing and persistent, and I know he would do his best to please you, even if, as a start, you merely put him to dust up the office, see to the stoves and make himself useful. I have told him to come up to your place on Monday at 9.30 a.m.

Yours very truly

B. Enys King

We see here evidence of a youngster who had made himself liked by a potential employer who in his turn was sensitive to the need to find a place of work for Tim that did not entail unnecessary travel expenditure.

A year or so later, Tim's diary entries continue to show a young man with a sense of social responsibility, and furthermore reveal his desire to take a look at what is going on in the big world around him. We can observe a loving

Tim, a confident teenager

family (of modest means) which well understands his growing feelings for the theatre. He shows evidence of easy social relationships, of a willingness to involve himself in community activity, and of a growing talent on the stage.

1911

January 2nd   Went to elocution at the Club.

January 4th   Walked to Clapham Junction and went to the Shakespeare Theatre to see Sinbad. *Then went to the Club, washed myself, and practised our play.*

January 6th   Smoked herbs with Cyril. Went to the Treat and gave our play. Saw conjurer.

January 9th   Len and I blowed [sic] *the organ for a wedding.*

January 11th   My 16th birthday. Had wrap from Mother and two shillings from Father.

January 14th   Went to Tooting, then caught the workman's tram to Waterloo. Went to the Lyceum to see Cinderella.

January 16th   Went blowing the organ, then to practice for concert where I tried my dresses on.

January 26th   Altering clothes for play.

Sunday Jan. 29th   Went to Mr Holland's class, then to Church. Had dinner [the midday meal, presumably], *then took Granny some down. To bible class, then to tea. Then Church. Then went for walk with Annie King, and went with Phoebe and Daisy and two more girls.*

February 6th   Went up to Club to get part for play 'The Jacobite'. Got John Duck.

February 11th Went to theatre to see Chocolate Soldier. [This is Oscar Straus's loose adaptation of George Bernard Shaw's *Arms and the Man*]

February 14th Went to Calico Printing Works for a job. No vacancy yet.

February 15th Went to theatre to see The Sign of the Cross.

February 21st To theatre for Charley's Aunt.

February 27th Started work at Dorset Road.

March 1st   To theatre for The House Opposite.

March 8th   Went to theatre with Fatty, one of the boys at the Printing Works. We saw The Sin of London.

March 15th   Theatre for East Lyne. [Presumably the melodrama *East Lynne*]

March 17th   Stayed indoors in the evening writing School Play.

March 21st   To the Masonic Hall where

Tim's Mother

18

I played John Duck in the play The Jacobite. *Very good.*

    March 22nd   To work as usual. Worked overtime till 9 o'clock. Sixpence.

    March 24th   To Theatre with Dad: Priscilla Runs Away.

    March 27th   I go to get part for new plays The Merchant of Venice *and* St. Patrick's Day. *I am to be Lieutenant O'Conner*

Clearly Tim, in his seventeenth year, is strongly interested in the theatre, and is already not only managing to see far more productions than one might expect, but is also acting and even trying his hand at writing in the dramatic medium. Life for him is beginning to flower, one feels.

    April 15th   Moved from Mostyn Dale, Mostyn Road to 12 Wilton Creascent [sic.].

    April 18th   Winnie Godfrey followed me home from work on her bike. Went to see Our Miss Gibbs. [Another musical, this time by Lionel Monckton. It had opened in January 1909 with a starry cast: Gertie Millar, George Grossmith and Gladys Cooper among others. Its settings in the White City and in Garrods, which everyone knew was Harrods, helped it to run for 636 performances. What a pity Tim does not give his opinion of this extravaganza. Perhaps his mind was on Winnie Godfrey, who presumably had not accompanied him to the theatre.]

Tim's Father

    April 22nd   Went to the Electroscope Picture Palace.

    April 25th   To theatre for The Arcadians. [This was Monckton's greatest success. It had opened at the Shaftesbury Theatre on April 28th, 1909.]

    April 29th   Bought boots for seven shillings and tenpence halfpenny.

    May 14th   Went to Wimbledon Theatre to hear General Booth

The diary continues to record the energetic doings of a young man with interests in the theatre and with the intention to seek out a reasonable career. By now he had gone to work at an establishment called Gordon's. In a couple of months' time he would make a real attempt to enter the theatre, but with no success.

    June 19th   Haircut 3d. [Three old pence: just over one decimalised penny.]

    June 24th   Fetched Granny home from Masonic Hall. Coronation of George V.

    July 14th   To a theatrical agency in London. No good. Bought shirt for two shillings and threepence, and three collars for tenpence.

    August 5th   Bought new suit

    September 1st   Started work at Berners as

Ledger Clerk: Six shillings and threepence a week.

September 19th   Got up, but never felt well, and fainted just as I opened the door. Doctor Collier came. Mrs Disney brought me biscuits and got medicine. Had to lie down all day.

September 21st   Went to Dr Collier for tonic, then called on B.S.C.and Co. re. Work. For walk all day over Morden. Met Lily Woods in evening.

September 23rd   For walk in morning calling at B.S.C. and Co. for wages. To theatre in afternoon with Len to see The Piper. *Getting sick pay eight shillings and fourpence. Then to theatre again in the evening by myself to see* Hamlet.

October 2nd   Finished writing play in pencil.

October 3rd   Saw The Quaker Girl. [Yet another Monckton score, which had opened at the Adelphi on November 5th, 1910.]

October 8th   To Church and Bible Class. Had row with all of them.

November 2nd   To theatre with Dad to see The Belle of New York. [This musical show had originally opened in New York in 1897. With tunes by Gustave Kerker, it had achieved only 56 performances in New York, but when it opened in London's Shaftesbury Theatre this story of a Salvation Army girl so delighted the British audiences that it ran for 674 performances, and continued very profitably into the provinces.]

Tim was still determined to acquire the skills necessary for a stage career: a fact illustrated by several small diary entries:

November 16th   Gave dad two shillings for banjo strings.

November 21st   To Mr Cameron for lesson on banjo, paying ten shillings and sixpence for lessons.

November 22nd To theatre for A Waltz Dream. [Oscar Straus's great, sentimental hit from 1907, which contained one of the most gorgeous of all late-Viennese waltzes 'Leise, ganz leise'. Miscasting and a failure in London to understand the idiom led to little success there, despite the earlier success of Straus's *The Chocolate Soldier*. The latter, of course, had the advantage of having sprung from a Shaw plot – *Arms and the Man*.]

November 28th   Met Gwen and went home with her. Had small row, and we gave each other up. [Gwen will continue to appear in his diaries for many years, though he certainly does not realize the fact at the time.]

December 12th   To banjo practice and to meet Gwen. She gave me a letter, which will be found in my box under 'Love'.

1912

January 11th   My 17th birthday. Gwen gave me a tie, and Mum two shillings and sixpence.

February 12th   Got part of Grumio in Taming of the Shrew.

March 7th   Had my first shave. Went to theatre for Floradora. [This must have been either a revival or a local tour: Tim, regrettably does not specify. The songs were by Leslie Stuart, already well-known for 'Lily of Laguna' and 'Soldiers of the Queen'. *Floradora* opened at the Lyric in November 1899, and ran a year and a half in London, somewhat longer in New York. Its most memorable number was 'Tell me, pretty maiden, are there any more at home like you?']

April 1st   With Dad to theatre for Taming of the Shrew. [No doubt the part he was later to play was observed with special care.]

April 6th   *To theatre. Saw* Romeo and Juliet.

One might be tempted to think that Tim was a model youth, always studying, working hard, keenly interested in the dramatic art and intending a thespian career if possible. But then:

May 28th   *Went into Rutlish Schools. Pinched sweets, etc.*
July 10th   *To theatre for* Tommy Atkins.
August 28th   *Moved from 4 Leigh Villas to number 2.*

Tim was very precise where money was involved. He begins September 1912 with a few financial notes, recording that he was 'still earning fifteen shillings and fourpence a week', that he had bought boots for eight shillings and elevenpence, a suit for thirty shillings (= £1.50) and a bioscope book for five shillings (= 25 pence). Was he, one wonders, in view of the book mentioned here, even contemplating a career in the cinema? Certainly he did bear a considerable similarity to Spencer Tracey in later life. An entry in October suggested that his chances on the stage were, at least, better than on the football pitch:

October 19th   *Played football for Millgreen Athletic against South Mitcham. Lost 10-2.*

His interest in Gilbert and Sullivan, however, flourished at about the same time. Sullivan had been dead for just over a decade, but Gilbert, that master of words (which Tim would certainly have appreciated) did not pass on until 1911:

October 19th   *During October I have seen D'Oyly Carte in* Patience, Pirates of Penzance, Iolanthe *and* Yeomen of the Guard.
November 26th   *To theatre for* The Country Girl. [Another of Lionel Monckton's tune-filled extravaganzas, which had opened in 1902 and ran for 729 performances in London before considerable international success.]

1913 found Tim becoming more and more involved with the theatre, not only as a spectator but also as a performer. He was working hard to acquire the necessary skills:

December 20th   *To Kingston for a dancing lesson.* [He remained a nifty dancer well into late middle-age.]

He is, in addition, becoming used to travel, being unafraid of lengthy walks when he could neither afford nor arrange transport. He seems to have been a keen student of several useful arts associated with the theatre, taking lessons on banjo and piano as well as his Terpsichorean adventures. There is little in the diaries to suggest any interest in politics except for a then common delight in annoying those ladies who sought to secure parliamentary representation for women. Perhaps he later felt a lingering regret at his attitude to the Suffragettes: significantly perhaps, he was years later to christen his younger daughter Ann Veronica, after the liberated heroine in H.G. Wells's novel of the same name.

1913
January 7th   *To a party at Mr Smith's house. He is Head Stableman to Vanderbilt.*

January 11th   My 18th birthday. Because it's Saturday I go to dancing lesson at 2.30.
February 4th   To piano practice at 7.15.
February 23rd For walk on Common with Cyril, etc. Suffragettes hustled.
February 27th Started work at Merton Printing Co., Dorset Rd. 8-7.
March 2nd   Went up the Common. Suffragettes assalted [sic].
March 11th   To theatre with Dad to see The Dollar Princess. *Very good.* [Tim now regularly gives brief judgments of what he sees, and sound judgment at that. Leo Fall's work had opened at Austria's Theater an der Wien in November 1907, and was a great advance on some of the musical offerings of the time. His melodies even influenced the young Jerome Kern, who actually supplied two songs for the American première. The somewhat altered London production proved hugely successful, running for 428 performances.]

March 15th   Cyril and I went to theatre to see The Merry Widow. *Good.* [If it seems surprising that Tim awarded a lesser accolade to the Widow than to the Dollar Princess, it must be remembered that the Widow suffered in Britain then, and still does, from a failure to appreciate the serious nature of Lehár's secondary romantic plot, which failure often makes the work seem too light-weight.]

March 24th, Easter Monday Caught 7.40 from Wimbledon to Waterloo, then the City Railway to Fenchurch Street, and then the London and Tilbury line to Southend. Got there at 10.30. Went out on a boat for 2 ½ hours. To Southend Hippodrome in evening at 6.30 (Zona Vevey, etc.) Then to beach again and caught 9.12 back, arriving home at 12.30.
March 28th   To Appollo [sic] *Picture Palace to see* Les Miserables.
April 1st   To theatre for Westwood Ho [sic]. *Very good, with Mr Matheson Lang.*
April 9th   Walked around with Territorials.
April 15th   The Importance of Being Earnest.
May 12th, Whit Monday   Went for ride to Sevonoaks [sic] *in Kent: about 33 miles via Croydon and Westerham on bikes.*
May 20th   I played Potter in Still Waters Run Deep *at Masonic Hall.*
June 9th   Went to Kinemacoler pictures at 6.30.
June 16th   Moved to Red House (Mr Rutter's).
June 24th   Moved to 195.
June 28th, Saturday To work, then home. Started for Hastings at 4.30 with Charlie True (by bike) via Purley, Caterham, East Grinstead, Heathfield, Battle, etc. Riding all night. Got to Hastings at 12.30. Then went to beach and sat on deck chairs, etc. Put bicycles up at 7 o'clock. Breakfast at 8.30. Then on cliffs and beach, etc., until 12.50. Then had refreshment and started back at 1.20 via St. Leonards, Bexhill, Pevonsy [sic] *and just by Eastbourne and Beachy Head. Had tea at Uckstead* [probably Uckfield] *at 5.30 till 6.20. Then via East Grinstead, Warlingham, Caterham and Purley. Got home at 11.20.*

Tim's concern for precise times and details, especially on a journey, was to make his later war diaries of special interest. His exhausting trip to Sussex seems to have taken its toll, however:

June 30th   Up at 6 o'clock. Then came home [from work, presumably] *and lay down until 9.30. Then to Doctor's, etc. Stayed indoors all the afternoon. Slept at our house.*
The diary does not make clear the form Tim's indisposition took. It appears not to have stopped him getting out and about during part of the following day!

July 1st   Stayed indoors in morning. Went round Ethyl's house in afternoon. Went for walk to Common in evening. Then home.

July 2nd   Stayed indoors all morning. Round Ethyl's house in afternoon and to Park. Then to hear band.

July 3rd   Indoors all morning and afternoon. Went to Doctor's at 7 o'clock, and then to N.D.F.S. [Presumably the National Deposit Friendly Society where, for a small regular sum, one could expect to receive some financial help in times of illness.]

Tim then records on several occasions that he is indoors 'learning his Part' in a play. This does not entirely exclude the company of the fairer sex:

July 12th, Saturday   To work. Indoors drawing, etc., till 6 o'clock. Then to Sports (Merton Boys' Club) in Hatfield Park. Spoke to Nora Rafferty and other girls. Then met Lily King at 9.30 and for a walk until 10.20. [The word 'walk' has above it a symbol –a star within a circle- that suggests a little more than perambulation.]

July 26th, Saturday   To work, then to Charing Cross Station and caught 4.30 to Headcorn, Kent. 46 ½ miles, fare seven shillings and eightpence. Arrived 6.15. Played Harwood and John Leyton in The Prince of Rogues *at the Headcorn Institute. Stayed the night.*

By now Tim was beginning to travel in order to play sundry stage parts. He never satisfactorily describes the process whereby he arrived at this activity, but the diary suggests that there was an element of professional employment about it. The impression is that some established performer (perhaps now beyond his prime) would employ a promising youngster like Tim to 'fill out' the other parts in a touring production, perhaps put on in a village hall. The itinerant professional was named Phillips, and Tim's entry for July 26th presumably recorded his first professional engagement. Regrettably we do not learn the value of Tim's fee.

July 27th   Up at 7.15 and went for walk. Breakfast with Mr Phillips. Then we caught 8.30 from Headcorn, arrived Charing Cross 10.50. Home at 12.20. Went for walk to Common in afternoon with Cyril, and by myself in evening. Spoke to two girls.

July 28th   To work. Then met Lily King and went for walk over Bunce's Meadows. [Here the special symbol!] *Home at 10.10.*

July 29th   To work. Lily King came into my house from 7.40 until 8.20 [then the same symbol].

July 30th   To work. Then went to hear band at South Park Gardens. Spoke to girls, and went home with girl named Kate.

August 2nd   To work. Stayed indoors all afternoon. Met Lily King at 7 o'clock, then went to theatre for White Slaves of London. *Then I met her again after I came out. Went for a walk. Home at 11.25.*

August 3rd   To Church in morning, and again in afternoon. Went for walk round Raynes Park and Cambridge Road to the Common. Spoke to Hope Foulsham and another. Then followed Edith Chappell and Ida Mott and some boys over the Common by Caesar's Well. Spoke to Edie.

August 4th Bank Holiday.   Mum, Dad and I went to the Zoological Gardens in the afternoon from 1.30 until 4 o'clock. Then I went to St Pancras Station and caught the 4.45 to Radlett, Herts (15 ½ miles). Walked to Shenley (2 miles) and played the parts of John Harwood and

Leyton in The Prince of Rogues *at Shenley Village Hall. Caught the 12 o'clock back to St Pancras (fare two shillings and sixpence); arrived there 1.10. Then had to walk back to Westminster Bridge, and caught tram at 3.20 a.m. to Tooting Broadway. Got home at 4.45, and went to bed at 5 a.m.*

At this point Tim's diary is full of work, piano practice, trips to the theatre (including *The Second Mrs Tanqueray*, which he describes as 'Good'), visits to the cinema, and encounters with many different girls. His personal ambitions as an actor are not forgotten, however:

September 13th   Got up at 6.30. Had bath etc. Caught 12.40 from Wimbledon, changed at Surbiton and Alton, arrived Tisted at 3.20. Walked to Aunt Annie's Horse and Groom. *Bed 10.30.*

September 16th   Rode to Selbourne [sic] in afternoon re. Cecil Phillips: 3 ½ miles. Walked there again in the evening and saw A Noble Brother.

September 17th   Walked to Selbourne in evening and played the Chief of Paris Police in The Black Vampire *at the Parish Hall. Dad and brother Harry came to see it.*

By September 21st he is back in Merton, making up for lost opportunities with the girls, including Phyllis who earns a sizeable secret code-mark. On September 23rd he went to Kennington to visit the Sinclair Stage Agency. Lily King got her asterisk on October 11th, on which occasion Tim records that he 'hit chap'. No reason is given. On October 13th he records that he played Scrooge in *A Christmas Carol* in Wimbledon, and the following day he is off on another (presumably professional) theatrical engagement:

October 14th   Caught bus to Charing Cross Station, then the 10.55 to Gomshall in Surrey, and to lodgings in Shere, arriving 12.30 at 4, Gomshall Road. Went to the Village Hall at 7 o'clock where I played a dumb soldier in The Fighting Parson.

October 15th, Wednesday   Went down to the Hall at 10.30. Tidied up. Rehearsal until 12.30. Dinner [i.e. lunch] and a walk in the afternoon. To Hall at 7.15 where I played Silas Mellish in The Mormon and his Wifes [sic].

October 16th   To the Hall at 11 o'clock, and again in afternoon. Played General Boomer in A Cheerful Liar. *Bed at 11.15.*

October 17th   Went to practise my knife-fight. In the evening played both Ritza and the Chief of Police in The Black Vampire. *Then packed scenery, and to bed at 11.30.*

October 18th   Up at 6.15 to load scenery at 7.30. Caught the 9.10 to London Bridge, and then to Gravesend for 12. Then I walked to Thorne, and stayed in my lodging writing all evening.

October 20th   Mr Bush and I rode to Gravesend on a cart to get scenery at 11 o'clock, then walked back. Put up scenery in the afternoon. In the evening I played Sir Gerald Kingston and Ben Chucks in Trail of the Serpent.

Tim is clearly fulfilling another professional engagement. He then plays two parts on October 21st, one on the 22nd, and another on the 23rd. On the 24th he watched the same company perform *Lady Audley's Secret*, but took no part.

October 25th   At 2.30 at the Hall I performed little sketches and songs for a children's matinee. In the afternoon I watched Thorne lose 7-1 to Highcliffe at football. In the evening I played Silas Mellish, then rode on the back of Mr Cook's bike to the station (4 miles). Caught the 11.39 to Charing Cross from Gravesend, then a tram to Tooting. Walked home arriving 2.30 a.m

October 27th   To work at Coles all morning. We all went on strike at 1.30. Walked to Hackbridge, had meeting. Guvnor gave in to us.

November 13th   To work in morning. Went to funeral at 3. Then tea. Took bus to Liverpool St. Caught 5.25 to Roxbourne (18 miles). Walked one mile to Wormley, Herts. Played part of Ritza in 'The Black Vampire' for Mr Phillips, and caught 10.55 back.

December 16th   Played part of Scrooge in A Christmas Carol.

December 26th   Cyril and I went to the theatre to see Crusoe. *Mistakes were frequent.*

1914

January 17th   To Daly's Theatre to see Gertie Millar in The Marriage Market.

February 5th   Moved from 195 to 'Ashington'.

February 17th   Played Samson Burr in The Porter's Knot *at the Masonic Hall.*

February 25th   Saw Fred Terry in The Scarlet Pimpernel.

March 21st   To Nelson Hall, Merton. Pictures awful.

March 28th   To Kingston Empire to see Harry Champion, etc.

These sample diary entries give some indication of the activities of a young man, full of life, and possibly destined for a career in the theatre. The following four months, however, led to the declaration of war in early August, and to the German occupation of Brussels around August 20th. Tim's diary makes no reference to these shattering political events. He is far more occupied with his theatrical progress and with the many girls with whom he 'went for walks', sometimes accompanied by a small symbol which presumably meant he received something 'extra' on these walks. To read the three-inch by two 'Reporter's Notebook' which serves as his 1914 diary is to be carried back to a carefree, if very busy, young world.

Tim's enlistment in the Army will come on November 9th and will be reported in terms similar to all his previous entries. There is no evidence of his having pondered the decision in advance. The following excerpts convey the flavour of what were later to be seen as momentous months. One suspects that many young men were similarly 'sleepwalking towards eternity'.

April 13th, Easter Monday   Cyril and I caught the 11.30 express from Waterloo to Weymouth via Southampton. 143 miles. Arrived 3 p.m. ...Caught 7 o'clock train back; had supper on train: two shillings and fourpence. Very friendly with people on the train.

April 28th, Tuesday To work until 12.30. Then caught 4.15 from Liverpool Street to Billericay. Walked to Rectory Hall, Stock, and played General Boomer in A Cheerful Liar. *Home at 12.30. (Took two hours from Essex.)*

May 9th, Saturday   To work. Then Reg and I met Catholic Choir at New Malden and we walked to Ashtead: 3 hours. Had dinner at the Leg of Mutton, 8 o'clock. Then concert until 10.45. Caught 11.05 back.

June 1st, Bank Holiday Monday   Up at 4.50. Cyril and I caught 6.30 to Waterloo and 7.15 to Lyme Regis via Axminster. 150 miles. Arrived 11.20...Arrived home after midnight, at 12.55.

June 13th   To Victoria Palace to see George Roby [sic], Lane and Maine (good)

July 18th   Took my 'Company' to Kingston in evening and gave the sketch A Merry

Muddle.

September 5th   To Trafalger [sic] *Square. Went to Savoy Theatre to see* Mr Wu. *(Matheson Lang).*

This was a period when Tim was managing to see many plays and musical presentations. He gives no indication of how he could afford these extravagances. On September 7th he saw *Faust* (presumably Gounod's opera). On the 9th the O'Mara Opera Company gave Verdi's *La Traviata* (Tim was there); and on the 14th he saw Offenbach's *Tales of Hoffmann* performed by the Carl Rosa Opera Company at Kennington Theatre. On the 26th at London Opera House he saw *England Expects*, starring Seymour Hicks.

October 8th   Spoke to Queenie Wordon and used 'phone'. Went to a rehearsal of the Edward Terry Dramatic Club off Regent Street in the evening.
October 17th   Belgium Flag Day. [A mention of the war at last!]
October 24th   Saturday   Cyril and I started cycling to Hindhead at 9 o'clock. Arrived 1.30. Went for a walk in the afternoon down the Glen with Dolly and Gwen Reid (Cyril's cousins). Walked to Churt.
October 27th   To Waterloo Station, watching soldiers, etc.
October 31st   To Woking Police Court re. riding bike without light. Fined two shillings and sixpence. Fare two shillings and ninepence. [This seems almost unbelievable in the 21st century, where one is constantly threatened by unlighted cyclists on town pavements]
November 9th To London at 9.30 and enlisted in the Ninth Battalion City of London (Queen Victoria's) Rifles. At the headquarters 56 Davies Street all day.

The deed is done. Tim is a soldier. His life is about to change in every respect save one: he will continue to keep a diary. As a result we are privileged to learn something of the life and thoughts of an ordinary soldier in that most terrible of wars.

'Queen Victoria's Rifles' was the designation of the Ninth Battalion of the London Regiment. QVR (as it was swiftly abbreviated) was effectively one of twenty-eight Territorial units brought into one Regiment as a result of a major reorganisation dating from 1908. All these various volunteer battalions were within the County of London (not 'City', as Tim writes). The QVRs were one of the first Territorial battalions to serve in France. They arrived at Le Havre on November 5th, 1914 and were involved in the attack on Hill 60 within the Ypres Salient in April 1915. There is a memorial to the Battalion actually on Hill 60. In February 1916 the First London Division was re-formed in France as the 56th Division, and the Queen Victoria's Rifles were absorbed into the 169th Brigade, fighting on the Somme, and at Arras, Ypres and Cambrai. In February 1918 it joined up with the 2/9th and became the 9th Battalion, fighting right up to the Armistice. This complicated history need not concern any but the pedant. Tim would certainly have had no understanding of it on joining; but later (as one can see from his diaries) he became deeply concerned at some of the amalgamations which took place.

CHAPTER THREE

NOW TIM'S A SOLDIER

Just why Tim decided to enlist on that particular day, November 9th, 1914, remains a mystery. Apart from the indignity of appearing in court for cycling without lights (and incurring a fine), the diaries running up to that date record a full, but normal, life-style. On Sunday November 1st he went to Church, and in the afternoon to Bible Class (where he reported speaking to Emily Foulsham and Winnie Turner). In the evening he went for a walk with his friend Cyril, mentioning the company of two girls, both called Violet (Violet Baggett and, as he put it, Violet --.) On November 2nd he and Cyril walked to King's Palace Picture House. He refers each weekday to 'Work', which gets no detail. On the 4th he saw Pygmalion, which he describes as 'Good'. On the 5th it was 'Singing Practice', and on the 7th he and Cyril went to the Charing Cross Road Picture Palace. On the 8th it was early morning Communion, followed by Morning Service, with a Bible Meeting at the Club in the afternoon. And on Monday 9th he went to London to 'enlist in the 9th Battalion City of London, Queen Victoria's Rifles, remaining at 56 Davies St., W (Battalion Headquarters) all day'. He records the details in a neat hand, in ink, in a black hardback notebook measuring about 3"x5" which served as his 1914 diary. He referred to the City of London, whereas the correct description of the regiment was the County of London. Then his new life began!

Nov.10th   Caught 7.25 to Waterloo.   Done Drilling at Hyde Park in morning and was inoculated in afternoon. Home 5.30 and to bed.

On the following day he had a walk in the morning, then *to Hackbridge in afternoon (to see Mr Coles)*. [No reason for this meeting is given.] *Went to Theatre in evening* The New Magdalene. *Sat with Nellie Peake and chap, etc.*

The pattern for the next nine days is: train to London, drilling in Hyde Park, and home again each night. On the 20th he records *Payed* [sic] *24/6* [about £1.25].

A somewhat less confident new recruit is photographed without his hat, but with his puttees

Nov 22nd Sun   Caught 7.53 (District) (Got uniforms etc). Home at 2.30

By November 23rd, he really was 'in the Army':

By rail to Headquarters, 56 Davies St., 7.20. Battalion marched to Victoria Station. Caught train 9.20 to Crowborough, then marched to huts (4 miles). Preparing beds etc., and lights out 10.

Immediately his life became that of a volunteer recruit as the Army 'knocked him into shape'. His days are recorded in a neat inked hand in the same tiny book, with little comment or complaint. The only sign of stress is to be seen in the fact that he had later to correct a few dates

Tim's diaries for 1911, 1915 and 1916. The modern ruler indicates the scale

where he had got 'out of step'. It appears that he inadvertently entered two November 19ths, and stayed wrong until November 30th, at which point he went back and corrected the entries. (He was using a notebook rather than a printed diary, so it was easy to make such errors.) The following entries are presumed correctly dated, following his revisions.

Tues Nov. 24th: Bugle for rising 6-30. Parade 7-15. Breakfast 8-15. Parade 9-30. Dinner [=Lunch] 2-30. Parade 3-15. Teas [or possibly 'Tens'] 5 Oclock. [His way of setting down details has been reproduced here. Could the 5 o'clock entry be intended as a reference to 'tents'? Interestingly he adds] *For walk to Crowborough in evening. Home 9 Oclock.* Clearly a fun-filled day had not exhausted his interest in seeing the locality; and he is happy to refer to his army bed as 'Home'.

November 25th and 26th followed the usual pattern, including visiting 'The Blue Anchor' in Crowborough. On Friday 27th he writes *Paid 4s 5p, and inoculated in afternoon.* Perhaps the sudden accession of wealth (about 23p) accounts for the fact that he 'with others' attended Crowborough 'Picture Palace' in the evening, 'Home 9.30'.

Sat Nov 28th   Bugle 6.30, up at 7.15. Lecture etc in morning. Feet and rifle inspection. In hut all day.

Sun Nov 29th   Church Parade in morning on our Ground. Rifle inspection. Went for walk in afternoon with Murcott. Spoke to girl in Crowborough. We met her and went to St John's Church, Wytham in evening. [Possibly Withyham]

Mon Nov 30th   Digging trenches in mud till 4.30. Indoors all evening.

On Thursday December 3rd he records 'I was hut Orderly all day', but nonetheless he walked into Crowborough in the evening where he 'spoke to girls, etc.' The 'etc.' is not qualified.

On Friday December 4th he was paid 8 shillings (about 40p). Sunday December 6th saw a Church Parade and Inspection at 9.15, after which he was free to visit the Y.M.C.A. for tea. What is revealed in Tim's diary is the thorough organisation of each recruit's day, which makes considerable demands but nonetheless allows a surprising amount of freedom in the evenings and on Sunday. The pay, though small, is regular; and members of the fair sex seem available if one makes the effort to seek them out:

Sun Dec 13th   In huts all morning. For walk in the afternoon to Y.M.C.A. Met Ada Frost at 4.45. Had tea in a cottage with her. Camp at 9.15. [No indication is given as to Ada's age. Was she perhaps a kind old soul who gave tea to 'the boys in uniform'?]

Wed Dec 16th   Inspection by Sir Ian Hamilton in morning. For night march 4.45 – 7.00.

Thurs Dec 17th For march and drill in morning. Short march in afternoon, and Choir Practice. To pictures in evening.

Fri Dec 18th   In hut all day (raining).

Sat Dec 19th   To St John's Camp (Fatigue work). Had dinner in Church yard. To Crowborough in evening with Puttock, and for short walk with Ada. [Who, presumably, was not, after all, a kind old soul.]

Sun Dec 20th   Church parade in morning on Golf Links. For walk in afternoon with Puttock round Crowboro' district; to tea at cottage with Ada Frost, then taxi to camp 9.15.

Tues Dec 22nd To Crowboro' Station with Fatigue party in morning 11.30 to 1.45. Choir practice in Y.M.C.A. in afternoon. In hut in evening.

Xmas Eve Dec 24th, Thurs   Advance guard, etc., in morning. Payed [Tim cannot decide how to spell that important word] *in afternoon. To town in evening (tea at Red Cross Hotel). Called back to camp 8 o'clock and had to parade at 9 p.m. with full kit for march, and back at 10.30.* [Tim doesn't, regrettably, say what form of 'call' got him back to camp. There were no mobile phones then!]

Xmas Day 25th Dec   Church parade 10.15. For walk with two others to Hurstwood. Dinner at 5 o'clock in camp. Concert all evening. Lights out 12 midnight.

Boxing Day, 26th Dec Sat   For 8 mile march in morning. (Got drenched.) In hut all afternoon. To Y.M.C.A. concert and tea in evening with Wallace.

Sun Dec 27th   Inspection by Colonel Berry. In evening with Cook for walk with two girls: Maggie and Nancy.

Mon Dec 28th   Fatigue work all day. To Y.M.C.A. concert in evening.

Tues Dec 29th   Attacking positions in morning, and route march in afternoon.

Wed Dec 30th   Outposts etc in morning. Short march and lecture in afternoon.

Thurs Dec 31st   To firing range in afternoon. Had concert in hut in evening (New Year's Eve.) I recited Shakespeare's Henry 5th Battle of Agincourt.

So ended 1914. Tim concluded by adding the following 'key' events at the end of his notebook:

August 3rd   War declared between England and Germany.

Nov. 9th   Enlisted in the 9th Batt. City of London, Queen Victoria's Rifles, 1st Reserve Battalion. Territorials.

Nov. 22nd.   Drafted to Crowborough, Sussex. Stationed in Huts at Brown Knoll.

1915

For 1915, Tim acquired a proper diary instead of utilising a notebook. Possibly because he was aware of the need for concealment, the diary was very small, measuring 3' in height and little over 2' in width. The title page proudly proclaims:

> Charles Letts's Waistcoat pocket diary for 1915, containing coupon for
> £1000 accident insurance with £2 per week Sickness Allowance.

Very useful for a soldier shortly to be drafted to the Western Front ! The diary has provision for a small pencil along the spine, but Tim usually managed to find ink. His sense of humour is shown on the page for Personal Memoranda, where, against Telephone Number, he writes simply 'Berlin'. He records his glove size as 6 ½, his size in boots as 8, collar size as 14 ½ , hat size as 6 5/8, weight as 10 stone, and height 5 ft 6 ½ inch. Where the diary prints the words 'In the event of this diary being lost kindly return to the above address' he writes 'T.G. Elliott, Homelyn, Merton Park.'

His entries in this minute diary are packed with little refinements which Tim clearly invented for himself. They even suggest, by implication, that he realized he may later wish to make swift reference to particular events, so he provides a set of index pages to special happenings. Was he, even then, contemplating a future in which he would write up his experiences, perhaps for publication? Who can say ? Certainly he takes great trouble to make this teeny, pocketable record easy to find one's way around. On the Memoranda pages which appear at the front of the diary, for instance, he inscribes 'key' dates, presumably written when he had completed the year so that all the entries for 1915 were made swiftly available to him. The first such date is:

Left Crowboro Camp May 14th.

The last of some fifty such entries is:

Enemy active with trench mortars Dec 28th.

Clearly during 1915 he is going to find himself in the front line.

Even the addresses which he inscribed with great care on the appropriate page of his diary display the geographical split which will be seen to have occurred in the coming year, as far as he is concerned.

-Mrs Whitmore, 223 Kingston Rd., Wimbledon
-Mr V. Whisker (or Whisher), 33 High St., Merton
-Miss G. Reed, 'Glenside', Beacon Hill, Hindhead, Surrey, Angleterre
-Madame Cailleux, Cultivateurs, Chipilly, Somme, France
-Miss G. Reed, Valency Lodge, Northwood, Middlesex
-Mr Elliott, 35 Dorset Road, Merton Park, Surrey.

One presumes that Miss Reed is special, and that she moved during 1915. Will Mme. Cailleux become a character in the real-life play in which Tim, the ex-actor, is shortly to perform a minor, but remarkable, role?

The first three weeks of 1915 are meticulously recorded. Life is getting repetitive, but Tim makes no complaint. Tuesday January 5th saw an inspection by a Major General [Kay? Fry? The entry is indistinct.] Monday January 11th would have been Tim's 20th birthday, but he makes no mention of it, recording only:

11th, Plough Monday. Morning, afternoon and evening in Hut, reading, writing, etc.

Tuesday 12th passed in a similar fashion, until the evening:

In Crowboro' in evening, and for walk with Ivy and Olive.

It appears that the Army no longer had immediate plans for Tim, who spent several days in the Hut, venturing out, generally, in the evenings:

Wednesday 13th To Crowboro' Picture House in evening with Ivy and Olive.

A week later, on the 20th, he writes:

Up at 5.30 and to Range. Firing and marking all day to 4.30. Fired 50 rounds.
Fri 22nd Jan. For 6 mile March in morning. Musketry and pay in Hut in afternoon. Concert in Hut in evening.
Sat 23rd Jan. To Range 9.30 till 3.30 Firing and Marking.
Mon 25th Jan. Double Co. Drill morning; March and Drill afternoon; in Hut all evening (boxing and reading).
Tues 26th Jan. Practised an attack Morning. Standing on Parade on Golf Course After-noon. Standing by for orders Evening.
Wed 27th. Attack and Charge Morning. Short March Afternoon. In Hut Evening (Boxing, etc.)
Thurs 28th. On Range 7.30 to 12.15 (fired 23 rounds). Cookhouse Fatigue Afternoon. In Hut in Evening (Waiting Orders).
Fri 29th. Quartermasters Fatigue 9 till 4.
Sat 30th. Attack and Charge Morning. March afternoon.

On Sunday 31st, after a Church Parade, he met his father, who had travelled from Merton :

Met Dad at Station 1.45. For walk with him all round till 6.45. Then with Murcott and girls.
Mon Feb. 1st. Attack in morning. On guard all night: 2 hours on and 4 off in Guardroom.
Tues Feb 2nd. On guard all day, and relieved at 4.15 p.m.
Thurs Feb 4th. Went for 20 mile route march. Started at 10; home 6.30. Route: Nutley, Ashdown Forest, Dinner [probably early afternoon], Colman's Hatch, Hartfield.
Fri. Feb 5th. Retreat and Attack (8 miles) in morning till 2.00. On guard at Detention Hut (4.45) – six prisoners. Hours of guards 4.45, 6.30, 10.00-12.30. (Rain)
Sat Feb 6th. Guarding prisoners 4.30-6.30 [presumably a.m.], and 1030-12.45. Left Guardroom 4.45. Went to Crowboro' in evening with rest of Guard.
Sun Feb 7th. Morning Church Parade and Inspection by Colonel Berry. For walk in afternoon; Murcott also in Y.M.C.A. Church in evening; spoke to Kate.

Mon Feb 8th   Platoon and Squad Drill in morning. Short route march in afternoon. In hut all evening (rain).

Tues Feb 9th   Started for Range 7 a.m. In huts again 9.40 (rain). Lecture in hut, morning. Route march, afternoon.

Wed Feb 10th   Started for Range at Old Lodge 7 a.m. In butts signalling, and fired 23 rounds. Saw second draft off 5 p.m. To Crowboro' in evening.

Thurs Feb 11th Inspection on Golf Links by Brigadier, and for 18 mile Route March via Groombridge and Eridge. Back at 6.30.

Fri Feb 12th   Attack in morning till 1.30. Paid in afternoon. 200 recruits arrived.

Sat Feb 13th   Escorted the body of Corporal Roe to station in morning. [There is no indication of how Cpl. Roe died.] *Soaked with rain. 200 men arrived.*

Sun Feb 14th   Hut Orderly all day. Went for walk down town at 5 o'clock, and for walk with girl named Rose. Back at 8.45.

Mon Feb 15th   Battalion Training all morning. Dinner on Common. Attack in afternoon, and back at camp 6 p.m.

Tues Feb 16th   Attack through Ashdown Forest in morning. Evening, pictures in Crowboro' with Binder.

Thurs Feb 18th For 20 mile Route March 9.30 to 6.15, via Sheffield Park, Dane Hill, and Nutley.

Sun Feb 21st   Church Parade on Golf Links. For walk in afternoon. Spoke to Lizzie Neve, and for walk with Lily Bramswell. For walk with Daisy Neve in evening.

Mon Feb 22nd An advanced Attack in morning under Brigadier.

Tues 23rd   Parades. 7.30 Physical Drill. 9.15 Fatigue. 2.00 Fatigue. 5 p.m. Fire Alarm. 6.00 Night Charge. Then in Hut.

Wed 24th   On Quartermaster's Fatigues all day till 6 o'clock, and to Cinque Port Drill Hall.

Thurs 25th   For 18 mile route march via Chuckhatch, Colmanshatch, Ashdown Forest and Nutley.

Much now seems repetitive to a reader of the diaries; but Tim continues to record each day in some detail.   Here are a few samples:

Sun 28th   Reveille 5.30. At Old Lodge Ranges till 4.45. Fired 23 rounds. To Crowboro' in evening for walk with Rose. Later spoke to Lizzie and for short walk with two girls.

More time was spent on the firing ranges than on musketry at the camp. On Friday March 5th he records:

At the range from 8.00 to 5.30. I fired 30 rounds to complete the Regulars' Course.

And on Monday March 8th he is at last allowed some leave:

Had Outpose scheme in the morning. Caught 6.01 p.m. from Crowboro' to Wimbledon via Groombridge and Clapham. Arrived home 9 o'clock.

Tues 9th March   Visiting various people in morning. To schools, etc., in afternoon. Tea with Aunt Ellen. For walk with Maria. To theatre 9 o'clock for 'Our Boys'.

Wed 10th March.　　　*To Aunt Sophie's and Mr Bartlett's in morning. For ride to Hackbridge and Sutton. Tea with Lizzie. For walk with Maria in afternoon. For walk with Hope, Emily and Nellie Foulsham.*

Thurs 11th March.　　*Caught 8.45 to Haslemere, then bus to Hindhead. Then to 'Glenside'. For walk with Gwen, Doris and Mrs Reed. To bed at 11.15.*

Fri 12th March.　　　　*Up at 8.30. Breakfast 9.30. For walk with Gwen and Dorry in morning to Grayshott and in the Glen. Caught 5.25 from Haslemere.*

Sat 13th March.　　　　*Visited Mrs Bartlett and Aunt Ellen. For walk at Clapham Junction. Caught 11.17 to Crowboro' via Eridge. Cleaned Hut, and to pictures in evening.*

The leave is over. But nearly three months are to elapse before Tim sets sail for France. The pattern of most days remains as before, with occasional entries revealing progressively 'warlike' or 'battlefront' training:

Mon 15th March.　　*Battalion Attack 10.30 till 3.45 (Blanks)*

Tues 16th March.　　*Company Attack Morning. Night operations 6 until 9.15.*

Wed 17th March.　　*With Company in morning inspecting trenches, etc. Kit inspection by Captain Wilton afternoon. Five-mile run in evening with others.*

Thurs 18th March.　　*An attack and company drill in morning. Went on guard 5.30 until 8 pm. Then in Guard Room.*

Fri 19th March.　　　*On guard midnight till 2 am, 6 to 8 am, 2 to 3 pm, 6.45 to 8.30 pm.*
 Guard then dismissed.

Sat 20th March.　　　　*Musketry on Minerature* [sic, perhaps Miniature] *Range (15 rounds) till 10.30. Marched to Rotherfield afternoon – Company Sports. Then to Crowboro'.*

Passion Sunday, March 21st, began with a Church Parade. The evening brought a walk with Daisy Neve. Friday 26th introduced 'Sight and Observation, and Distance Testing'. Palm Sunday, the 28th, began with the customary Church Parade, but during an afternoon walk Tim 'met two girls at Jarvis Brook'. The evening brought 'a walk with Daisy'.

Mon 29th March.　　*Bayonet Instruction 9–10. Lecture 10-12. Marched to Nutley 1.30 and attacked back to Range. Made second attack, and home 9.45.*

There is little evidence of time-wasting by the military authorities, or of resentment by the soldiers. The last day of March was typically packed:

Company Drill in morning. Bayonet instruction Noon. 4 mile run in afternoon. YMCA concert in evening (good). [Tim had, by now, started to make a value judgment about the entertainment, as he was wont to do when visiting the London theatres.]

Easter Day 4th Apl.　　　*Morning – YMCA Hut. Afternoon - ride in car to Rotherfield, Marks Cross, etc. Night - Walk with Elsie Holden and her friend.*

Easter Monday 5th Apl.　　*Trench digging in the morning. Walked to Groombridge in afternoon. Met Elsie Holden and her friend 6 pm and went for walk with them.*

Wed. 7th Apl.　　*Reveille at 4 o'clock. Caught 6.30 from Crowboro' to Ore. Fired rounds in Fairlight Glen. Dismissed in Hastings 3 o'clock and caught 5.55 to Crowboro'.*

Fri 9th Apl.   Paraded 8.15 for Field Day. Marched by Buxted and Uckfield. Home through Maresfield, arriving back 8.10.

Wed 14th Apl.   Fire control etc in morning. Inspection etc in afternoon. Night operations start 8 pm. Releaved [sic] those in trenches etc. Back 12.15, just after midnight; bed at 1 am. [Tim's fatigue after so long a day no doubt contributed to the rare spelling error.]

Thurs 15th Apl. March through Colemans Hatch and Ashdown in morning, and then attack through Nutley.

The following day Tim had more Fire Control instruction, followed by inspections of his rifle and of his no-doubt-aching feet. On Saturday April 17th the morning was spent on Company drill, after which he had a short leave:

Caught 1.47 to Clapham Junction.   Home at 4.45. He then saw Dorothy Taylor, and, for good measure, went for a walk with Marie Santo in the evening. The following morning, Sunday 18th, he went to the 8 am communion at the Parish Church, then fitted in several social calls: *for walk with Marie on the Common, and with Cyril and Bert in the afternoon.* He caught the 7.10 back to Crowborough camp in the evening.

Mon 19th Apl.   Field Day. Attack in the morning, skirting Nutley. Back at 5 o'clock. To YMCA in the evening.

What is interesting to the present-day reader of these diaries is the discovery that the Army clearly made strenuous attempts not only to see that budding soldiers were well-trained and fit, but also to ensure that they had leisure and spare-time activities. In addition, considerable freedom to 'roam' was allowed, and was certainly appreciated by Tim. We have no way of knowing whether he was typical: to some it was perhaps Purgatory. What is certain, though, is that if there were disastrous mistakes in the pursuit of our military aims, they were made at the highest level, rather than further down the chain of command, where dedication both to duty and to 'other ranks' is evident (by implication) in everything Tim wrote then. The simple entry for Thursday April 22nd 1915 is a case in point:

Brigade day. Attack, etc. Back at 2.15. In hut for inspection in afternoon. YMCA Concert in evening, with London Turns.

The demands made on these young trainees were considerable. Consider the entries for 23rd and 24th April:

23rd: Drilling on St John's Camp in the morning. Pay, etc., afternoon. Paraded 7.30 pm for Night Operations. Marched by Nutley. Had Charge, etc.

24th: In camp again at 12.15 am. Lights out 1 o'clock am. Battalion Drill, etc., in the morning. To Groombridge in the afternoon [presumably at leisure] *and Crowboro' after 7pm.*

Despite the demands being made of 20 year old Timothy Elliott, he was able to continue the interest he had shown in his teens in the wider world around him:

Sun 25th Apl.   Parade at Parish Church 10.00-10.45. Walk to Rotherfield to tea in afternoon. To Crowboro' Wesleyan Church in evening.

Mon 26th Apl. Divisional Day. Marched to Maresfield and attacked back (7.45 until 1.30). Inspection, etc., in afternoon. To Crowboro' Fair in evening with Boyd.

Thurs 27th Apl. Orderly all day. Trench-digging all morning. In hut in afternoon, and to Fair in evening, where spoke to Olive and Ivy.

Wed 28th Apl. Battery and Company work in morning. Musketry in afternoon. Writing in hut at night.

Thurs 29th Apl. Up at 5.15. Brigade route march through Nutley, Maresfield, Buxted and Hurstwood. Concert at YMCA in the evening.

That concert was well earned. The march must have covered at least fifteen miles, probably on very variable surfaces. Even so, Tim was to put the skills of walking to good use on Sunday, May 2nd:

Caught 10.42 to Tunbridge Wells. Walked from there to Groombridge via Langton Green (taking one and a half hours). Then for walk with two girls. Then [unreadable, perhaps Weald Green]. *Caught 8.45 home* [i..e. back to camp].

Mon 3rd May. Brigade Day. Back at 3 o'clock. To YMCA Concert in evening (Bontoff Magician).

Tues 4th May. Battalion Attack, and dinner [= lunch] *in field. Back at 4 o'clock. Concert in Hut in Evening. (Orderly). Bed at 10.45.*

Thurs 6th May. Brigade route march to Coleman's Hatch, Hartfield, Whythyam [Withyham], *etc. Back at 1.30. YMCA Concert in evening.*

Fri 7th May. Company training in morning. Inspection, etc., in afternoon. YMCA evening (Farewell to General Fry). Lights out 11.00.

The following day brought some really important news which, surprisingly, appears in brackets! The presumed consequence of this news was a spot of well-deserved leave:

Sat 8th May. Cleaning hut all morning. (Selected for Expeditionary Force draft.) Medical inspection in the afternoon. Caught 7.35 to Wimbledon. Arrived home 10.30. Spoke to Cyril.

Sun 9th May. For walk in morning, and to Aunt Ellen's. Walked on Wimbledon Common in afternoon. With cousin Nellie in evening, and for walk with other girls.

Mon 10th May. To Merton Abbey with Harry [his brother] *8 o'clock. To Aunt Ellen's, and for ride with Marie* [a bike ride, presumably: this was not *Downton Abbey*]. *Saw Ethel and Lizzie and Marie in afternoon. With Dad to station, arriving Crowboro' 7.27.*

The short leave was over, and life at the camp returned to its demanding routine.

Tues 11th May. Brigade Route March 8.30 to 1 o'clock, through Groombridge, Eridge and the Cross: 12 miles. For walk [good feet at this point, obviously] *with Chantry in evening.*

Wed 12th May. Company work in the morning. To Crowboro' in evening with Wilmott Randall Shilston. [That name clearly struck Tim as worth recording in full. Or did he fail to punctuate three fellow recruits?]

Thurs 13th May, Ascension Day. Reveille 5.30. Standing by in hut and packing up all day. Concert at YMCA in evening. Sitting by fire till 12 pm.

It's impossible to decide whether after so long a day Tim then made a rare confusion between am and pm, or whether his day was not yet over. The entry that follows is therefore somewhat ambiguous.

Fri 14th May. In hut till 1 am. Then to Crowboro' Station. Caught 2.30, arriving at Ipswich 9.15. Put in billet with Leroy [unclear: could be Derry] at Mrs Richardson's.

Sat 15th May. Parade at 6.45 till 7.15. Morning Parade 9.15. Went for march to Bealings. Rifle inspection in afternoon. In town all evening. [Little and Great Bealings lie north-east of Ipswich, near Woodbridge.]

Sun 16th May. Church Parade at St John's, Ipswich. Then for walk in town with Sutton. Ditto afternoon and evening. Spoke to various girls.

Tim is now based near Ipswich, and the routine continues not unlike that which obtained in Crowborough. The following entries are examples of what Tim recorded daily.

Mon 17th May. Physical drill 6.45 to 7.15. Breakfast at 8. Parade 9.15. Platoon and Squad Drill on Golf Course till 1.30, and afternoon 3-6. With various girls in evening.

Tues 18th May. Indoors all day (rain). Lecture 11-12 St John's Hall. For walk in evening with Elsie. Roll Call 9.30.

Wed 19th May. Brigade operations till 2 o'clock. Rifle inspection in afternoon. For walk round town in evening.

Thurs 20th May. Brigade Orderly from 7.30 am to 8 pm. For walk to Ipswich in evening.

Whit. Mon 24th May. Empire Day. Roll call 10.45. Physical and Company work in morning.

Wed 26th May. Route march through Nacton and Levington from 9 am to 2 o'clock. Battalion went on night operations.

Fri 28th May. Physical 6.15 to 7.15. Draft paraded for equipment all morning. Pay in afternoon. To town in evening with Dorothy. Home at 11.30.

Sat 29th May. Draft inspected by Brigadier, etc. in the morning. To station at 4 o'clock. Then with Elsie and to pictures. Then with Dorothy.

Sun 30th May. Met Dorothy Smith and other girl (Kate) and for walk with them in the morning. With Dorothy afternoon and evening.

Mon 31st May. With Company in morning. Kit inspection by Colonel in afternoon. In town in evening, and for walk with Dorothy.

Tues 1st June. Company training in morning. Lecture, etc., afternoon. For walk in town in evening, and with Elsie Sheldrake.

Wed 2nd June. Physical lecture by Doctor 10-11. Then route march round town. To Ipswich Baths afternoon. For walk with Elsie Sheldrake night.

Thurs. 3rd June. Brigade route march 8.30 through Tuddenham and Bealing. Back at 1 o'clock. Inspection in afternoon. For walk with Dorothy Smith in evening.

Fri 4th June. Reveille 5 am. Paraded at 6.20. Left Ipswich at 8.15, arrived Liverpool Street 10.45. Marched to Waterloo 12.40, arrived Southampton 2.20. Then to rest camp and town.

Sat 5th Jun. Drawed rifles and swords morning, and kit, etc., afternoon. To Baths in evening. Then tea and for walk round town with Tuck. Spoke to girls. [A rare grammatical error; and 'swords'? That's certainly what is written in ink.]

36

Sun 6th Jun.   Breakfast 8.30. For walk to town and on pier with Scottie. Marched from Camp 2 o'clock, and left Docks at 5 pm for France, escorted by Destroyers.   In bunk at 9 pm.

Mon 7th Jun.   1915. Arrived in France 1 a.m. Boat left again 10 am and anchored out at sea until 4 pm. Then started for Rouen down river. Arrived there 10.30 pm.

Tues 8th June.   Marched off boat at 7 am, to Territorial Base Depot, Rouen. Under canvas there.

So, that's it! Tim has his feet on French soil. This is what all the training has been for. Reading his diary has revealed many details of that training, and of his leisure activities in Sussex and Suffolk. It also reveals a young man who has been able to absorb the punishing routine without either complaint or backsliding. There are no value-judgments, simply a concern to record accurately and succinctly the pattern of each day. How will he face the months ahead of him?

Now Tim is in France

Wed 9th Jun.   Inspection in morning. Left camp at 4.30 and caught train at Rouen 7.30. Half an hour's halt at Abbeville about midnight.

Thurs 10th Jun. Continuing journey through Boulogne and Calais, reaching Bailweld. Reninghelst 3.30 pm. [Possibly Bailleul and Reningelst, which is west-south-west of Ypres.] Marched to dug-outs at Scottish Woods at night.

Fri 11th Jun.   Morning inspection by Major Dickens. Resting in afternoon. Left for trenches at 8.30 pm at St Elois. Under Russell Jones (in Q2).

Sat 12th Jun.   Stand to arms at Dawn. 2 am breakfast. Sleep in daytime on and off. On Water Fatigue at 11.30 pm. To Voor Mezeele.

Sun 13th Jun.   Back in trenches at 1.30 am. Breakfast 2.30 am. Shelled heavily 7.30 to 8.30am Trench routine till 8.30 pm. Then Guard and Stand to Arms.

The last two entries slip easily by in the reading; but as one comprehends the timings and the implications behind the simple exposition, one realizes the appalling reality of trench life in 1915 near Ypres.

Mon 14th Jun.   Breakfast at 4.30 am. Digging trenches in Q3 all day. On guard at 5 pm

Tues 15th Jun.   Digging trenches from 12 midnight to 1.30 am. Breakfast at 3.30. On guard 4 am, then sleep 1 ½ hours Then writing letters, etc. Trench-digging again at 10 pm, under heavy fire.

Wed 16th Jun.   In trench again at 1.45 am. Breakfast at 3.45, then sleep for two hours. Resting all day, but trench digging again at 10.30 pm.

Thurs 17th Jun. Back in trenches 1.30 am. Breakfast at 3.15. Sleep three hours, then usual day work. Relieved at dusk by B Company.

Fri 18th Jun.   Reached Scottish Woods 1 am. Sleep till 5 am. Resting all day, and bed at 10 pm.

Sat 19th Jun.   Breakfast 9 am., then resting all day. R.E. Fatigue to R1 trench at 9.30. Reached S. Woods again at midnight.

Sun 20th Jun.   Breakfast 9 am, then resting all day. Left at 10 pm for trenches at St Elois. [St Eloois, just south of Ypres.] Occupied Q2 at 11.30 pm.

Mon 21st Jun.   Breakfast 3.30 am.   Sleep 6 am to 3.30 pm.   Usual trench duty, then extending rear trenches from 10 pm to midnight.

Tues 22nd Jun. Breakfast 3 am. Sleep 5 am to 9.30 am.   Usual trench routine. I then volunteered for Post Fatigue to Voor Mezeele 8.15 to 10 pm. Then on guard.

Wed 23rd Jun.   Breakfast 3 am. Trench guard 7.15 till 9.30 am. Enlarging communication trench 3 till 5 pm. Left for Scottish Woods at 11 pm.

Thurs 24th Jun. Reached Scottish Woods at 12.15, and slept 1.30 to 8 am. Trenching 11 am to 3 pm. For walk to Dickebusch [Dikkebus] in evening. Fatigue 9.30.

Fri 25th Jun.   To bed at 1.30 am. Digging during the day. Dug-outs flooded owing to heavy rain in evening. Fatigue 9.30 to 6 on No 2 Trench. Up all night.

Sat 26th Jun.   Sleep impossible owing to water. Breakfast 10 am. Then resting all day. To Dickebusch for lunch. 9.30 Fatigue to R1 Trench in evening.

Sun 27th Jun.   Breakfast 10 am. Resting all day. Short service at 6.30 in Woods. Fatigue to Q3 trench at 9.15. To bed at midnight.

Tues 29th Jun.   Rifle inspection 1.15 pm. Went with Davis to Dickebusch 4 to 7 pm. In Q2 trenches in evening.

Wed 30th Jun.   Standing to, 1.30 to 2.30 am. Breakfast at 3 am. Renewing trenches mid-day, and also at night.

Thurs 1st Jul.   Breakfast 3.30 am. Completing trenches in afternoon. Guard 1 till 2 am.

Fri 2nd Jul.   After guard, breakfast 3.30 am. Left for Q3 trench at 10.30. Filling sandbags till midnight.

Sat 3rd Jul.   Walking about till 2.30 am. Breakfast 4 am. Resting all day.   To Dressing Station Voor Mezele, and stayed there all night.

Sun 4th Jul.   Up at 3.30, for walk round village, and then breakfast at 8.30. Sent to Scottish Woods by the M.D. (neuralgia). Before M.D. at 4.30 with sprained foot. Resting.

Mon 5th Jul.   Rifle inspection 11.30. Resting all day, then went before the M.D. at 5 pm with sprained foot. Hanging about till midnight.

Tues 6th Jul.   Exploring Chateau 3 am to 4 am at St Eloi. On aeroplane guard 8 till 10 am and 2 till 4 pm. Fatigue in evening to R1 trench. Back at Scottish Wood 1.15 am.

Wed 7th Jul.   To bed 2 am. until 3.30 am. Then to Chateau with Davis. Breakfast at 7.30. Writing letters during the day. To Dickebusch in evening, then to Q2 on Fatigue.

Thurs 8th Jul.   Breakfast 9.30. Rifle inspection at Noon. Writing in the afternoon. To trenches at 10 pm, and relieved other QVR [Queen Victoria's Rifles]. Then on Post Fatigue.

Fri 9th Jul.   Stand to 2 till 3 am. Sleep 4 till 9 am.   Guard 11 to 12. Usual trench routine. Fatigue and Guard all night.

Sat 10th Jul.   On guard etc from 12 am. Stand to Arms from 1.50 to 4.30. Five German sap blown up at 3.30. Slight attack. Sleep 5.30 am till 1.30 pm.

Sun 11th Jul.   Digging 12 till 1.30 am.   German bombardment at 5.30.   West Kents evacuate Q1 trench, but return. Post Fatigue in evening, and to Scottish Woods.

Mon 12th Jul.   To sleep 2.30 am. Breakfast 9.30 am. Digging, etc., 3 pm to 5 pm and 6.30 to 7.30. Fatigue to Q3 at 9.30, and rebuilding trench parapet.

Tues 13th Jul.   Left Q3 at 1 am, arriving at Scottish woods an hour later. Breakfast at 10. Digging 4 pm till 6, and 7 to 7.30. Fatigue at 9.30 to Q 2 & 3.

Wed 14th Jul.   To Woods and sleep 2 to 5 am. Digging 2.30 to 5 pm. Fatigue R.E to Q1 trench in evening. (Rain)

Thurs 15th Jul. Dug-outs flooded. Sleep 2.30 to 3.30 am. Then walking about, etc., to dry. Breakfast 10 am. Wet conditions all day. On Ration Fatigue 9.30 pm to Q2.

Fri 16th Jul.   Snatches of sleep owing to wet weather. Speaking to various fellows who arrived at Woods. (Draft of 50). Dug-out very wet. (No sleep.)

Sat 17th Jul.   To Q2 11 pm. Very wet weather (little sleep). Breakfast 9 am. To Dickebusch in afternoon with Davies and Grover. Then Davies and I went to Headquarters in Voor Mezele.

Sun 18th Jul.   Guard till 1 am. Stand-to 2.10 to 3.10 am. British Bombardment 8 till 10 am. Then filling sandbags. [At this point Tim is having a spot of trouble with his pen making ink-blots, but the script is still decipherable.]

Mon 19th Jul.   Standing-to 2.30 to 3.20 am. Breakfast 4.15 am. Water Fatigue to Voor Mezeele 2.15. Filling sandbags at night.

Tues 20th Jul.   Filling sandbags till 1 am. Stand-to 2.30 to 3.20 am. Breakfast 9 am. Trench work all day. Left Q2 for Q3 trenches at night.

Wed 21st Jul.   In trenches at St Elois all day. Relieved at 10 pm by H.A.L. [possibly H.A.C. or H.A.1] *Brigade. Marched off 11 pm. Q.V.R. arrived at Oudrodorn via Dickebusch at 12 midnight.*

Thurs 22nd Jul. Arrived at Reninghelst 3 am. Breakfast at 11.30. I act as Batman to Mr Farmiloe all day. Marched from Camp at 8.45 via Boeshepe. [This last place-name is badly blotched, but is inscribed legibly on the opposite page, with an arrow indicating to what the name refers. Tim appears to have got a better nib, or better ink, and is taking pains to see that his record is as accurate as he can make it. Amazing with all that marching and lack of sleep.]

Fri 23rd Jul.   (Weather terrible). Arrived at Steenvorde at 1 pm, and billetted in a farmhouse. Woke at 10 am.   Then assisting in house and in Officers' Mess. To Steenvorde in evening. Dinner at 8.30.

Sat 24th Jul.   Breakfast 9 am.   Assisting in Farm [word indistinct] *in morning. Lunch 2 pm. To Steenvorde in afternoon. Tea 5pm. Dinner at 8.30. Had merry night.* [So Tim had what looks a 'normal' day, though one would like to know in what way the night was 'merry'. I suspect it refers to a generous supply of wine.]

Sun 25th Jul.   Breakfast 9 am. Usual work at Farm. To town in afternoon and evening. Bed at 1030.

Mon 26th Jul.   Usual work at Farm.   To Steenvorde in afternoon. Waiting at table for Dinner. Bed 10.30.

Tues 27th Jul.   Usual work at Farm. Steenvorde in afternoon. Bed 10 pm.

Wed 28th Jul.   Usual work at Farm. Steenvorde in evening. Bed at 10.30.

Tim, now with greatcoat and cane, giving a good imitation of an officer; not a good idea in the front line as officers were often targeted by snipers

Thurs 29th Jul. Usual routine of work at Farm. Battalion went for Route March and Drills. To bed at 11 pm.

Fri 30th Jul.   Usual routine of work at Farm. Preparing to depart in the afternoon. Dinner 8 pm. Bed at 11.30.

Sat 31st Jul.   Breakfast 7 am. Left Steenvorde at 8.30 am - arrived at Godwaersvorde station 10 am. Left in train at 11 am, arrived Corbie at 12. [To judge from the next entry this would be midnight, implying a lengthy train journey. Corbie is east of Amiens, near the junction of the Ancre and Somme rivers.]

Sun 1st Aug.   Left Corbie station 12.30 am, arrived at Farm La Neuville 1.15 am. To bed 4am, up at 10 am. To Corbie in afternoon. Spoke to Isabel.

Tim has arrived in the area loosely described as The Somme. What a resonance that name has! One suspects that his few days of relative normality (before his journey to an area destined to become part of legend) will soon seem just a distant dream. He has, however, (as we see from the last three words of his entry for August 1st) wasted no time in making contact with the natives.

General Sir Douglas Haig, mounted statue in Montreuil. His conduct of the coming Somme Offensive has come under detailed scrutiny by many military historians, but here, in Montreuil (where he later made his Headquarters), his statue shows every inch the patrician Commander-in-Chief. In World War II the Germans took delight in destroying this fine equestrian representation, but it has been carefully restored and now looks over a fountain in the little town's main square

A rather blurred wartime snapshot showing Haig's statue destroyed by the German invaders in WW2

CHAPTER FOUR

NOW TIM HAS REACHED THE SOMME

Monday August 2nd, 1915, was an English Bank Holiday. Timothy Elliott, of the Queen Victoria's Rifles, was not in England to enjoy it; but he could hardly have failed to notice the fact because printed in his tiny diary for that date are the words "Bank Holiday". And his entries, made in a clear, inked script, suggest that he was well-pleased with his lot at that moment:

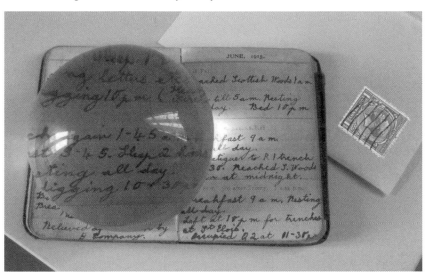

Tim's 1915 Diary, with magnifying lens, and postage-stamp to give scale

Mon 2nd Aug. Usual work at Farm. [Alas, he does not enlarge upon that word "usual".] *For walk into Corbie in afternoon with Soar. Dinner at Farm in evening at 9.30 (tres bon). Bed 11 pm.*

Tues 3rd Aug. Regiment left Corbie at 11 am and marched to Ribemont (Somme), [Ribemont is in the Somme region, but is on the Ancre.] *arriving at 2 pm. Inspection 3 pm. Then into billets at Farm.*

Wed 4th Aug. To Town etc in morning. Backing up afternoon. March from Ribemont 8 pm, arriving at Bray outskirts 12 midnight. [This march would have been eastwards, keeping just north of the Somme river, travelling in the direction of Péronne.]

Thurs 5th Aug. To bed in Farm at Bray 2 am. Up at 10 am, and to Officers Billet. Usual work in the Mess, and for a walk in town in evening.

Fri 6th Aug. Up at 8 o'clock. Usual work in Mess. Changed Billet during day to Main Road. Bed at 11 pm.

Sat 7th Aug. Up at 7.30 am. Usual Mess work, and for walk in town. Bed 11 pm.

Sun 8th Aug. Up at 7.30. Usual Mess work. Went fishing with Lieuts. Farmiloe and Caley in afternoon on the River Somme. Also for walk in town. Bed 11.30 pm. [It hasn't taken Tim long to be on good terms with two commissioned officers.]

Mon 9th Aug. Up at 7.30. Usual Mess work. Dinner 7.30. Bed at 10.30.

Tues 10th Aug. Usual Mess work. Lunch 1.30. Dinner 7.30. Bed 11 pm.

Wed 11th Aug. Usual Mess work. Fishing in afternoon with Mr Farmiloe and Mr Caley till 8 pm. Dinner, and bed at 10.30.

Thurs 12th Aug. Usual Mess work. Fishing in afternoon with Mr Farmiloe and Mr Caley till 8.30. Dinner, and bed 10.30.

One wonders whether Tim's life could possibly get better. It could !

Fri 13th Aug.　　　*Usual Mess work. In Town in afternoon, and to concert at Filles Ecole in evening.   Dinner, and bed 11 pm.*

Sat 14th Aug.　　　*Usual Mess Work. Fishing in afternoon with Mr Farmiloe. Bed 11 pm.*

Sun 15th Aug.　　　*Usual Mess work. Packing-up afternoon. Left Bray-sur-Somme at 9 pm. Bois Billon 11 pm. To sleep in dug-out 12 pm.*

Mon 16th Aug.　　　*Mess work, etc in Wood. Resting all day. To bed at 11.30.*

Tues 17th Aug.　　　*Usual Mess work. Reading and writing. Bed 11.30 pm.*

Wed 18th Aug.　　　*Usual Mess work. Packing-up in afternoon. Left Wood at 9.30 pm with Lieut Farmiloe and Company. Arrived in Reserve trenches 11 pm.*

Thurs 19th Aug.　　Assisting Lieut Farmiloe in trenches at Carnoy. [Carnoy is east of Albert on the Péronne road.] *Rat hunt in evening. Shelled by Germans 4 till 5 pm. Drew rations, and bed 10.30.* [The idyll is ended by rats and shells.]

Fri 20th Aug.　　　*Breakfast 9.30 am. Usual work. With Lieut Farmiloe in his Hut 4 till 7 pm. To bed 11.30.*

Sat 21st Aug.　　　*Breakfast at 9.30 am. Usual work. Rat hunt in evening. Bed 10.30 pm.*

Sun 22nd Aug.　　　*Breakfast 9.30 am. Usual routines. Helping Captain Renton, Lieuts Farmiloe, Eeles and Rashly* [possibly Rashby] *in evening.*

Mon 23rd Aug.　　　*Breakfast 9.30 am. Usual routine. Dinner 8.30 pm. Rat hunt 10 pm. To bed at midnight.*

Tues 24th Aug.　　　*Breakfast 9.45. Usual routine. Dinner 8.30. Rat hunt 10 pm. To bed 11 pm.*

Wed 25th Aug.　　　*Breakfast 10 am in Officers' Dug-out. Living with them all day. To bed 10.30.*

Tim's familiarity with the officers was, I suspect, unusual, and is not explained except insofar as he occasionally seemed to act as a sort of Mess-servant. In his diary he is careful always to accord them their rank, or to refer to "Mr" so-and-so, even during the occasional happy days when they went together to use the Somme for its proper purpose, fishing.

Thurs 26th Aug. Breakfast 9.30 am. In dug-out writing, etc., during day. Marched off at 11pm.

Fri 27th Aug.　　　*Arrived at Neuville Bray-sur-Somme 1 am. Had supper, and then to bed 2.30am. Breakfast 10 am, then to Bray. Writing letters evening, and bed 11.45.*

Sat 28th Aug.　　　*Rain. Walked into Bray in afternoon with Rowland.   Marched off 7.30 pm, arriving in Fire Trench 10.30.*

Sun 29th Aug.　　　*Usual routine in Fire Trench all day. Left for Carnoy to get rations at 8.30. Led party back through woods 11 pm.*

Mon 30th Aug.　　　*Raining all day. Waiting on Officers at each meal.*

Tues 31st Aug.　　　*Breakfast 10 am. Usual trench work. Went for rations in evening with Wiggins. Bed 11.45.*

Wed 1st Sep.　　　*Waiting on Officers for all meals. Went for rations with Rowland. (German Shelling.)*

Thurs 2nd Sep.Rain all day. Mud in trenches awful. Waiting on Officers at dinner 8 pm.

Fri 3rd Sep.　　　*Rain all day. Germans shelled wood in rear of dug-outs. Went for rations 9.30. Back at 11.45 pm.*

Sat 4th Sep.　　　*German attack at 8 pm, but repulsed. (2 killed) For rations 9.30. Bed midnight.*

Sun 5th Sep. Breakfast 11 am. Usual trench work, and preparing to depart. Left Carnoy at 11 pm leading the Platoon.

Mon 6th Sep. Arrived in La Neuville Bray 1.30 am. Supper, and bed 2.30. Breakfast at 11am.. Usual Mess work, and to Bray.

Tues 7th Sep. Breakfast 10 am. Usual Mess work. Lunch 2 pm. Dinner 8.30. Shooting rats, and Bed midnight.

Wed 8th Sep. Breakfast 10 am. Usual Mess work. Listened to Band in evening. Dinner 8.30pm. Bed midnight.

Thurs 9th Sep. Breakfast 10 am. To Bray in morning. Packing-up in afternoon. Left Bray 8pm, arrived Carnoy trenches 10 pm.

Fri 10th Sep. Breakfast 9 am. Usual Mess work. Reading, etc. To bed 10.30 pm.

Sat 11th Sep. Breakfast 9 am. Usual Mess Routine. Dinner 8.30 pm. Left Carnoy 10.30 pm. Arrived La Neuville Bray midnight.

Sun 12th Sep. Bed 1.30 am. Breakfast 9.30 am. To Bray etc in day. Usual Mess work. To bed 11 pm.

Mon 13th Sep. Breakfast 9 am. Mess work and to Bray during day. Packed up. Marched off at 8 pm., arriving in trenches 11 pm.

Tues 14th Sep. To bed 1 am. Usual trench work. Trenches situated to left of Carnoy in Bois Talus and district.

Wed 15th Sep. Usual Trench work. Heavy French bombardment in Arras direction, north of Q.V.R. C Company strength is 150 men.

Thurs 16th Sep. Usual Trench work. French bombardment continues North and South. C Company Q.V.R. are holding 500 yards of Trench.

Fri 17th Sep. Usual Trench work. French bombardment continues. German rifle-Battery blown up by British.

Sat 18th Sep. Usual Trench work. British shelled German lines very effectively in afternoon. Bed 11.30 pm.

Sun 19th Sep. Usual trench work. Germans shelled trench in morning. (Probably revenge for previous day.)

Mon 20th Sep. Usual trench work. French bombardment continues. (Two Companies of Q.V.R. are holding 1,300 yards of trench.)

Tues 21st Sep. Usual Trench work. Kitchener's South Wales Borderers arrive in trenches for instruction. Q.V.R. left at 10 pm for rest.

The detailed entries of the past week contain no suggestion as to how Tim acquired all this information about numbers, distances, the French, and so on. The surprising fact is that he did have these details, whether they were right or wrong, and was prepared to include them in a written record which no-one saw fit to censor. Or did everyone in authority fail to spot that his diary-keeping was going on?

Wed 22nd Sep. Arrived in Bray 12.30. To bed 2 am. Breakfast 11.30 am. For walk in evening. Dinner 8.30 pm. Bed 11.30.

Contrary to popular belief that little was done for the troops' comfort at the time, one notes that when they have left the front line 'for Rest' and arrive in a relatively safe place after midnight, the time for breakfast is adjusted accordingly, and Tim feels happy to take a walk before the meal he now confidently calls 'Dinner'.

Thurs 23rd Sep.   Breakfast 10 am. Usual work, and listened to Band in Evening. Packed up 7 pm. Left Bray 10 pm. Arrived at Billon Bois midnight.

Fri 24th Sep.   To sleep 1.30 am. (British lines shelled by German Artillery.) Held [as] *reserve in Wood for impending events.*

The phrase 'for impending events' is well-chosen, as the following understated entries demonstrate.

Sat 25th Sep.   Usual routine in Wood. (Weather rain.) 1 Company are mining under trenches towards German lines.

Sun 26th Sep.   Usual Routine. French advance 2 ½ miles on our right in Champagne district. Service at 5 pm. Our sapping continues.

Mon 27th Sep.   Felling trees etc Morning. The British advance and take village of Loos left of Arras. [Presumably Loos-en-Gohelle, halfway from Amiens to Péronne.]

Tues 28th Sep.   Felling trees etc. Visited guns of 119th Battery R.F.A. 18-pounders hidden in Wood. French Cavalry active.

Wed 29th Sep.   Usual Routine. All ground captured is held in spite of counter-attacks. British held up at Souchez.

Thurs 30th Sep.   Usual Routine in Wood. Revolver Practice Afternoon, and packing up. Also to Bronfay Ferme. Left Billon Bois 8 pm. Marched through Etinehm [sic].

Fri 1st Oct.   Arrived at Chipilly 12.30 am. Billeted in Farm. To bed 2 am. Breakfast 10.30 am. Usual Mess Work. For walk in Chipilly. [On the Somme, halfway from Amiens to Péronne.]

Sat 2nd Oct.   To Company Billet at 12 midnight. Then writing letters etc. Bed 2 am. Breakfast 10.30 am. Then to Chipilly walking round.

Sun 3rd Oct.   To bed 3 am. Breakfast 10.30 am. Tea with Madame and Jeanette, etc. in afternoon. Dinner 9 pm. Then writing letters etc. till midnight.

Mon 4th Oct.   Breakfast 9.30 am. Fishing in afternoon in the River Somme with Captain Waller, Captain Cox and Subalterns. Dinner 10 pm.

Tues 5th Oct.   Bed 1 am. Breakfast 10 am. Fishing with Mr Farmiloe at river by Café de la Marine. Had dinner in evening with Madame, etc.

Wed. 6th Oct.   Bed 1 am. Breakfast 10 am. Fishing etc during the day by Café de la Marine. Dinner at 10 pm, and jolly evening. [The last four days have shown young Tim doing what he could always do well: getting on with people of higher rank.   It was to stand him in good stead in later life.]

Thurs 7th Oct.   Bed at 1 am. To Cerisy in afternoon with Rowland and Millard. (Saw Jermain.) [Possibly "Germaine" ?] *Dinner, and bed 12 pm.*

Fri 8th Oct.   Breakfast 10 am. Packing up and left Chipilly at 5 pm., passing through Etinehm at 6 pm, and arrived in Bray at 7 pm. Unpacking etc, and bed at midnight.

Sat 9th Oct.   Engaged part of day packing up. Also for walk in Bray. Good time in evening. Bed at midnight.

Sun 10th Oct.   For walk in Bray, etc., and packing up ready for trenches. Left Bray at 5 pm, and arrived in trenches (Carnoy) at 8.45.

Mon 11th Oct.   Artillery active on both sides. Bombs thrown by K.O.Y.L.I. at intervals. [Presumably Kings Own Yorkshire Light Infantry.] *Some very effective.*

Tues 12th Oct.   Enemy shell Valley in rear of Fire Trench. Damage normal.

Wed 13th Oct.   *Enemy rather active with Rifle Grenades. Parapet damaged. Heavy French bombarding on right of our line.*

Thurs 14th Oct.   *Small shells in morning. Huns blow up three mines, and open with rapid fire at dusk. It is easily repulsed, and no damage done.*

Fri 15th Oct.   *Arrived in Bray late on previous night. To Ecole Chambers in evening with Terry and Elms to see Concert party.*

Sat 16th Oct.   *Buying various things during day. With Terry and Elms in afternoon. Dinner at 9 pm.*

Sun 17th Oct.   *Making various purchases at different places in day. With Terry in afternoon talking to [gap] also evening.*

Mon 18th Oct.   *To various places in Bray during day. To Concert at 5 pm with Terry and Elms. Then to dinner 9 pm.*

Tues 19th Oct.   *To Mill and with Mr Familoe in morning. In Bray for walk. Dinner at 9 pm and merry evening.*

Wed 20th Oct.   *Various visits in Bray. Left for Support trenches at Carnoy 5 pm.*

Thurs 21st Oct.   *In Head Quarters dug-out at Carnoy. Aerial Torpedoes used by Enemy at Night.*

Fri 22nd Oct.   *Head Quarters all day. Left for trenches in evening. Situation normal in 41 and 42 trenches.*

Sat 23rd Oct.   *To Carnoy in Morning with Rowland for Officers' rations and water. Enemy shell Valley in rear of First Line.*

Sun 24th Oct.   *To Carnoy in morning. Heavy fire both sides. Captain Waller wounded and three men killed.*

Mon 25th Oct.   *Rifle Grenades on both sides. One man wounded.*

Tues 26th Oct.   *Situation Normal.*

Wed 27th Oct.   *Weather bad. Enemy active with Rifle Grenades. Parapet and Officers' dug-out damaged.*

Thurs 28th Oct.   *Raining all day. Heavy enemy fire in evening, and one of our mines blown up.*

Fri 29th Oct.   *Heavy shelling in Morning on our Trench. Parapet blown in. Repaired later. Relieved at 8 pm, and left with Terry.*

Sat 30th Oct.   *In Bray all day. To 'Whiz Bang' Concert in Evening with Terry and boys.*

Sun 31st Oct.   *Mess work in Bray. For short walk in Afternoon. Dinner at 9 pm and merry evening.*

Mon 1st Nov.   *In Bray all day. Listening to Band, etc., and to 'Whiz-Bangs' in evening with Terry.*

Tues 2nd Oct.   *To Bray etc all day, also with Millard, etc. Dinner 9 pm.*

Wed 3rd Nov.   *In Bray all day. Listening to Band, etc. Dinner at 9 pm.*

Thurs 4th Nov.   *Packing up in morning. Left Bray at 4.30 with limber for Carnoy. Arrived at trenches 39-40-41 at 8 pm.*

Fri 5th Oct.   *Went to Carnoy in morning with Hawkins for water. Heavy bombardment to left of 40 trench.*

Sat 6th Nov.   *Heavy bombardment continues to left. Firing at Hun aeroplane in afternoon.*

Sun 7th Nov.   *Bombardment continues. Kings Own Scottish Borderers 1st trench badly damaged.*

Mon 8th Nov.   *Bombardment continues. Some of our shells fall short on our first-line trench.*

Tues 9th Nov.   *Enemy very active with small shells. (Weather bad.)*

Wed 10th Nov.   *Our artillery shell first line of enemy trenches. (Raining.) Left trenches at 7 pm with Sgt Major Sheriff for Bray.*

Thurs 11th Nov.   *In Bray doing various things.*

Fri 12th Nov.   *In Bray all day. 'Whiz-bangs' in evening with boys. Merry evening.*

Sat 13th Nov.   *In Bray generally.*

Sun 14th Nov.   *To see Hall in afternoon. Spent jolly evening.*

Mon 15th Nov.   *General business in Bray. To 'Whiz-bangs' in evening. Dinner at 9.15. Snowing.*

Tues 16th Nov.   *Preparing to leave Bray for trenches. Left at 4 pm with Limber. Arrived in trenches at 9 pm.*

Wed 17th Nov.   *Trench mortars used frequently by Huns. Very little damage.*

Thurs. 18th Nov.   *Nothing to report. Situation normal.* [It's interesting to see what has become "normality" !]

Fri 19th Nov.   *A few cases of frostbite reported. Shelling on both sides.*

Sat 20th Nov.   *Very heavy explosion in Hun's trench. Cause unknown. Talking heard in enemy trenches in evening very plainly.*

Sun 21st Nov.   *K.O.Y.L.I. opened rapid fire in afternoon. Weather very misty.*

Mon 22nd Nov.   *(62nd Regiment) Three Germans with bombs attempted to bomb listening post in trench 37. All killed and brought in.*

Tues 23rd Nov.   *Relieved previous night at 6 pm. Rode back on limber with Sergeant Major Sheriff. To C.Concert* [sic].

Wed 24th Nov.   *In Bray general business.* [Tim is getting to be quite a tease with his unspecific entries relating to the town of Bray.] *Dinner 9 pm and merry evening.*

Thurs 25th Nov.   *Bombs dropped on Bray by enemy aeroplanes. Damage slight. To Carnoy Support Line. Mines 'blown up'. Huns* [sic]

Fri 26th Nov.   *Continuous bombardment on our left. More bombs on Bray. Seven British aeroplanes go over enemy's lines.*

Sat 27th Nov.   *Bombardment continues on our left. Snow in morning and heavy frost at night.*

Sun 28th Nov.   *Water carts frozen – great inconvenience caused. Lieut Farmiloe and I left for first line trench in evening.*

Mon 29th Nov.   *Heavy firing on our left. Lieut Familoe and I left trenches in afternoon. (Raining hard) Arrived in Bray soaked.*

Tues 30th Nov.   *In Bray on general business. Out with 'Boys' in evening paying visits.*

Wed 1st Dec.   *In Bray with Lieut Farmiloe. Writing all night.*

Thurs 2nd Dec.   *Lieut Farmiloe left for England at 3.30 am. I went to bed 4.30 am. To 'Whiz-bang' Concert in evening.* [Has Tim made a rare error in putting "a.m." when "p.m." initially seems more likely? I prefer to think he is literally correct and that his "I went to bed 4.30 am" follows on from the previous "writing all night" entry.]

Fri 3rd Dec.   *In Bray on rest.*

Sat 4th Dec.   *In Bray on rest. C.Company came from trenches.*

Sun 5th Dec.   *In Bray on rest.*

Mon 6th Dec.   *In Bray generally. To Whiz bangs in evening.*

Tues 7th Dec.   *Ditto.*

Wed 8th Dec.   *Ditto.*

Thurs 9th Dec.   *In Bray generally. To 'Whiz-bangs' in evening. General and Staff present.*

Fri 10th Dec.   In Bray generally.

Sat 11th Dec.   Packing up things. Company left for trenches in evening. Lieut Farmiloe returns from leave.

Sun 12th Dec.   In Bray Morning. Left for trenches in afternoon with Lieut Farmiloe. (Trenches in awful condition – mud and water.)

Mon 13th Dec.   Seven British Aeroplanes return from Enemy lines. Artillery fire both sides. Byles wounded.

Thurs 14th Dec.   German machine gun sweeps Valley behind our trenches. Answered by British fire. R.E Officer wounded.

Wed 15th Dec.   Machine gun continues. Trenches become worse. Dug-outs continually falling in.

Thurs 16th Dec.   Dug-out falls and buries men in 'Fleeche' [sic]. Robinson killed. Left trenches in Evening and went to Supports. Carnoy.

Fri 17th Dec.   Arrived in Bray early morning with Officers, Captain Cox and Lieut Farmiloe. In Billet all day.

Sat 18th Dec.   Usual business in Bray. To Whiz-bangs in evening. (Mr Farmiloe left Company.)

Sun 19th, Mon 20th and Tues 21st Dec.   Usual business in Bray.

Wed 22nd Dec.   Packing in morning. Left for trenches in afternoon. Arrived in evening. (Acting Runner.)

Thurs 23rd Dec.   To Carnoy with report with Elms 8 am. Mine fired at Fricourt. Artillery dual [sic] both sides.

Fri 24th Dec.   To Carnoy with report. Enemy shell our support lines, etc. Overland with messages to Platoon Commanders 39-40-41 trenches.

Sat 25th Dec.   Digging etc in trench. Enemy active with rifle grenades. Shelling at intervals. (Damage slight.) [That was a really jolly Christmas day.]

Sun 26th Dec.   At 5 am led party of Duke of Wellingtons to 40 trench from Carnoy. Heavy bombardment started by British at 11 am.

Mon 27th Dec.   More sniping than usual. To Carnoy with report. British bombardment continues at Huns lines. 10 am over parapet with messages.

Tues 28th Dec.   [Tim's little diary reminds him that today is "Holy Innocents".] To Carnoy with report. British resume bombardment at 10.30 am. (Mud still deep in trenches.) Relieved in evening. Arrived Bray 8.

Wed 29th Dec.   Rest and usual Business. To Whiz-bangs in evening.

Thurs 30th Dec.   Usual work. With Rfn Cocks in Bray. Dinner 9 pm.

Fri 31st Dec.   Writing letters etc. Waiting at Head Quarters dinner evening. With orders to Sgt Major Sheriff. Then to Estaminet 11 pm.

And so ended 1915. While Tim was at the Estaminet did he, one wonders, find time to flip open the little card advertisement at the back of his tiny diary? Had he done so he would no doubt have smiled at its imitation handwriting which read:

Note   To ask my Outfitter to show me latest patterns of 'Viyella' for my next Shirts and Pyjamas.

Presumably at a later date, Tim made a quick 'ready-reference' occupying three front pages of this minute diary. Here he put some fifty 'key' dates, e.g. Left Crowboro' Sussex May 14; In trenches St Elois June 11th; Arrived at Chipilly Oct 1st.

CHAPTER FIVE

TIM'S WAR CONTINUES INTO 1916

Tim's 1916 diary is identical in format to that for 1915: Letts Diary and Notebook for MCMXVI. This year Tim begins with his name and address: *T.G.Elliott (3418) Q.V.R. C. Comp'y B.E.F. France.* He has entered his Personal Memoranda as: *Size in Boots: 7; Size in Collars 6 ⅝; Weight 11 stone.* The Addresses page has only one entry: *Miss G. Reed, The Bungalow, Wheeler Street, Hedges, Maidstone, Kent.*

His diary entries begin relatively calmly, bearing in mind that two opposing armies are trying to destroy each other: just, as it were, up the road:

Sat Jan 1st.   For walk in Bray. Resting from trenches. Rather merry evening.

'Merry', appropriately for New Year's Day, indicated (in all probability) a little alcoholic lubrication. But very quickly we are reminded of the reason for his being where he is:

Sun 2nd Jan.   Bray shelled in afternoon by Enemy. To concert in evening, and then had jolly time with the Boys.
Mon 3rd Jan.   Left for trenches beyond Carnoy. Heavy rifle fire along railway and 41 trench. Enemy active with mortars.
Tues 4th Jan.   Bray shelled. To Carnoy with report. British shell Enemy 1st trenches. Enemy reply heavily. Observing shots and reporting. On parapet with Capt. Woolly V.C.

It's easy to see why Tim should proudly make reference to Captain G.H. Woolley (not Woolly), the first Territorial Army officer to be awarded the Victoria Cross. Woolley was the son of a London curate. Destined eventually for the Church, he gained a commission in the 9th (County of London), Battalion of Queen Victoria's Rifles - the very regiment in which Tim had enlisted. On April 17th 1915 (on which date Tim, as part of his training in Sussex, was firing some rounds at Fairlight, near Hastings) the British had captured Hill 60, a low rise south of Ypres. As the Germans counter-attacked, Second Lieutenant Woolley's Company was sent to take additional ammunition to the British defenders. Casualties were very heavy, but Woolley refused orders to withdraw until his Company was relieved. Relief eventually came, but only one-tenth of the 150-strong contingent arrived back. For conspicuous gallantry, Woolley was award the V.C. The award citation stated that he was the only officer on the hill at the time, and that he and his men resisted all attacks, despite heavy shelling, bombing and machine-gunfire. In the eight or so months since the event, news of the action and of Woolley's award would certainly have reached Tim and the other QVR Riflemen in the Somme region; so it is no surprise to find him taking some pride in 'observing and reporting' alongside so brave a gentleman. To be 'on the parapet' under fire, however, might have truncated the diaries somewhat ! But both Tim and his illustrious companion survived the day. Regrettably Tim does not say how Woolley came to be there in early January. Probably he did not know when he wrote the entry whether the eminent Captain (who had been promoted without need of the intervening rank of 1st Lieutenant) was to be a permanent fixture or was simply 'passing through'.

Wed 5th Jan.   To Carnoy with report. Aeroplanes very active. Artillery rather quiet. With messages on Parapet. Lewis guns very active. [The Lewis machine-gun, with its characteristic rotary ammunition-feed, was a fine, easily carried weapon. Coincidentally, my own father was a Sergeant Lewis Gun Instructor during the immediate post-war occupation of Germany.]

Thurs 6th Jan.   To Carnoy with report. With messages to Platoons re. Patrols in front, etc. Trenches very bad.

Fri 7th Jan.   To Carnoy with report with Rifleman Sheppard. Artillery very active on Carnoy, etc. With messages to 39 – 40 – 41 T. [= trenches]

Sat 8th Jan.   To Carnoy with report with Rfn Elms. Numbering trenches, etc. Relieved evening. Heavy bombardment over Fricourt.

Sun 9th Jan.   Moved to another billet in Bray. Heavy artillery fire on our left front.

Mon 10th Jan.   Attending to Lieut Mackay at his billet in Rue D'Albert. To Whiz-bangs evening. Artillery fire continues on our left.

Tues 11th Jan.   Packing up in morning. Left Bray 3 pm, arrived in Sailly-Laurette at 7 pm via Corbie Road. Slept in billet with Lieut Mackay. [Jan 11th was Tim's 21st birthday, though he makes no reference to the fact.]

Wed 12th Jan.   Various business in Sailly-Laurette. With Rfn Foster in evening to farm and téte a téte [sic] *with Aundriette.*

Thurs 13th Jan.   In Billet Morning. Listening to the Divisional Band in the Square in afternoon. Then Dinner.

Fri 14th Jan.   Usual work morning. With Riflemen Rolland, Elms and Millard afternoon to Football Match at Sailly-la-Sec. B.V.G. Company Draw 1 – 1

Sat 15th Jan.   Work and writing letters. Listening to Band in Square. Then with Foster. Large Dinner in evening.

Sun 16th Jan.   Church Parade in Morning. To Chipilly with Boys in afternoon to see Madame Cailleux. Also had talk and café with Jermain.

Mon 17th Jan.   Usual business and writing letters during day. With Madame and Monsieur Lefèvre. (My Billet)

Tues 18th Jan.   Listening to Band, etc, also writing letters in my billet.

Wed 19th Jan.   To see Football match in Afternoon. C Company 2, B Company 0. Had party in Evening to celebrate Millard's Birthday. [This entry makes it rather surprising that no-one, as far as we can read, thought to celebrate Tim's 21st a few days earlier.]

Thurs 20th Jan.   In Billets all day, writing letters, etc.

Fri 21st Jan.   In Billets, etc. Listening to band in afternoon.

Sat 22nd Jan.   Parade at 9.45. Kit inspection by Col. Dickens, and Platoon drill. Watching Boxing in afternoon.

Sun 23rd Jan.   Packing up Morning. Left Sailly-Laurette 2 pm, by bus with Lieut Mackay. Arrived at Montigny 4 pm via Corbie. Work in Chateau.

Mon 24th Jan.   Reveille 6 am. Work in H.Q. Grenade School. To Béhencourt in morning. With Warwick.

Tues 25th Jan.   Work in Chateau and to Café. For walk to [blank: presumably because he intended to check the place-name later, but omitted to do so]. *In a cottage at Béhencourt afternoon. In evening to Café and to Chateau.*

Wed 26th Jan.   Work in Chateau. To Café [blank]. *In Cottage at Béhencourt Afternoon. To Café at Montigny in Evening.*

Thurs 27th Jan.　　For walk in morning to Beaucourt-sur-L'Hallue, and afternoon to Esbart and Bavelincourt, and Café at Béhencourt.

Fri 28th Jan.　　In Montigny generally and Café etc.

Sat 29th Jan.　　Work in Chateau Morning. With Royal Scot to Beaucourt and Béhencourt and in various Cafés etc. all afternoon and Evening.

Sun 30th Jan.　　To Béhencourt in Morning. Listening to Band in Afternoon. To Cottage with Boys, and Concert at Chateau.

Mon 31st Jan.　　Work at Chateau. Then with Royal Scot for walk to: St Gratian, Querri, Pont-Noyelle, Frechencourt and Concert. Tea at Cottage Montigny.

Tues 1st Feb.　　Parade 10 am, then for walk with Royal Scot to Mollien au Bois, Villers Bocage and Raineville Returned to Montigny 7 pm. [Tim's several references to 'Royal Scot' were at first taken to refer to an unknown soldier of a Scottish regiment. By now, however, Tim would surely have been using his name; so I infer that maybe some mother surnamed Scot decided to christen her little babe 'Royal'.]

Wed 2nd Feb.　　To Béhencourt Morning. On Ambulance Car in afternoon to Frechencourt, and isolated in Cottage.

Thurs 3rd Feb.　　For walk with contacts in morning to Béhencourt. In house all day.

Fri 4th Feb.　　In house all day.

Sat 5th Feb.　　For walk with Contacts in morning to Béhencourt. In house all day. [The last four days have an air of mystery. Was Tim suspected of carrying a nasty illness which took him to an isolated hospital, from which only other 'contacts' were allowed to walk with him?]

Sun 6th Feb.　　In Cottage opposite with Madame and Denise. Then marched with R.A.M.C. to Allonville. [Just N.E. of Amiens.] For walk with Sgts. K.O.S.B. and R.W K. Evening. [The mystery continues unexplained.]

Mon 7th Feb.　　Under canvas at Allonville. Watching aeroplanes at aerodrome. In tents all day.

Tues 8th Feb.　　For walk in morning. In tents all day.

Wed 9th Feb.　　To Coisy in morning for walk. Watched in afternoon: R.A.M.C. 0, D.C.L.I. 2. In tents after.

Thurs 10th Feb.　　To Petit Camon in the morning. In tents all day.

Fri 11th Feb.　　For walk round village in morning (raining). In tents all day.

Sat 12th Feb.　　To Petit Camon in morning. In tents all day.

Sun 13th Feb.　　Walk round village. In tents all day.

Mon 14th Feb.　　Carried Lieut Cave's body, 4 Squad Royal Flying Corps, to ambulance. Marched to Poulainville. [Just north of Amiens. A small 'x' is inserted after the word 'ambulance', but no explanation is given.]

Tues 15th Feb.　　For walk in morning. In tents all day.

Wed 16th Feb.　　Left Poulainville in morning. Marched via Amiens. Lunched at Dreuil-s-Ancre, then via Picquigny to Soues [?] (Terrific hailstorm and rain). Billeted in Cottage.

Thurs 17th Feb.　　For walk to La Mesge in morning. In Cottage all day.

Fri 18th Feb.　　For walk with Sgt Gibson, Kings Own Scottish Borderers, to Crouy. (Raining hard). In Cottage all evening.

Sat 19th Feb.　　To Hangest-s-Somme in morning via Beachcourt [sic]. Watching football afternoon R.A.M.C. With a Warwick in evening to Reincourt.

Sun 20th Feb.　　Left Soues 12 noon. Then in Café at Hangest. Caught 3.55 train to Longpré-s-l-Somme. Then by bus to Citerne, and walked to Fresne 8 pm.

Mon 21st Feb.   Rejoined Regiment at Fresne. For walk with Cocks and Crick to Oisemont in afternoon. In Cottage etc. all evening.

Tues 22nd Feb.   In Fresne generally all day.

Wed 23rd Feb.   In Cottage with Madame. Also with George to his Billet.

Fri 24th Feb.   In Cottage and Fresne - heavy snow storm.

Fri 25th Feb.   Various duties. Heavy snow storm. Dinner in evening with Madame and Monsieur, and Musical Evening at Mess.

Sat 26th Feb.   Snow continues. Various duties. Dinner with Madame and Monsieur at my Billet.

Sun 27th Feb.   Moved from Fresne 9 am via Huppy. Lunch at Liercourt and Pont-Remy. Via Franciéres to Ailly-le-Haut Clocher. (Delayed with snow) 8 pm.

Mon 28th Feb.   For walk in Ailly-le-haut-Clocher. Various duties. Ecriere etc dans le maison de Bellard Dubourguier. [Tim tries out a little (not very accurate) French.]

Tues 29th Feb.   In the town etc, and seeing things in general.

Wed 1st Mar.   In town during day. Visited Church etc. Also in House with Monsieur and Madame Bellard Dubourguier.

Thurs 2nd Mar.   In Town and various houses during the day. Spoke to Ernescille Dulin.

Fri 3rd Mar.   In Town generally.

Sat 4th Mar.   In Town and Billet generally.

Sun 5th Mar.   Watched Rugby Match in Afternoon.   Q.V.R. v. 1st London Regiment. Q.V.R. won 6-5.

Mon 6th Mar.   In Billet all day.

Tues 7th Mar.   For walk with Elms and Reid in afternoon to Bussus. Had café etc, also beaucoup liqueurs evening.

Wed 8th Mar.   In Billet all day.

Thurs 9th Mar.   With Fernande Morning and Afternoon in house. Writing letters, etc in evening. Bed 11.30.

Fri 10th Mar.   Reveille 6.30 am.   With Fernande in Cottage all morning.   Billet all afternoon. Met W. Divall 12th London. T. [sic]

Sat 11th Mar.   In Ailly-le-Haut generally. Watched Football afternoon Q.V.R. v Rangers (Lost 3-0.) Making preparations for departure in Evening.

Sun 12th Mar.   Left Ailly-le-Haut-Clocher 8.30 am, and marched via Bernaville to Fienvillers. Arrived 3 pm.

Mon 13th Mar.   In various Farms etc during the day at Fienvillers. With Elms and George in Evening. Meals with Madame. Fire in evening.

Tues 14th Mar.   With Aundréa etc in Farm morning. With Elms for walk to Condas in Afternoon. Mr Farmiloe arrived evening.

Wed 15th Mar.   Left Fienvillers 9 am. Arrived Doullens 1 pm. To Station in afternoon. With Elms and Burley in Cafés Evening.

Thurs 16th Mar.   Left Doullens [north of Amiens] *at 9.30 am. Marched through various Villages and arrived at Houvin* [S.S.E. of St Pol; E.N.E. of Frévent] *3.30 pm. To Café in evening.*

Fri 17th Mar.   Various 'business' in Houvin. To Café with Elms and Burley. Writing letters.

Sun 19th Mar.   In Houvin – H. Generally. Writing letters, etc. In Café in Evening.

Mon 20th Mar.   Usual work. With Cocks in Morning to Magnicourt. To Café etc in Evening. Dinner 9.30 pm.

Tues 21st Mar. Usual business in Houvin. Inspection of Billets by Brigadier Coke. To Café in evening.

Wed 22nd Mar.   In Houvin generally. To Cafés etc and writing letters.

23rd and 24th Mar.   Ditto

Sat 25th Mar.   In Village generally. To Café in evening with Elms.

26th to 30th March. In Village generally.

Fri 31st Mar.   Left Houvin 6 pm, arrived at Frévent 7.30 pm. Meal at Café and slept at Rest Hut in Frévent.

Sat 1st Apl.   Reveille 4.30 am. Breakfast 5.55. Caught train 6.30 am. Route: Doullens 8 am; Longpré [W.N.W. of Amiens] *at 10; Amiens 12 (Lunch); Rouen 6 pm; Le Havre 10 pm. On H.M. 'Viper' 11 pm.*

Sun 2nd Apl.   Boat reached Southampton 8 am. Train to Waterloo 10.20; Home at Noon. With Violet Chennel, Dad, Annie etc rest of day.

One is impressed, reading the above entries, by the efficiency of the railways and the ship which took Tim home for a period of Leave. How fortunate he recorded places and times.

Mon 3rd Apl.   Visited Firm and various people in Wimbledon during day. To Theatre in evening with Dad. What Happened to Jones. *Saw Mary, Ida and various others.*

Tues 4th Apl.   Visited Audrey Butter and Cousins in morning. Lunched with Cyril and caught 2.44 to Maidstone 4.50.   Home and 'Cinema' with Gwen and Mrs Reed.

Wed 5th Apl.   In Maidstone with Gwen and for walk on Boxley Quarries. To Music Hall with Gwen and Mrs Reed.

Thurs 6th Apl.   To Business with Gwen. Caught 9.30 to Victoria 11.30. Home at noon. Visiting afternoon. To Party in evening with friends at Aunt Ellen's.

Fri 7th Apl.   Visited Mr Jagger and others. Tea with Mrs Bartlett. Saw Mr Bowman 7 pm. Caught 8 pm to Sutton. Evening with Mrs Truelove.

Sat 8th Apl.   Caught 6.45 to Merton Park and 10.45 to Maidstone. With Gwen all day. Caught 9.45 to Victoria.

Sun 9th Apl.   Saw Audrey, Marie and others. With dad and others to Waterloo. Caught 4.30 to Southampton. Boat Archangel *left docks 7.30 pm. (Smooth passage on Channel)*

Mon10th Apl.   Arrived Le Havre 2 am. Then on train to Rouen, Amiens, Longpré and Doullens. Reached Frévent [north of Doullens] *9.30. Slept there in 'Rest Hut'.*

Tues 11th Apl.   Breakfast at Café 8 pm. Reached Houvin-H by 'lorry' at 11 am. Usual business.

Wed 12th Apl.   Generally in Houvin-Houvigny .

Thurs 13th Apl.   Parade 3 pm. Extension order Drill, etc. Usual work.

Fri 14th Apl.   To Frévent in morning (Lunch there). Usual work.

Sat 15th Apl.   Usual work. To Brasserie in evening with Crick and Elms.

Sun 16th Apl.   To Frévent with Crick and Elms. Had tea, etc in Café. To Cinema in evening. Then to Estaminet. Back at 8.30.

Mon 17th Apl.   Left Brigade Headquarters at 10 am by bus, arrived at Noyelle-Velle 11.30. In Hut with Lieut Farmiloe.

Tues 18th Apl.   Trench Howitzer Course commenced. To Noyelle-Velle during day. Slept in French Hut.

Wed 19th Apl.   To Avesnes during day. Also again in evening   and went to Cinema (Raining hard.)

Thurs 20th Apl.   To Avesnes-Le-Comte in morning. To Noyelle-V evening, and then to Hut.

Fri 21st Apl.   *Left Noyelle-Velle at 11 am by bus. Arrived Houvin-Houvigny 12. To Café etc evening.*
Sat 22nd Apl.   *In Houvin and Café etc.*
Sun 23rd Apl.   *Ditto. For walk with Elms in evening.*
Mon 24th Apl.   *Houvin.*
Tues 25th Apl.   *Ditto.*
Wed 26th Apl.   *C. Company Sports in afternoon. Tea etc on Field. Brasserie evening.*
Thurs 27th Apl.   *Houvin-Houvigny.*
Fri 28th Apl.   *Ditto. (General Townshend surrenders at Kut.)*

That entry for April 28th is remarkable. It appears to be written with the same pen, in the same hand and at the same time as the word 'Ditto', yet the usual date given for Townshend's surrender is a day later. How did that news reach a Rifleman so very swiftly, even allowing for his easy relations with a Lieutenant?

Major- General Charles Vere Ferrers Townshend (1861-1924) was descended from a Field Marshal and himself went to Sandhurst. As early as 1884 he served on the expedition to the Sudan; and by 1911 he was a Major-General. He commanded the Sixth Indian Division when it was sent to Mesopotamia in 1915. Ordered to advance up the Tigris and capture Baghdad, he took Amara on Jun 3rd 1915. By 28th Sep his troops had taken Kut. Against Townshend's advice, he was instructed to proceed to Baghdad. Continuing to follow the Tigris, he reached Ctesiphon (25 miles from Baghdad) where his advance was halted by a large Ottoman force commanded by a German Field Marshal, Baron von der Goltz. Having lost some third of his men, Townshend returned to Kut on December 3rd, pursued by the Ottomans, who laid siege to the town. A message reached Townshend's superior, General Nixon, stating that the defenders of Kut had only a month's supplies; but in the event it was not until April 1916 that supplies were exhausted. Several relief expeditions were all defeated by Goltz's forces, and Kut was surrendered on April 29th.

Townshend was well treated by his captors, living on a comfortable island near Istanbul, and given the use of a Turkish Navy yacht. His defence of Kut (though unsuccessful) was rewarded by the award of a K.C.B. After the war, he was for a time Member of Parliament for The Wrekin (1920-1922). When, however, it was learnt that more than half his gallant troops had died in Turkish captivity while he had lived in comfort, his stock fell and he was blamed for the failures at Kut and Ctesiphon. He died in relative penury in 1924.

Sun 30th Apl.   *In Houvin Houvigneul. To Café evening.*
Mon May 1st.   *Regiment left Houvin-H 9.30 am. Packing morning. Left Houvin-H 3 pm by bus,* [travelled east] *arriving at Givenchy-le-Noble 4 pm.* [Quite why Tim had such preferential treatment is not, at this stage, made clear.]
Tues May 2nd.   *Living at Chateau. Parades 9.40 and 2.15. On course at 56th Divisional School of Instruction.*
Wed 3rd May.   *Parades at Chateau 9.30 and 2.15. Then to Avesnes le Comte with Berry. To B.E.F.C. and to Cinema in Evening.*
Thurs 4th May.   *Parades 9.30 and 2.15. To Avesnes-le-Comte at 4 pm. To B.E.F.C. for tea. Then to Cinema in Evening.*
Fri 5th May.   *Parades at 9.30 and 2.30. To Givenchy at Cafés etc in Evening.*
Sat 6th May.   *Parades at 9.30 and 2.30. To Ambrines in Afternoon with Cheshire. To different Cafés etc in Givenchy in Evening.*

Sun 7th May.   *Parades 9.30 and 2.30. To Lignereul with Cheshire in afternoon. Then on to Grand Rullecourt via Blavecourt. Back at 9 pm.*

Mon 8th May.   *Parades 9.30 and 2.30. For walk in afternoon to Manin, also in evening to Epicerie.*

Tues 9th May.   *Parades 9.30 and 2.15. To Manin in evening in Epicerie and Café. (Raining all day.)*

Wed 10th May.   *Parades 9.30 and 2.15. To Manin with Cheshire in evening in Epicerie.*

Thurs 11th May.   *Parades as usual. To Avesnes le Conte with 'Queen's Westminster'. Went to Cinema.*

Fri 12th May.   *Parades 9.30 and 2.15. Supper in Givenchy.*

Sat 13th May.   *Parades as usual. To Lignereuil in evening.*

Sun 14th May.   *Parades as usual. To Grand Rullecourt via Lignereuil and Bavlincourt with 'Cheshires',*

Mon 15th May.   *Parades 9.30 and 2.15. To Manin in Epicerie.*

Tues 16th May.   *Parades as usual. To Avesnes le Conte via Lignereuil and Wood de Robermont with Q.W.R., and to cinema.*

Wed 17th May.   *Parades as usual. To Manin in evening and in Epicerie. Back at Chateau 9.30.*

Thurs 18th May. Parades as usual. To Avesnes via Bois Robermont and to Beaufort in evening. At Chateau 9.30. [Tim now has the French 'Bois' in his vocabulary: See May 16th for comparison.]

Fri 19th May.   *Parades as usual. To Avesnes le Conte, and in cinema.*

Sat 20th May.   *Parade 9.30. In Avesnes and Beaufort in evening. Home via Wood.*

Sun 21st May.   *Parades as usual.*

Mon 22nd May.   *Parades as usual. Givenchy le Noble.*

Tues 23rd May.   *Packing up. Left Chateau on bus 4.30. Halt at Gaudiampré. Arrived Sailly au Bois 8 pm. [Midway between Doullens and Bapaume.]*

Wed 24th May.   *Sailly 2 ½ Kilometres from Trenches. Left at dusk (8.30), arrived Hebuterne (600 yards from Trenches). Shelling at intervals.*

Thurs 25th May. In reserve at Hebuterne . Left with Lieut Farmiloe 8.30 pm. On Ambulance car to Sailly, arrived at Bayencourt 11 pm.

Fri 26th May.   *To bed at 4 am. Went to Sailly. Heavily shelled: 3 killed and 30 injured. Left for Hebuterne with Fleetwood.*

Sat 27th May.   *Heavy shelling by Huns. In reserve at Hebuterne. Very much aeroplane action.*

Sun 28th May.   *Moved to Support line in Hebuterne. Very heavy Bombardment by Enemy 10.30 pm till midnight. Heavy casualties.*

Recently Tim seems to have rather enjoyed exploring French villages, but Hebuterne is a far less healthy spot in which to find oneself. Yet his diary entries remain factual, and very much in the same tone as before.

Mon 29th May.   *Sleep at 3 am. Heavy shelling all day at intervals on both sides. Casualties.*

Tues 30th May.   *In trenches all day (Y50). On guard from 8.15 pm till 3.15 am [sic]. Patrol over parapet to Sherwood Foresters 11pm and 1 am.*

Wed 31st May.   *On guard in trench Y50, and patrol to S.F. at 11pm and 1 am Heavy shelling during night. Heavy losses.*

Thurs 1st Jun.   Relieved at 4 pm and returned to Hebuterne in Support. Shelling on both sides continues.

Fri 2nd Jun.   Shelling continues on both sides during day.   9.30 pm commenced digging new fire trench 300 yards in advance of old.

Sat 3rd Jun.   Enemy opened on us with shrapnel and shells at 1 am. Left new trench at 1.30. Laying cable in C trench in afternoon. Heavily Shelled.

Sun 4th Jun.   Our artillery opened heavy bombardment on Enemy at midnight, and shelled till 2.30 am. Effective.

Mon 5th Jun.   To Sailly au Bois with Rfn Tidey in afternoon; returned at 4 pm. Artillery less active. Acting for Lieut Fielding.

Tues 6th Jun.   In Hebuterne all day. Artillery quiet.

Wed 7th Jun.   Ditto

Thurs 8th Jun.   French aeroplane brought down.   Relieved by London Scottish.   Left Hebuterne 12.45, under shrapnel fire. Marched to Alloy via Pas [?] *(20 kilos)*

Fri 9th Jun.   In Alloy on rest. Living in canvas hut. (Rain). In Cottage with French people for café [= coffee] in evening.

Sat 10th Jun.   Ditto. Also with Elms, Neale and Terry.

Sun 11th and Mon 12th.   In Alloy.

Tues 13th Jun.   Left Alloy at 6 pm.   Marched via Pas [?], Enu and Souastre, arrived Hebuterne at midnight.

Wed 14th Jun.   In support at Hebuterne. Occasional shelling.

Thurs 15th Jun.   British shell Hun line with heavy guns at intervals all day. (Daylight-saving commences in Army.)

Fri 16th Jun.   Brith [sic] *continue heavy shelling on Hun line. Left at 3 pm for Sailly, arrrived at Hebuterne 10 pm.* [This entry doesn't seem to square with the entries for the 13th and 14th.]

Sat 17th Jun.   Shelling on both sides. Huns very active with trench mortars.   Great aeroplane movement by Briitish and French.

Sun 18th Jun.   Usual activity both sides. Huns use Minenverfers. A large number of shells on Hebuterne.

Mon 19th Jun.   Usual activity.

Tues 20th Jun.   Hebuterne shelled. Usual activity.

Wed 21st Jun.   Through first line trenches with Terry. Enemy shell with high explosives. Left Hebuterne 4.30 pm. Arrived Halloy.* [Could that be the correct spelling of previously-mentioned Alloy?]

Thurs 22nd Jun.   Resting in Halloy. Usual business. Under canvas.

Fri 23rd Jun.   Ditto. British commence bombardment.

With remarkable prescience Tim speaks of the British *commencing* a bombardment. Does he sense, accurately, that *this* particular bombardment is the prelude to something big? His simple accuracy in choice of words no doubt echoed the reasoning of the Germans, who soon realized that this particularly prolonged bombardment should be seen as a warning to prepare a strong defence. Their preparations would, in a week, reap a dreadful harvest of British and French casualties.

CHAPTER SIX

THE FIRST BATTLE OF THE SOMME

Once the British army was committed to a major offensive intended to over-run the strongly fortified German forces, a very simple plan was instigated as a sort of hors d'oeuvres to the main course. The enemy would be pulverized by a prolonged artillery barrage which would render them incapable of resistance. That was the plan; and Tim observed it in action as the shells whistled over his head. The sheer quantity of explosives delivered along the fourteen-mile British front would, it was assumed, eliminate the defences: the barbed wire, the trenches and the dugouts.

And although many of the million-plus shells were duds, and others did little damage as they landed in soft mud, there was confidence that the carefully-planned sequence of events would carry the day (or, to be more accurate, 'days'). On June 24th 1916 mainly shrapnel-shells ensured that the maximum discomfort and injury was caused to any German soldier in an exposed position. The following day the type of shell was predominantly high-explosive, fired from howitzers, aimed at destroying the fortifications themselves and maximising the terror occasioned to the defenders. Gas shells added to the permutations available in order to cause maximum death, injury and terror.

Occasionally the shelling would stop, in order that probing raids could be made across No Man's Land. These raids were intended to report on the damage done to the fortifications, and to capture a few prisoners for interrogation. In the churned-up landscape around the German lines, these reconnaisances were rather less informative than might have been hoped. Aerial observation by Royal Flying Corps planes from Vert-Galant, however, reported huge explosions from German ammunition-dumps at Pozières, Longueval, Mametz Wood and Montauban, all presumed to be caused by accurate bombardment. So some auspices were judged positive, even though attempts to secure aerial photographs of the effects of the shelling on German lines were less successful. Surprisingly both sides were able to call on many locally-sited aircraft which could harass ground troops and positions, or undertake observation missions. Trenchard, later to be regarded as the real father of the Royal Air Force, initially had 185 machines, the Germans rather fewer, probably around 130.

Tim knew that an attack seemed imminent, and his entries were succinct and to the point:

1916

Sat 24th June   British bombardment intensifies.
Sun 25th June   British bombardment continues.
Mon 26th June   Concert in evening. British bombard heavily.

And in the midst of all this build-up, he recorded a change of position:

Tues 27th June   Bombardment continues. Left Halloy and arrived at St Amand. [East of Doullens; N.W. of Hebuterne.]
Wed 28th June   Preparations made for attack, but afterwards cancelled. In St Amand.

This cancellation of the actual infantry onslaught was caused by a combination of heavy rainfall during June 28th and the fact that the ability of the German defenders to respond to the small probing raids brought a growing realization that even the mighty artillery activity had, perhaps, been less than 100 percent effective.

Thurs 29th June   Viewed the 9.2 Howitzer heavy guns. Standing by ready to move off.
Fri 30th June   Preparations for attack. Q.V.R.s left St Amand practically at full strength.
Waiting in trenches. Shelling heavy.

Although Tim could not have known the precise plan of attack, he certainly would have observed that nearly all his immediate comrades were now waiting in their trenches . He would realize that 'something' was imminent; and he knew that their preparations implied that they were simply waiting for the order to go 'over the top'. Meanwhile the final decision was being taken to commit twenty-six British divisions (and, incidentally, fourteen French) to over-run the German lines to a depth of some two kilometres on day one. Some comfort was taken from the knowledge that only six German divisions were facing the British, and it was assumed that they were no longer capable of putting up any serious resistance.

What is not generally appreciated today (except by those who have served in the infantry) is the fact that the 'charge' could not possibly imply that young, fit men would run like athletes towards the (presumably obliterated) German defences, for the simple reason that most of the British infantry carried about 70 lbs of equipment. The rifle and bayonet were only part of it. There were also between 100 and 200 rounds of ammunition, a steel helmet, and the wherewithal to survive after a successful advance: food- packs, filled water bottles, and so on. Many even carried picks and shovels, essential for repairing any trenches captured, and changing the direction they faced. For most of the participants, the 'charge' was quite a difficult and slow-moving affair.

Tim's simple report of the day's work (written, presumably, when he returned to the trench from which he had scrambled) describes his experience that day in very few words:

Sat 1st July   Charged at 7.30 am. Took three German lines, but Retired in afternoon,
or rather the few of us who were left.

With his companions he was among the few who actually went a long way towards achieving their objectives. But was ever so momentous a date in history given such a movingly simple immediate written description as 'Retired in afternoon, or rather the few of us who were left'? On that day, British losses were beyond comprehension, as the Germans, alerted to the attack by the cessation of the mighty bombardment, mowed down the advancing troops as a reaper might scythe a field of corn. British and French artillery had used 3,000 guns to deliver over 1½ million shells. In addition, mines had been fired in tunnels excavated underneath German positions. It was assumed that this 'preparation' would ensure that the infantry assault would be virtually unopposed. In the event, the Germans had taken shelter in their carefully-constructed concrete bunkers, and had judged precisely the right time to emerge and man their machine-guns. The attack was a disaster. The giant craters caused by the explosions under the German trenches (which had been remarkably successful in killing, injuring or vapourizing many defenders) proved to be hazards in which Germans and British later died side-by-side. The British suffered 58,000 casualties on that first day, of whom nearly 20,000 were killed.

Tim took part in the 'charge'; and (in his own words) was 'one of the few who were left'. His entry for the following day shows how swiftly a tide can turn:

Sun 2nd July   Huns Shelled us heavily in Morning. Truce in afternoon for an hour. Left our battered line and arrived at Bayencourt. [I can find no formal reference to this hour's truce on July 2nd. Who called it? Who agreed to it? Was it intended for burial of the dead? Or for the recovery of any remaining living injured? Tim's short reference does not make any assessment of the reasons for this cessation of 'activity', nor of the uses to which the truce was put. It has been stated, however, by A.J.Coates in his book *The Ethics of War* that numbers of German machine-gunners were so appalled by the extent of the carnage their work had caused among the attacking British and French troops that they could not bring themselves to shoot the retiring remnants in the back. Could this chivalry have led to the negotiation of a brief local truce, unsupported by authority from the higher echelons of command?]

Mon 3rd July   Congratulations by General - . [For once Tim did not, apparently, know who was congratulating him!] *Bayencourt shelled.   Left there at 5 pm.   Arrived at St Amand 6.30.*

Tues 4th Jul   Resting in St Amand. Congratulations by Corps Commander.

Wed 5th Jul   In St Amand.

Thurs 6th Jul   Left for trenches, just on outskirts of Fonquevillers in Evening. (Rain. Our usual luck.)

Fri 7th Jul   Trenches all day.   Left at 11.30 pm with Mr Farmiloe. Arrived at St Amand. [Mr Farmiloe had, it seems, also survived the first day's slaughter.]

Sat 8th Jul   With our transport all day.

Sun 9th Jul   Left at 6 pm. Caught bus at Souastre and train at Doullens to Frévent. Four hours in Frévent, then train to Auxi-le-Chateau. [N.E. of Abbeville, WNW of Doullens.]

Mon 10th Jul   Living at No. 54 Rue d'Hesdin. Parade at 9 am. (Course of training.) 3rd Army School of Instruction.

Tues 11th Jul   Breakfast 7 am. In Auxi-le-Chateau with Foster.

Wed 12th Jul   Parade at 9.40. Practised Charge with Indian Cavalry. Concert in Evening.

Thurs 13th Jul   Extended order attack followed by 'Charge'.

Fri 14th Jul   In Auxi-le-Chateau all day.

Sat 15th Jul   Caught 3 pm train, arrived Abbeville 4.30. Slept at Hotel de Lampe Rouge. (Had glorious time. Have written enough.) [Imagination runs riot !]

Sun 16th Jul   Walk in Abbeville and caught 1 pm train to Auxi-le-Chateau. For walk in evening.

Mon 17th Jul   Usual routine in Auxi-le-C.

Tues 18th Jul   Ditto. Band in attendance.

Wed 19th Jul   Working on trenches in morning. Concert in evening at Hotel de Ville.

Thurs 20th Jul   In Aixi-le-Chateau. For walks with Wilson and Foster.

Fri 21st Jul   Ditto.

Sat 22nd Jul   Parade 10 am for attack [practice, presumably]

Sun 23rd Jul   In Auxi-le-Chateau. With Wilson and Foster.

Mon 24th Jul   Parade 9.30, for Attack. In Auxi for evening.

Tues 25th Jul   Parade 10 am. Attack and Charge. In Ville all evening with Boys.

Wed 26th Jul   Various business in Ville during day. Concert at Marie [Mairie?] *in evening. Spoke to......*[illegible]

Thurs 27th Jul   Usual parades in Auxi during day. Listening to Band. In Café Beaudoux. Evening with Georgette and Jeanne.

Fri 28th Jul   *Usual parades. Listening to Band. In Estaminet evening with usual people.*

Sat 29th Jul   *Train to Abbeville at 3 pm. For walk in town etc: and in various Restaurants. Passed night at A.S.C. Camp X. (Rather cold.)* [This entry, and especially the 'X', is not explained. Was it simply no. 10 Army Service Corps Camp?]

Sun 30th Jul   *In Abbeville, etc, all morning. X. Caught 1 pm to Auxi-le-Chateau. To Church service at Marie* [Mairie?] *6.30. Spoke to Georgette, etc.*

Mon 31st Jul   *Orderly Room 9-10 am with L/c Wilson (London Scottish). In Town in evening.*

Tues 1st Aug   [For several pages the ink is very much fainter.] *Usual business in Auxi-le-Chateau with London Scottish.*

Wed 2nd Aug   *Ditto. To Concert in Evening by 'Artist Rifles' (very good).*

Thurs 3rd Aug   *Parade at 8.40 for various trench work. In Town evening.*

Fri 4th Aug   *Digging Snipers Range in Morning. Mr Farmiloe gave Dinner in Evening. (Had fine time.)*

Sat 5th Aug   *Packing up. Left Auxi-le-Chateau at 3 pm (by train). Arrived at Abbeville 4.30. In Y.M.C.A.*

Sun 6th Aug   *Left Abbeville 4.45 am. Via Frévent and Doullens. Arrived at Saulty 12 mid-day. Rode to St Amand.*

Tim seems, therefore, to have had about five weeks away from the horrors of the front line. But now he is approaching it again, and this time he is to enter trenches 'in front of Fonquevilliers'. This would place him in the northerly sector, in an area which, at the start of the Somme attack, had been chosen for a feint. The idea was that British troops in that area should capture Gommecourt, incidentally tying down enemy forces who might otherwise have been moved to beef-up their defences further south. Since the German positions in this area were particularly well situated, the losses among the attacking British had been exceptionally heavy, even by Somme standards; and possibly Tim, having had a period of relative rest and recuperation, was one of many later brought up to plug gaps.

Mon 7th Aug   *In Village. Left St Amand 6 pm. Arrived via Bienvillers in trenches in front of Fonquevilliers* [sic. Normally Foncquevillers].

Tim is now to have rather more than a week sitting uncomfortably in a trench taking in the sights and sounds of battle.

Tues 8th Aug   *Sleep at 3 am. British Bombardment continues heavily on the right.*

Wed 9th Aug   *Sleep at 2.30 am. Bombardment continues. Enemy active with Minnenwerfers, etc.*

Thurs 10th Aug   *Bed at 2 am. Bombs and Grenades exchanged each sides. Machine guns also very active.*

Fri 11th Aug   *Bed at 2 am. Bombardment continues on right in direction of Pozières.*

Sat 12th Aug   *Bed at 3 am. Usual machine gun activity on both sides. Trenches shelled.*

Sun 13th Aug   *Bed at 2 am. Enemy active with Grenades. Fonquevilliers shelled.*

Mon 14th Aug   *Bed at 2 am. (Rain) Aeroplanes active on both sides.*

Tues 15th Aug   *Bed at 1 am. (Rain) Relieved at 4 pm, and arrived at Bienvillers.*

Wed 16th Aug   *In Bienvillers all day on various work, etc. Patrol of Indian Lancers here. Our artillery active.*

Thurs 17th Aug   In Bienvillers. Huns dropped about twelve shells here. No great damage. Old Lady and Yvonne very nice people.

Fri 18th Aug   Left Bienvillers at 7.30 pm. (Shelling continues.) Arrived at Gaudiempré 9pm. March all night.

Sat 19th Aug   2.30 am. In Beaudricourt. Digging in morning. For walk in evening with Jackson.

Sun 20th Aug   In Beaudricourt. To Estaminet evening, and card party.

Mon 21st Aug   In Beaudricourt. To Irvigny with Fryer. Preparations for departure.

Tues 22nd Aug   Reveille 4 am. Left Beaudricourt 6.30 with Battn. Ariived at Viller L'Hopital via Bourquemaison and Barly 1 pm.

Wed 23rd Aug   Reveille 4 am. Left Viller L'Hopital at 6.30 am and arrived at Agenvillers 4pm. Via Auxi-le-Chateau, etc.

Thurs 24th Aug   In Agenvillers all day. Living in Cottage with Lieut Farmiloe.

Fri 25th Aug   Usual Work in Agenvillers. (Rain)

Sat 26th Aug   Agenvillers. (Rain). Lunch in field. Night Operations.

Sun 27th Aug   Agenvillers. (Rain)

Mon 28th, Tues 29th, Wed 30th Aug. Agenvillers.

Thurs 31st Aug   Packing up.

Fri 1st Sep   In Agenvillers [Then an unexplained small star.]

Sat 2nd Sep   Reveille 3 am. Entrained at St Riquier 10 am. Arrived at Corbie 1 pm. For walk in town in evening.

Sun 3rd Sep   Left Corbie [on the Somme, east of Amiens] *at 2.30 pm. Marched to Camp on outskirts of Albert. Spent night standing in heavy rain. (No shelter)*

Mon 4th Sep   Usual Camp life in 'Happy Valley' all day. Heavy Bombardment in progress on the Front.

Tues 5th Sep   23 Observation Balloons on Somme front. [How does Tim know that?] *Bombardment continues.*

Wed 6th Sep   Left Camp in 'Happy Valley' 5 pm. Marched to Bronfay Farm for rest. March continued all night. Under shell fire.

Thurs 7th Sep   Arrived in abandoned Hun trenches 1 am. Left at 6 pm and relieved London Scots in Leuze Wood 10 pm. Spent awful night in hole.

Tim's diary has, at this point, recorded what seems to be virtually continuous but pointless movement from one place to another. However, the fact that he has now arrived at Leuze Wood suggests that the travel was far from pointless, and in all probability was aimed at threading a path for him and his immediate comrades to the spot where a major operation needing more men on the ground was in progress. Shifting men around to respond to rapidly changing situations was far from easy: they needed somewhere to sleep each night, for instance, no matter how uncomfortable the pillows on which they figuratively laid their heads.

On August 18th the Germans had launched a counter-attack from their positions in Leuze Wood. This time it was their turn to be mown down by machine-gun fire. The fighting then became intense, with huge losses on both sides. Some of the worst casualty-lists of the war were compiled during the battle for Leuze Wood, which on September 6th was eventually captured by men of the territorial London Scottish Regiment, of the Royal Irish Fusiliers and of the Devonshires. The following day, two hours before midnight, the 'London Scots' were relieved by Tim (and a few others). Tim, having endured a long march under shellfire, spent the rest of that awful night in a hole. It would not be long before he was to see action again.

Fri 8th Sep   *Heavy shelling continues. I accompanied Lieut Farmiloe on to 'No Man's Land' re. 'new trench' for assembling before 'charge'.*

Sat 9th Sep   *Q.V.R. attacked at 5 pm (casualties heavy). Succeeded in holding Hun trench in spite of great resistance. Shelling terrible.*

The diary does not make clear precisely what area was being attacked, but it could well have been German lines in front of Ginchy. This village, or what remained of it, was finally occupied on September 9th/10th.

Sun 10th Sep.   *Violent Bombardment continues all day (both sides). Q.W.R.* [sic] *attacked at 7.30 am and 3.30 pm, and failed both times. Left trenches 10.30 pm.*

Tim's battalion was now moved some three miles eastwards to the (comparative) safety of Fricourt, where he even found time to take in a performance by the Divisional Band and another by the 'Bow Bells' Concert Party. It was to be but a brief respite.

Mon 11th Sep   *Arrived at Camp (Fricourt) 4 am. Divisional band and 'Bow Bells' (Concert Party) in attendance.*

Tues 12th Sep   *Left Citadel Camp in afternoon, and arrived at Camp near Billon Wood. Standing by for orders to move up.*

Wed 13th Sep   *Waiting orders. Marched off at 6 pm and relieved Devons. (Rain). Heavy artillery duel both sides all night.*

Thurs 14th Sep   *Our position is just in rear of Combles, and to the right* [=East] *of Leuze Wood.*

Fri 15th Sep   *French make an attack on our right with success. Shelling continues. 'Caterpillars'* [modern term = 'Tanks'] *used in action against Huns.*

Tim was absolutely on the ball in mentioning Caterpillars. The first use of tanks was indeed on that very day. Their introduction was, however, botched. As early as 1915, Haig had placed the order for a thousand, accurately judging the potential of what was then called a 'Machine Gun Destroyer'. Asquith could only promise his War Committee that sixty-two would be available for what was to be their first time in action, namely the attack planned for September 15th. Immediately prior to the attack about half that number had been made ready near Trones Wood before being spread out along the front line. Eighteen finally went into action. There seems little doubt that they produced terror among the German defenders: there were accounts of enemy troops fleeing before the machine-gun fire of the new armour-plated monsters; and the strategically-placed village of Flers, some four miles north of Tim's position, was swiftly occupied by the New Zealanders who had caterpillar support. It must be said, though, that despite the deployment of the 'secret weapon' many German machine-gunners were able to get into position to inflict huge casualties on the advancing allied troops; and it has to be concluded that greater effort should have been made to secure many more caterpillars. Their impact was severely limited by the wide dispersal of the few available. Furthermore, half their number suffered mechanical failure, sometimes caused by enemy shellfire. The handful that kept going forward advanced at least a mile, suggesting that far larger numbers could have had a devastating effect on the outcome of the battle. As it was, Haig decided on a standstill of four days to enable some relief to be brought to the exhausted troops. Tim's notes echo that reality:

Sat 16th Sep *Still heavy shelling. Our casualties mount up. Troops beginning to feel effects of biscuits and water, and of bad weather.*

Sun 17th Sep *No hope of being relieved. Feeling bad myself, but only wounded men may go to Hospital.*

Mon 18th Sep *Can eat no food whatever. Lying in hole all day feeling 'done in'. Relief does not come.*

Tues 19th Sep *Fire in Combles. Heavy shelling all round. Waiting for relief force. Still cannot eat.*

Wed 20th Sep *We are told to hang on for a few more days. Troops are well-nigh done. So am I.*

Thurs 21st Sep *Still cannot eat. Germans coninue to shell our positions, with heavy stuff. We reply firmly.*

Fri 22nd Sep *Weather seems better. Eat rations today for first time. Huns send over Tear Shells. We wear Smoke Helmets.*

Sat 23rd Sep *Will the Relief Force ever come? Our artillery continues to bombard effectively.*

Thus for well over a week Tim and his platoon were 'taking it' unrelieved, in bad weather and with totally inadequate rations. His simple entries make clear the unspeakable nature of trench warfare at that particular time, with some of his most pessimistic entries during the entire war occurring from September 18th to 21st. Despite their exhausted state the men were then required to renew the offensive:

Sun 24th Sep *Carried out Bombing raid on Huns lines. Casualties continue always. Our artillery excellent, also aeroplane service.*

The excellent aeroplane service had, unknown to Tim at the time, secured sufficient control of the skies above the trenches to obtain clear photographs of the German positions. This intelligence enabled tactical planning of the next attacks to be based on information hitherto unavailable except by dangerous probing reconnaissance missions on the ground.

Mon 25th Sep *Attacks carried out with great success. German prisoners continue to give themselves up. (This is War.)*

Tues 26th Sep *Germans evacuate Combles. We follow them up. We are relieved at last and march back.*

Wed 27th Sep *Arrived early morning in old Hun trenches in front of Méricourt. Left at 3 pm and arrived at Méaulte [just S.S.E. of Albert] 6 pm. In Billets. (I am a Runner.)*

Méaulte was the headquarters of Lieutenant General the Earl of Cavan, whose 14th Corps had, on the 25th, launched a determined and successful attack on Morval and Lesboeufs, where, in a recent previous attack, Captain Harold Macmillan had been seriously injured, but was ultimately rescued and survived to become, one long-distant day, the Prime Minister who gave new meaning to the words 'You've never had it so good'. General Sir Douglas Haig visited to discuss progress; but Tim, now a runner, had more immediate problems that needed attention:

Thurs 28th Sep *In Méaulte all day. (Deliver various dispatches.) Feet getting very bad. Raining on and off. Very heavy Bombardment at night.*

Fri 29th Sep *Paraded sick with feet. Marched off at 3 pm and arrived in abandoned Hun trenches. Had good dug-out.*

Sat 30th Sep   Left at 3 pm and arrived via Guillemont [East of Albert, NNW of Péronne] *in trenches at Lesboeufs* [North of Combles]. *Relieved Sherwood Forresters* [sic]. *(Some rest.) Feet are awful.*

Complaints are few in Tim's diaries; but clearly his feet are giving him great pain. Nonetheless for the next week or so he records several moves and some action ('We bomb Hun trenches'). He comments on the exhaustion both he and his comrades share (Oct 2nd), but his remark about the effect of prolonged rain on the trenches (also October 2nd) tells only half the story. Haig was determined that another huge 'Push' should be made in order to capitalise on the fact that German positions had been overrun, leaving the enemy with only hastily-prepared and inadequate defences, and thus making possible a rapid advance to the Bapaume Ridge area. More than a week of sustained rain, however, made the deployment of artillery (necessary for preliminary bombardment) impossible. Sporadic probing attacks were made; but as far as Tim was concerned his luck was to run out on October 8th. (Or was his luck to be seen as continuing in that his absence from the front line at so difficult a time was indeed fortunate?)

Sun 1st Oct   In trenches all day. Viewed recently occupied German line. Heaps of dead in dug-outs. Large quantities of shells and ammunition left. We bomb Hun trenches.
Mon 2nd Oct   Artillery duel very heavy. Rain commences and continues all day and night. Trenches awful. (Men knocked.)
Tues 3rd Oct   Rain continues, also shelling. Relieved at 3.30 pm under shrapnel fire. Arrived at Carnoy 12 midnight in dug-out.
Wed 4th Oct   Left Carnoy 8 am. Arrived at Citadel Camp, Fricourt [just East of Albert] *9.30 am. Cleaning up all day. (Mud everywhere.)*
Thurs 5th and Fri 6th Oct   In Camp at Citadel. (Same task.)
Sat 7th Oct   Left at 8 am. Arrived in Reserve Trenches at Ginchy 11.30 am. Left at 7 pm and arrived in trenches in front of Guillemont.
Sun 8th Oct   Took trenches in front of Lesboeufs 4.30 pm. Took more bombs up. Wounded in face by shell 6.30 pm.

For the rest of his life the damage to his sight was evident. He later found bright lights very troubling to the damaged eye, and as a result preferred domestic light-sources to be well shaded. In October 1916, however, his medical treatment seems to have been exemplary, and his comments upon it are very favourable:

Mon 9th Oct   Reached R.A.M.C. Trones Wood. Then by car to 48th C.C.S. Wound inspected by M.O. and re-dressed. Waiting for ambulance trains.
Tues 10th Oct   Left [departed] *in Red Cross train 2 am. Arrived at 18 General Hospital, Camiers* [just North of Le Touquet] *8pm. In bed 9.30 pm.*
Wed 11th Oct   In Bed all day. G Ward, No. 13 Bed. Inspected by M.O. and eye specialist.
Thurs 12th Oct   In Bed all day. (Nurses exceedingly good and attentive.)
Fri 13th Oct   Out of bed. Walking about Camp. (Am not allowed to smoke owing to my eye, but unfortunately I disobey.)
Sat 14th Oct   Inspected by Colonel and passed for No. 6 Convalescent Camp.
Sun 15th Oct   Left Camiers 4.30 pm (car). Arrived at No. 6 Convalescent Camp, Etaples. [Just east of Le Touquet, south of Boulogne.] *Placed in 22 Hut, H Company.*

Mon 16th Oct   Paraded before Colonel 9.30 am.   For walk in afternoon with 'Queens West Surrey'. To Lecture in evening. (Scouts Hut.)

Thurs 17th Oct   Short march in morning.   Lecture in afternoon. To Concert at Y.M.C.A evening (Slow).

Wed 18th Oct   Inspected by Eye-Specialist. For walk after. Concert in evening at R.C. Hut. (Very good.)

Thurs 19th Oct   Inspected by M.O. in morning. To Cinema in afternoon. In Expeditionary Force Canteen in evening.

Fri 20th Oct   March along Coast in morning. Left No.6 C.C. 4 pm and arrived at Details Camp, Etaples.

Sat 21st Oct   Assisting in E.F.C. and in Church Army Hut in the morning. Left Etaples 5 pm in cattle trucks, but occupied 1st Class carriage near Abbeville.   [Tim knew how to make the best of a bad job !]

Sun 22nd Oct   Arrived at Le Havre via Rouen 4.30 pm (Docks). By tram to Surfleur [Harfleur?] *Arrived at No.8 I.B.D. 15 Camp. 6 pm.*

Mon 23rd Oct   Révielle 5 am. [Suddenly Tim mis-spells a word he usually gets right. Was he a little more shaken by the experience of being wounded than his diary reveals?] *Breakfast 6 pm.* [Another mistake, for sure.] *Inspected by Colonel and Red Cross. YMCA Concert in evening.* [The entry for Oct 23rd may suggest apprehension at the possibility of a return to the trenches, from which he had just narrowly escaped with his life. Such little mistakes may well occur when one is preoccupied with unhappy musings. Had it perhaps occurred to him that his luck might be running out?]

24th Oct   Constructing Machine-gun Range on C.T.S. [?] *in morning. To Concert in evening at Y.M.C.A. (rather slow).*

Wed 25th Oct   Continuing Machine-gun Range on C.T.S. all day. In evening with 'Boys' in various Huts.

Thurs 26th Oct   In Camp generally all day with Gander, Ballard and Mclere [sic].

Fri 27th Oct   To C.T.S. in morning. In Camp afternoon. In Catholic Hut in evening with Boys.

Sat 28th Oct   Packing up, and in Huts. Left Harfleur and marched to Havre. Entrained at 12 midnight.

Sun 29th Oct   Arrived at Rouen 8 pm. In Rouen and Rest Hut all day. Left Rouen at 5 pm.

Mon 30th Oct   Via Abbeville, Etaples and St Pol, arrived at Béthune. By trucks to La Gourgue. [Although Tim is going to have some trouble spelling *La Gorgue*, it is clear that following a lengthy period away from the worst excesses of the Somme action he has now reported for duty in a new general location on the River Lys.] *In Billets there at 9 pm.*

Tues 31st Oct   In La Gorgue Estaires [sic] *in morning with Boys. Left at 3 pm and arrived in trenches at Neuve Chapelle* [NE of Béthune on D171 to Armentières] *7 pm. On Guard.*

Although in no sense was Tim a 'special case', his immediate despatch from the trenches on being wounded and his efficient removal to a safe area for hospitalization suggest there was an effective back-up which was staffed by concerned healers. The trains seem to have been running, and Tim's travels are as exemplary as his treatment. Despite military blunders by senior officers, one can see why Tim finds little to complain of beyond the mud, the snow, the cold and the danger, all of which he seems to accept with remarkable stoicism.

Wed 1st Nov   Stand-to 5.30 to 6.30 am. Improving trenches. Shelling on both sides: trench mortars and grenades.

Thurs 2nd Nov   Usual Activity. Aeroplanes overhead. On sentry duty at 119 and 138 posts, also Patrols. Wire party in front.

Fri 3rd Nov   Usual Guards etc. Relieved by Q.W.R. at 4.30 pm, and then to Billet in Bout-de-Ville at 7.30 pm.

Sat 4th Nov   Rifle Inspection. For walk in afternoon to La Fosse with Smith and Williams.

Sun 5th Nov   Raining. In Estaminet in Bout-de-Ville in evening. French dancing, etc., and musical evening.

Mon 6th Nov   Rifle Inspection. To'Bow-Bells' in evening with Boys at La Gorgue (Good). Arrived back 10 pm.

Tues 7th Nov   Batman to Captain Daniell, D.C.L.I. Living at Headquarters.

Wed 8th Nov   Usual business at HQ.

Thurs 9th Nov   Rilieved Q.W.R. in trenches 11 am. In dug-out HQ. [Again, Tim makes a surprising spelling error. Is this a sign of worry, apprehension, nervousness, poor vision as a result of injury?]

Fri 10th Nov   Building-up dug-out. Activity on both sides with Trench Mortars, etc.

Sat 11th Nov   Ditto

Sun 12th Nov   Usual business in trenches. Aeroplane activity by us.

Mon 13th Nov   Heavy shelling with Minenwerfers etc by Hun.

There is something about the diary entries during the past fortnight that suggest Tim was, for the first time, seeing little plan in the daily grind. His entries no doubt accurately describe his experiences of each day, albeit briefly, but whereas he had hitherto perceived the larger picture, now he seems to be rather 'out of touch'. The area in which he now finds himself presents new problems, and (perhaps unsurprisingly) he appears unaware that on November 13th a 'final' assault was launched in dense fog by some 40,000 troops along both banks of the River Ancre with the aim of capturing Beaumont-Hamel, St Pierre Division, Serre and Beaucourt. Although many Germans were taken prisoner, losses were heavy on both sides. Among the dead was Sergeant Hector Munro, better known as the brilliant writer, Saki.

By November 15th both Beaucourt and Beaumont-Hamel were in British hands, and two days later the snow began to fall. Despite the treacherous conditions, by the 19th St Pierre Division was also taken. As the assault petered out in mud, fog, swirling snow and bitter cold, Serre remained in German hands. Tim continued to record his own private view of the alternative battleground upon which he was now fighting. The Somme offensive was grinding to a muddy halt, and without his assistance. He is treading the ground of another area of France; but the opposing forces are still German, and their weapons are familiar:

Tues 14th Nov. and Wed 15th Nov   We are active with trench mortars etc. Huns also busy with Minenwerfers.

Thurs 16th Nov   Relieved at 3 pm. [Accurate spelling returns.] *Arrived at HQ Billet near Croix Barbe. In Estaminet evening.*

Fri 17th Nov   In Riechbourg St Vaast. Usual business. Aeroplane activity.

Sat 18th Nov   In Vielle Chapelle with Gaby Doleeze. Estaminet in evening. (Sing-song). To bed 1 am.

Mon 20th Nov   Another good day in Reichbourg St Vaast [sic].

Tues 21st Nov   Left at 3 pm and relieved Q.W.R. in trenches at Neuve Chapelle.

Wed 22nd Nov   Usual trench life. In Vielle Chapelle with Bowman.

Thurs 23rd Nov   Daring activity by our aeroplanes. Hun very active with shrapnel, etc.
Left trenches with Capt. D.

Fri 24th Nov   In La Gorgue. Saw Captain Daniell off at 1 pm. To Bow-Bells in evening.

Sat 25th Nov   Living with Saw in La Gorgue. To Bow Bells in evening.

Sun 26th Nov   In La Gorgue morning. Left at 3 pm and joined A Company at -----.   In Estaminet in evening.

Mon 27th Nov   Left at 3 pm and arrived at La Gorgue. For walk in evening to Belle Vien etc. In Billet 8 pm.

Tues 28th Nov   Inspection etc during day. To Bow-Bells in evening with Smith.

Wed 29th Nov   Parades for Drill, Physical, Bayonet fighting, etc. 9 am and 2 am. [pm?].
With Smith in evening at La Gorgue.

Thurs 30th Nov   Ditto

Elsewhere, the Battle of the Somme had gone off the boil. What we now know is that it petered out during November 1916, not least because the rain, snow and mud made fighting virtually impossible. General Haig had ordered repeated attacks, many of which were repulsed with heavy casualties. By the end of November British losses (killed, wounded or taken prisoner) reached some 420,000. The French had lost 200,000, while the Germans had lost around half a million. Our advance during several months of blood-letting amounted to about eight miles at the deepest point. While he had been involved, Tim had taken a dangerous part, and had survived. Now he was in a different part of the Front Line, some miles to the north, still in France, but much nearer to what remained of 'plucky little Belgium'.

WINTER 1916-1917
All Quiet on the Western Front?

By the end of November 1916, even the most gung-ho officers on both sides must have known that the war was not going to end swiftly. The same realization must have come to the men, who could also calculate that there would be plenty of time for them to become casualties. Some (very few) simply refused to fight any more, and of that few a sizeable number were shot for cowardice. (Surprisingly, the Germans executed fewer than any of the other major combatants: they would make up for such laxity in the 1939-45 sequel!) There were some attempts at mutiny. Among the British one such, centred on Etaples in 1917, became famous with the publication in 1978 of William Allison's book *The Monocled Mutineer*, and its adaptation for television some years later. It was alleged in the book that a Chesterfield man named Percy Toplis was a leader of the insurrection, and that he was shot dead some time later by police back in Britain, possibly to avoid the publicity of a trial. (It has to be said that many who have investigated the facts of the case are convinced that Toplis was, in fact, nowhere near Etaples at the time of the mutiny.) In the case of our French allies, it is now acknowledged that their haemorrhage at Verdun led to acts of defiance among the thousands of troops who were required to march to certain extinction; but at the time these facts were suppressed.

The majority, however, simply 'carried on', and tried to make the best of a bad job. Tim's first entry gives some indication that this was his view of the situation.

1916

Fri 1st Dec   Acting Batman to Lieut Poolley 'pro tem'. To 'Bow-Bells' in evening with Smith.

Sat 2nd Dec   In La Gorgue doing various things all day. With Smith etc evening.

Sun 3rd Dec   Assisting in A Company Officers Mess all day (Acting Waiter). Also D company.

Mon 4th Dec   In Billet most of the day. To Estaminet in evening.

Tues 5th Dec   Usual day in La Gorgue. 'Bon Fête' day in France preceeding St Nicholas day. 'Some Fun' today.

Wed 6th Dec   In Billet and also in Estaminet 'Au Commerce' with Rogers and Bowman. Lunch at Headquarters. Usual supper in Maison.

Thurs 7th Dec   In La Gorgue with duty in Mess. To Battalion Concert in evening.

Fri 8th Dec   Usual day in La Gorgue. To Bow Bells in evening, and supper at Billet.

Sat 9th Dec   Left La Gorgue 10 am and relieved R.W.R. Situation rather quiet.

Neither the British nor the Germans quite knew what to do for the best after the terrifying losses each had suffered during the battles at Verdun and by the Somme. Although there had been some British advance, no major objective had been obtained: even Bapaume remained in enemy hands. Although losses continued to be suffered by both sides (some as a result of courts martial which decreed death penalties for desertion) Tim was able to describe the situation when he entered the trenches in his new area of France as 'rather quiet' (December 9th). The Germans then decided on two courses of action that were to prove crucial as the conflict later evolved: first, they embarked on total submarine warfare; and second, they withdrew on the Western Front to new defensive positions. The former decision would ultimately bring the power of the United States into the war against them. The latter enabled the British to make substantial advances with very little fighting. But first Tim had to survive what, to him, were 'close shaves', even though they may have been relatively minor aspects of the immediate waiting-game. (See from Dec 21st 1916 to Christmas Day.)

Sun 10th Dec   *Usual trench life. Left for coal in morning. (Weather wet.)*

Mon 11th Dec   *Usual trench life.*

Tues 12th Dec   *Left trenches with Lieut Pooley, and arrived at Riez Bailuel* [Bailleul]. *Snowing heavily. To La Gorgue.*

Wed 13th Dec   *At Brigade Grenade School. On duty in Mess all day. To La Gorgue.*

Thurs 14th Dec   *Duty on Mess all day at Riez Bailluel* [sic; getting near!].

Fri 15th Dec   *In Estaminet all day. Left at 6 pm with Brooks, and arrived at Croix Rouge in evening.*

Sat 16th Dec   *Transferred to C Company. Batman to Lieut Sedgely in Pont du Hem.*

Sun 17th Dec   *Usual business in Pont du Hem.*

18th and 19th Dec   *Ditto*

Wed 20th Dec   *To La Goruge* [sic] *and Estaires. Usual day in Pont du Hem. To Estaminet with Sheldon and Surtees, also in café.*

Thurs 21st Dec   *Packed up and left Pont du Hem. Arrived in 1st line trenches 1 pm. Heavily shelled with Minenwerfers all night.*

Fri 22nd Dec   *Still being heavily shelled. Enemy enter our trench. Prisoners taken.* [It is not clear by whom.] *Many casualties.*

Sat 23rd Dec   *Everybody on the alert. (Sleep impossible). Enemy continues to shell our trenches. We reply heavily.*

Sun 24th Dec   *Situation same as previous day. D and part of A Company retire, trenches blown beyond repair.*

Mon 25th Dec   *C Company still 'hang on'. Heavy shelling continues on both sides. (What a cheerful Christmas.)*

Tues 26th Dec   *Usual 'strafe' in morning. Left with Mr Sedgely 12 noon. Arrived in La Gorgue. (Supper in café)*

Wed 27th Dec   *At Divisional Bayonet School. Various business in La Gorgue. To 'Bow Bells' with Wilson.*

Thurs 28th Dec   *Usual daily routine. On bicycle to Riez Bailluel and Pont du Hem in evening.*

Fri 29th Dec   *Acting Caterer to School all day. Also temporary Batman to Lieut. Madement 'Rangers'.*

Sat 30th Dec   *At Bayonet School. To various Cafés and Estaminets.*

Sun 31st Dec   *Caterer for the Mess all day. Also in various Estaminets, etc.*

1917

Tim was in northern France as 1917 began, and he purchased (or was given, or otherwise acquired) a French *Agenda*. It is twice the size of his English diaries for 1915 and 1916; and a glance shows at once that he intended to utilise the extra space to give a fuller account of his daily activities. He seemed to revel in using French words for the days of the week.

Janvier 1. Lundi (Circoncision)   Acting Caterer for the Divisional Bayonet School at La Gorgue. In various Estaminets during day. On the whole am having rather a busy time.

68

2. Mardi   *Nothing exceptional to report. Usually go out and visit Estaminets with Clarke of the 'Rangers'. Have an occasional chat with Lady at our Billet.*

3. Mercredi   *Nothing special to report today. Usual daily routine. Clementine from the Estaminet speaks English lovely for a self-taught girl.*

4. Jeudi   *Things are very slow. Spoke to Blanche. She seems quite nice, but there are better.*

5. Vendredi   *Am having a day off today. To Bow Bells in evening with Clarke. Had a chat with Evelyn who seems a very nice and sensible girl.*

6. Samedi   *Spent rather a busy morning in La Gorgue, packing up and clearing up. Said goodbye to various acquaintances and left in the evening, arriving in Merville* [west of Lille on the River Lys] *about 7.30 pm. Am in Billet with Lieut Sedgely and like it very much.*

7. Dimanche   *Lieut Sedgely and I are living in a very nice house on the outskirts of Merville. The people are very good and speak English. The little girl Margerite* [sic] *is very pretty (5 years). I walk into Merville, quite a fine town. The Officers and Sergeants of C Company had a dinner in evening and I waited at table for them.*

8. Lundi   *To Merville in the morning. The French people are very decent company and I spend much time with them. To Estaminet as usual. (Why not!) With Lieut Sedgely in evening.*

9. Mardi   *To Merville in morning. Also in Estaminet. (Benedictine is very good.) I feel downhearted there are no letters for me. Heavy bombardment by our guns. With Lieut Sedgely in evening.*

10. Mercredi   *Awake at 9 am. To Merville in morning. Received present from Gwen, also photos from Doris. Bombardment continues. Sitting with Lieut Sedgely in his room all the evening, talking and writing letters.*

11. Jeudi   [Tim's 22nd birthday.] *Packing up in morning, preparatory to going to hospital with Lieut Sedgely. We wait all day, but the Ambulance car fails to put in an appearance. Spend the evening with Lieut Sedgely in his room writing letters and doing other odd things.*

12. Vendredi   *Once again I pack up. The car is timed for 10.30 but it turns up at 12 am. We arrive at the 1/2 C.C.S. Merville at 1 pm (just in time for dinner). Handed over all kit and made myself useful. Went out with Surtees, Floriette* [?] *and Hearn in evening. (What a night!)*

13. Samedi   *In the Hospital. (Officers' Servants.) Revielle* [sic] *6 am. (What hopes!} Breakfast 9 am, Dinner 1 pm, Tea 5 pm, and very nice too. I should like this for the duration of the War. It is snowing and raining heavily. Went to Y.M.C.A. in evening and saw* Dick Whittington *played by R.A.M.C. Rather on Amateur side, but fair.*

14. Dimanche   *Have met Stroud of the R.F.A. who knew Dad quite well. To Y.M.C.A. in afternoon for writing. Spent good evening with Stroud and Colonel Cameron's servant (Lincolns). Spoke to Alice in one Estaminet. Not so bad. Usual type of French girl. (16)*

15. Lundi   *Packing Officers kit ready for departure to Base. To Merville Station by lorry, and helped carrying stretcher cases on to Ambulance train. Saw Officers off and returned to C.C.S. Tea 5 pm. Spent evening with Mac (R.F.A.) and Lincoln (Vizor) making a tour round various Estaminets. (Not a bad time.)*

16. Mardi   *Breakfast 8 am. Paraded at 9 am. Left C.C.S. at Merville and arrived at staion. Caught 11.30 train to La Gorgue. Visited old friends there and stayed with transport. To Bow Bells in evening* Alladin [sic] *(Very good.) Then to Madame - for supper, and chatted to them till 9.30 pm. Then to bed.*

17. Mercredi   *Made my own Reveillé at 10 am, then went to Baths in La Gorgue, and also visited Estaminet. Packed up at 1.30 and left with ration party. Arrived in Laventie* [East of Merville, towards Lille] *in time for tea at C.Company Mess. Expect to return to Company, but am not certain yet. Weather awful – snowing all day.*

18. Jeudi   Reveillé 8.45 am. I return to C.Company as expected. Spent the afternoon with Boys at Headquarters. To Estaminet in evening with Cpl Reed and L/Cpl Noble. (Hot red wine is very nice.)

19. Vendredi   Paraded at 8.30 am. Marched to trenches at Laventie Sector. Working and clearing trenches, etc. Our artillery send over plenty of shells and shrapnel, and the Hun replies feebly. Returned to Laventie 3 pm. Spent jolly evening with Reed, Noble and New Zealanders. (Sing-song)

20. Samedi   Packed up in morning, and for stroll in Laventie. We arrive in trenches at Laventie Sector at 2 pm. I am warned that I have been selected with eleven other men to hold a post in the German line as they have retired in parts owing to the trenches being flooded. (Now for a rest.)

21. Dimanche   It is too cold to sleep. Have breakfast at 3.30 am, then cross 'No Man's Land' and reach German trench 5.30 am. At 6 am a party of Huns attempt to take our position, but we drive them off with rapid fire. We are on the alert all day. They shell us, but cannot hit our post. Relief party arrives at 6 pm. We get halfway back across 'No Man's Land' when the Huns start heavy Bombardment.

22. Lundi   Luck favours us and we reach headquarters safely. Am now temporary H.Q. Runner. (Casualties last night 5 killed, 17 wounded.) Distance across top 400 yds to Irma post. Took draft of new men to C.Company. Then with orders to C, A and D company. Enemy capture Bertha post. I leave headquarters with Colonel Renton for the trenches.

23. Mardi   We arrive in front line before Bertha post. Arrangements are made to recapture it. Our artillery open with 18-pounders, but fall short. At 4.45 am three Platoons advance and capture the post. Quite a successful operation. I return to H.Q. with Col. Renton, arriving there at 7 am. (Sleep for a while). Then with Orders to B.Company. (Still freezing hard.)

24. Mercredi   Our casualties are ten killed, 35 wounded. Occasional shelling all day. Took Lieut Coles to D.Company. Huns commence bombardment on our advanced positions and first line which becomes more intense during evening. I go to D, A and E Companies with Orders. Reinforcements are called up. Our casualties have now reached 22 killed and 150 wounded. We retain Posts.

25. Jeudi   Still standing ready in case of attack. To B.Company with Orders. Huns comparatively quiet during day, but shelling commences on both sides during the night. Our posts in German line suffer heavily, and 'Bertha' has to be evacuated for a time. To B.Company with Orders. (New Colonel arrives, C.B. Follett.)

26. Vendredi   We are relieved by 2nd Londons, who sustain losses while relieving. Arrived in Laventie 12 midi with HQ Runners. Take various messages. Capt Hadden takes command of C.Company, and I return as his Batman. In Mess in evening.

27. Samedi   In Officers Mess at Laventie, two miles behind the line. Huns commence heavy artillery fire in evening which continues on and off all night. (Celebration of Kaiser's Birthday). Hun aeroplane flies very low over Laventie.

28. Dimanche   Huns drop heavy shells in morning near Billet. To Estaminet in evening with Shuttleworth, and met some of the Boys there. Dinner 8 pm.

29. Lundi. Inspection of Billets by General Gough [General Sir Hubert Gough, Commander of the Fifth Army, no less.] *Usual work in Mess. Nothing exceptional to report except for a few shells dropped into Laventie. (Still freezing.)*

30. Mardi   *Parade at 9.30 am for inspection by Colonel. Usual work in Mess. Huns drop a few more shells. Writing letters, etc.*

31. Mercredi   *Nothing startling. Another Hun aeroplane and a few more German shells.*

Fevrier. 1. Jeudi Start for trenches early in morning. Nothing of any importance to relate. Artillery active after dark. Wiring parties out.

2. Vendredi   *Usual trench life. I am cooking for Officers in a cramped little dug-out. Terribly cold at night. Still freezing hard. Rations might be better.*

3. Samedi   *Conditions much the same as previous day. Send a man each day to Laventie to buy extras. How cold it is. We have hot rum each night, and what a God-send.*

4. Dimanche   *Our artillery are very busy today in the trenches throwing aerial torpedoes at the Hun. Enemy send eighteen-pounders in return (Whiz-bangs), but fail to find our machines. Today is Sunday, and so there is the usual 'strafe'. Still freezing hard.*

5. Lundi   *Our men evacuate part of our front line whilst we fire trench mortars at the enemy, who reply ineffectively. We are shelled with Gas shells in evening, and have a few men gassed. Have just heard rumour that America has joined us.*

This last entry is intriguing in that the United States did not actually declare war on Germany until April 6th, 1917. Presumably even the men in the trenches had picked up strong indications that America's patience was running out regarding continued attacks on shipping, particularly by German submarines. (The sinking of the *Lusitania* had cost over a hundred American lives.) President Wilson's demand for an immediate cessation of such activity had been briefly complied with, but then attacks recommenced, leading to a swing in American public opinion which had initially preferred non-involvement in a European war. Information which led the British soldiery to believe that 'the Yanks were coming' (soon, if not immediately) would be heartening in the conditions of bloody stalemate prevailing in early February. It is possible that news had reached them of the Zimmerman Telegram which was linked to a reinstatement of submarine activity by the Germans and an attempt by them to enlist the help of Mexico should the U.S.A. enter the war. The British had probably been delighted to intercept that telegram, which was immediately passed to Wilson, and may have encouraged him to see where his allegiance should lie.

6. Mardi   *The day passes with an occasional burst of artillery fire. Parties out wiring all night.*

7. Mercredi   *Relieved by 2nd Londons. Left trenches at 11 am and arrived in Laventie. Busy with various work in Billet. We have quite a nice bed in kitchen. One mattress and blankets to bed early.*

8. Jeudi   *Usual day's work in Laventie. Aeroplane activity. Heavy Bombardment on both sides in evening. All soldiers in Laventie stood-to at 5 pm.*

9. Vendredi   *The lady of the house is very nice indeed. In Estaminet opposite Billet for a while. Artillery very busy.*

10. Samedi   *In Estaminet with Surtees. To Boxing contest in afternoon. Kramer wins twice. Heavy shelling on both sides in evening. Shell drops in Quartermaster's Stores. In Mess all evening.*

11. Dimanche   *Our aeroplanes active in morning. Just my luck: all leave is stopped. Usual time in Estaminet, etc. Artillery active.*

12. Lundi   To Estaires and La Gorgue during day. Visited various people I knew in La Gorgue. Arrived in Laventie at 3.30 pm. T.D.S. call at 6.30 pm. Rather big dinner in evening (5 Captains and 5 Lieut.)

13. Mardi   To Baths with Capt Hadden and Lieut Hallifax [sic]. *Visited relations of people at my Billet. Spent quite a good time there. We buy a Primus* [small stove, presumably] *for 35 Fr. Awfully jolly evening in -* [damaged page, but following words readable] *Table Gramophone.*

14. Mercredi   Packed up, and in Estaminet during morning. Relieved 2nd Londons. Arrived in trenches in afternoon. Fauquissart. [?] Occasional bursts of artillery during night. Great quantity of smoke rises from Hun line due to Aeroplane bomb.

15. Jeudi   Weather still very cold, but not quite as bad as previous time. Huns use Minenwerfers and we reply with Trench Mortars and 'Toffee Apples'. Heavy bombardment during night some miles away in Ypres direction.

16. Vendredi   Huns continue to 'put over' Minenwerfers on our right. Thaw has set in and things are very sticky once again. Heavy bombardment all night towards Armentières. Patrols out, also wiring parties.

17. Samedi   Rather quiet during day. At 10 pm our Artillery with trench Mortars commence intense bombardment on Hun lines. Enemy reply rather heavily for over half an hour. Rain starts and hampers operations. L.R.B. enter German lines and penetrate to 2nd trench. Six prisoners and many [Germans] *killed. Our losses slight.*

18. Dimanche   Rather a lull after the storm of last night. Trenches are in awful condition. Occasional bursts of artillery fire. Also a few Minenwerfers from Fritz. Patrols reconnoitre during evening.   Also go to Bertha Post and find it unoccupied by Enemy.

19. Lundi   Our trench mortars find it convenient to dispose of a few dozen shells to Fritz (much to my annoyance). Rain has now set in. A very violent artillery duel lasts throughout the night on our right flank.

20. Mardi   We start packing up fairly early and leave trench about 10 am. Relieved by 2nd Londons. Arrive in Laventie 11 am. Still raining hard. Billetted in one of our old Billets opposite 'Hospice Toulouse'. Met Shelly etc in café.

21. Mercredi   To Baths in afternoon with Capt Hadden. With Charlie Surtees and Jack Kissean in evening in Café Français. Back to Billet and spent merry time with Gramophone.

22. Jeudi   Nothing special to report except rumours that we are all leaving this position very soon. Spend evening writing letters. All Officers dine out.

23. VendrediTo Estaires and La Gorgue in afternoon in trap with Monsieur of our Billet. Spent rather quiet evening in Billet. Bombardment on the left. Gas shells dropped on trenches.

24. Samedi   To Brasserie St Louis for bath in afternoon. Spoke to Marie Louise in evening, also some of the fellows. Rather large dinner 8.30 pm in C.Company Mess. Surtees queer. [The probable implication is that he ate too much.]

25. Dimanche   Packing up. Left Laventie in morning and arrived in trenches at Tilloloy. German machine-gun very active so we 'keep low'. Our guns are noisy all the afternoon, and the Huns are not too quiet, however.

26. Lundi   Huns shell all round Headquarters with 5.9 shells. Machine-gun sweeping surrounding ground mostly all day. Heavy bombardment by our artillery started at 9.45 pm (on left). Wiring parties out all night.

27. Mardi   We move along to the right taking over part of L.R.B. front. Enemy still active with machine-guns. Aeroplane activity. Rather quiet night. (Am sleeping in oven in ruined house.)

28. Mercredi   Activity with long-distance shells by our artillery. Officers of West Yorkshires visit trenches. Usual machine-gun firing. I view Auboss ridge [?] and surrounding district from Observation Post (German line). Not too noisy at night.

Mars Jeudi 1   We are relieved by West Yorks 1.30 pm. Arrive in La Gorgue 3.30pm. To 25 Rue de Béthune. Very busy for while. Found Lucien very nice little girl (age 8 years). To bed fairly early.

2. Vendredi   Reviellé [sic] 6 am. Battalion moved off at 9.30, and marched via Merville, Colonne-sur-Lys, arriving at St Floris 12.30 pm. (Am quite tired out, but luckily the Lady of our Billet is very nice indeed.) In Mess all evening. Raining.

3. Samedi   Battalion marched off 9.50 am via St Venant, Lillers, Burbures, Vernes, and arrived at Pressy [?] 5 pm. (Everyone dog-tired.) We get fine Billet in Village School-house. Madame very nice indeed, also her daughter Ogestine. (Have quite a nice chat.) I retire not looking forward to the next day's march.

4. Dimanche   Treking is awful. Battalion march off at 8.30 am via Tangry, Wavrans, and numerous other villages. Arrived at Willeman 4 pm. (Feet are awful. I don't think I can walk another step.) We are billeted in old-fashioned French farm, charming place. People very reserved.

The Battalion has marched the best part of 50 kilometres in a south-westerly direction in three days. No wonder Tim comments that he doesn't think he can walk another step, and that his feet are awful! But there's more leg-work to come. Tim manages, however, to find an alternative that's acceptable to his superiors.

5. Lundi   Snowing hard. Battalion marches off 9.30 am. I follow behind in transport waggon. Route – Wail – St Georges – Le Quesnoy – Ragnaville. We spend lot of time getting suitable Billet as we are staying here for three weeks. Most of the people very miserable, but we manage to find Billet.

6. Mardi   2 am. Orders arrive – Regiment will march off 10.30 am. (Just our luck.) Route – Cherienne – Fontaine L'Etalon – Quoeux – Flaravesnes – Bachimont – to arrive at Rougefay early in the evening. Our Billet this time is in the Ecole et Marie [Mairie], and we sleep in the Schoolroom. The old Schoolmaster is awfully obliging.

7. Mercredi   Once more we pack up. Battalion march off at 9.30 am. I go with transport, driving R.F.A. mule most of the way. We arrive at Ivergny via Bouquemaison and other villages at 4 pm. Iverny [sic] is an awful place – we have rotten Billet. All the people seem terribly mean.

8. Jeudi   We march off again at 9.30 am, and although we are tired out anything is better than Ivergny. We march through Sus St Leger –Sombrin – Barly – Bavincourt – and arrive at Gouy en Artois in evening. [i.e. marching eastwards, but with an unexplained deviation southwards to Bavincourt.] I drive mule; my foot has long given out. Heavy snow and wind the whole way. Terribly cold. Billets here are not too good.

9. Vendredi   Can it be true? We are not marching off again. Gouy en Artois is about 3 kilometres behind the line and 9 kilos on the right of Arras. ['On the right of Arras' does not mean due east, but 'on the right' as far as the line of trenches facing the enemy is concerned. Gouy-en-Artois, to be specific, lies some fifteen kilometres west of Arras, and is about 3 km east of Barly, which is about 4 km east of Sombrin.] Not a very nice place, it is very difficult to buy anything. Most of the people here are very trying. C'est la guerre.

10. Samedi   In Gouy-en-Artois all day. Parade at 2.30 pm for instruction on new system of attack. Pay 4.30 pm. Heavy guns very busy. More rain and mud.

11. Dimanche   Life awfully monotonous at present, and conditions make matters worse. We are expecting to move into the line at any time. Drafts of men continue to arrive very frequently --- What does it mean? (I know.)

Tim's entry for March 11th is very telling. One might expect monotony to be welcomed rather than described as 'awful'. He is clearly referring to the monotony of his free time, which by implication he contrasts with the varied activities he had enjoyed on his 'days off' in previous areas of France. He clearly associates the drafts of new men with an impending 'Big Push', with its dangers and uncertainties.

12. Lundi   Parade at 2.15 pm. Raining All the time. Nothing special to report but rumours, rumours – nothing but rumours. Guns are very busy. Our next move will be under cover of darkness.

13. Mardi   Nothing at all startling. I expect <u>that</u> is to come. Battalion strenuously practising new method of attack. ('Nuff said.') Observation balloon is above us. I meet another old friend from the 2nd Battalion.

14. Mercredi   We are off !! Packing up etc. Regiment march off 6 pm and arrive in Arras via Beaumetz and Dainville at 11.30 pm. (17 Kilo's). Guns are very active. Our Billet is in rather a large House and the old lady is not bad.

15. Jeudi   Bed 3 am. Heavy gunfire. Not many soldiers allowed in streets of Arras during day -- it is 600 yds behind trenches and under observation. Went out in evening. It is a fine town, but knocked about rather badly. Regiment in the trenches digging, etc.

16. Vendredi   To bed at 2.30 am. Our guns very busy. Breakfast 12 midday. Great aeroplane activity. In Arras walking round in evening. This part of town has escaped most of German shells. Busy all night.

17. Samedi   Bed at 3.30 am. Heavy bombardment by our guns. Walk round town in evening. The Cathedral has suffered badly – only one wall standing, and area all round in heaps of ruins. Great aeroplane activity.

18. Dimanche   Germans are retiring in front of Arras, and we give them intense bombardment to help them along. Many fires can be seen in their lines as though villages are being burnt. We pack up immediately and follow them up. We arrive in Achicourt [just SSW of Arras] passing prisoners in awful condition. Our guns continue to bombard.

19. Lundi   We spend a little while packing up and off we go again. Marching over rough ground we spend a miserable night in the trenches about a mile behind Beaurains [south of Arras]. (In enemy hands and shelled to the ground.) It is raining hard and we are in a hopeless mess and find it difficult to discover way about. No sleep at all.

20. Mardi   We advance still further beyond Beaurains, occupying enemy 1st, 2nd and 3rd lines. Huns manage to blow a few of their Dug-outs up before going, but not too many. Their trenches are good. I am now living in one of their dug-outs about 30 feet below the ground. Five entrances (3 blown in) and over five rooms to it. I feel safe.

21. Mercredi   I get a few hours sleep after 3.30 am. I explore dug-out during morning and discover heaps of interesting articles. Our artillery are exceedingly active. Men are very busy wiring, digging and reversing parapets, etc. Advance trenches are also being started.

22. Jeudi   Our casualties are few. Light field guns are now well advanced. One battery is put out of action. The Huns shell Beaurains and trenches. Manchesters make a successful raid on our right. We are busy with long-distance shells. Huns appear to be holding their positions with machine-guns only.

23. Vendredi   I try to make myself acquainted with the maze of old Hun trenches. We carry on the good work of consolidating our new positions. Shall not be sorry when we are relieved. A few 'Bosch' shells fall near enough to our dug-out. Very little sleep.

24. Samedi   Aeroplane activity. One of ours brought down after battle in the air. Fritz finds it convenient to strafe our latrine. 'General Windup' expects the Huns to raid us tonight so there is no sleep whatever. I wander with Capt Hadden and Capt Symes round trenches left of Neuville Vitesse. We are enfiladed by Fritz. We send out raiding party.

25. Dimanche   We put our watches on one hour. Slowly the time passes. We stand in the trenches all through night and morning until dawn. Fritz has <u>not</u> attacked. I sleep from 9am. to 1.30 pm. but am still awfully tired. Fritz obliges with a few tear shells. Our guns are also busy moving up into new positions. Recconoitering [sic] parties are also busy.

As the watches are moved on an hour Tim seems to have acquired a more literary style, even introducing some intended, and one unintended, touches of humour. Some progress on the ground has brought, perhaps, an initial hope that things might at last be moving in the 'right' direction so far as the war is concerned. Yet do I detect some cynicism creeping in about the quality of leadership back at Headquarters, wherever that might be?

CHAPTER EIGHT

TIM'S WAR CONTINUES IN THE SPRING OF 1917

A s Tim now has more available diary-space to fill each day, he is seizing the opportunity to take his imagined reader rather more deeply into the realities of life in, and out of, the trenches. One gets the impression that he carries a certain determination that a record will be kept of the life he is living. Was it his wish, should he survive, to work on these day-by-day details at some later stage, but with the assurance that his memory shall not play him any tricks? Or were his daily observations simply his way of giving some meaning to the apparently meaningless slaughter of which he was a part ? Whatever his motivation, it is astonishing that he was able, often in extremely unsuitable circumstances, to maintain a clear, handwritten account, in ink. The paper in his 1917 *Agenda* was extremely thin; and he seems even to be taking care that his ink was not excessive, for fear that it would leech through and ruin the following page.

This, for sure, is the diary-record of a man who was a determined diarist. His observations demanded recording; and to miss a day would clearly have been, in some way and in his own eyes, a sign of failure. It is no surprise that he continued this discipline throughout his entire life. I know, indeed, from experience, that he passed the same determination to his daughter (my wife) who makes a note of the minutiae of our life together which gives some form of permance to the fleeting moment, whether it be happy, sad or simply monotonous.

1917

Mon March 26th The rain has now converted these trenches into glorious ditches making it awfully difficult to navigate ones voyages. We are going to be relieved tonight. (Cheers) Guns on both sides warn each other they still have a few shells left. I arrive in Auchicourt [presumably Achicourt] *and roam about in the rain on various jobs. We turn in between wet blankets.*

Tues Mar 27th   The day passes much the same in Auchicourt except for one thing:- Loads and loads of ammunition and other War materials are coming each night into Auchicourt and other parts in preparation for 'future events'. The Huns drop a few long-distance shells into the Village. (No great damage.)

Wed Mar 28th   Digging trenches in evening. (Battalion). Rather bad weather. Guns active on both sides. We expect to be relieved soon.

Thurs Mar 29th   We go the Baths at Agny but do not get a bath. Am feeling pretty queer, and go to bed about 6 o'clock.

Fri Mar 30th   Up at 8 am. (Am still feeling very queer.) Spend very bad day. Parade sick. Arrive at 2/3 London Field Ambulance. Temp 102.2. Stay there for six hours, then by car to Train Station at Bavincourt [WSW of Arras]. *Put to bed on stretchers.*

Sat Mar 31st   Temp 101. Left for 43rd C.C.S. near Saulty. In bed (stretcher) all day. (We are living under canvas, and as it is raining all night I cannot say things are exactly comfortable.)

Sun 1st Apl   Temperature has now gone down, consequently the Red Cross Train arrives and clears all bad cases to the base and perhaps to Blighty. [He does not mean that his own temperature has fallen back, as initially appears, but that the weather has got colder.]

I shouldn't like to miss the Offensive Eh! What! I make the most of plenty of blankets and a shelter. I shall not be here long.

Mon 2nd Apl   There is nothing special doing, except that one minute I am marked to be sent down to the Base, and the next they think better of it. Really I seem destined to remain in this country of France. Heaps of lorries and other transport is continually making its way toward the line.

Tues 3rd Apl   The usual day in a Casualty Clearing Station. Today there seem to be more stretchers passing covered by the 'Union Jack'. The C.C.S. is erected in the grounds of a fine picturesque Chateau doubtless lent by the owner to the British Red Cross.

Wed 4th Apl   I spend the morning in No. 12 Ward reading, etc. I am informed that I am now better so am sent to Convalescent (No. 6 Tent). Another occupation is added to my already numerous list, this is grave-digging in the British cemetery on yonder hill. (Fifteen are buried.)

Thurs 5th Apl   I spend the morning with others pulling down our 'Church'. We put this up again in another place. Dinner! (I pass no remarks.) I journey in a lorry over an awful road the other side of Saulty for stones which are brought back and dumped in the C.C.S.

Fri 6th Apl   Spend an exceedingly busy day bringing in wounded from Ambulances and carrying them to various wards. I take through in particular a wounded Hun who looks very fat and healthy but very young. (Wounded in shoulder.)

Sat 7th Apl   Roadmaking in morning, and judging from its appearance I come to the conclusion that navvying is not one of my successful accomplishments. There is an evacuation of wounded etc in afternoon, and we are all very busy getting them on to the train. In the Reception Room until 8 o'clock. Then to bed.

Sun 8th Apl   Working in Reception Room on various odd jobs in morning. It is a glorious day. Sun shining, and signs of approaching Summer. For walk with Hewitt in afternoon to Warlancourt, and spent interesting time in grounds of Royal Flying Corps. To Saulty in evening with Old Soldier. In Estaminets, etc.

Mon 9th Apl   I am returned to No. 12 Ward once again (Sick). What a contrast in the weather today. Snow, rain and awfully cold. Heaps of wounded arrive today. I retire to sleep once again on those awful stretchers. Oh, what an uncomfortable bed they do make.

Tues 10th Apl   Quite a number of German wounded have arrived. Most of them are either young or rather old. Life at this C.C.S. is rather dull, but better than the trenches. Weather continues bad. Spend evening playing games, etc.

Wed 11th Apl   It is snowing hard. A consignment of wounded arrive. Spend the time assisting in Wards. According to all accounts we are doing very well in the Arras attack, but at what a cost. More wounded arrive and continue to pour in.

Thurs 12th Apl   Trains are continually coming in to evacuate all wounded. I am very busy in Ward. No improvement in weather. Spend evening playing games. Also amuse the boys with a mouth-organ given to me by a Hun prisoner.

Fri 13th Apl   Quite a fine day today. Spend the morning pottering about the Ward. I am ordered by M.O. to return to Convalescent, however I remain in the Ward, and also pass the night there. Scores of wounded continue to arrive. I am lucky not to be in the trenches.

Sat 14th Apl   Another fine day. I am now establshed as gardener in the C.C.S. Yet another occupation added to my already numerous list. A large number of Q.V.R. arrive wounded. Their attack appears to have been unsuccessful. To bed in Convalescent Ward.

Sun 15th Apl   Raining all day. Evacuation of wounded at 6.30 am. I helped them but it was awful turning out of bed. Working in the C.C.S. all morning. Playing card [sic] in afternoon. Ditto in evening.

Mon 16th Apl   I carry on in the C.C.S. with my friend 'Durham' – he is a very nice fellow, but I cannot understand half he says, however we get along very well together.

Tues 17th Apl   I am now assisting on the 'Incinerator'. Perhaps it may be objectionable but under consideration preferable. Another day of rain and snow. The Cavalry are returning. Playing cards in evening with R.E. 3rd London R.B.

Wed 18th Apl   C'est la même travailler aujourd'hui. Raining all day. An evacuation of wounded. To Salty [sic] in evening with R.F.A. To Cinema also in Y.M.C.A. Arrived in Camp 11.30 pm.

Thurs 19th Apl   An evacuation of Convalescents in morning. (I do not happen to be one of them but Hewit does.) Working in grounds of Camp in morning. Wheeling wounded to Train all afternoon. (Raining) To Y.M.C.A. in evening – met Tom Edwards and others.

Fri 20th Apl   I am detailed for night duty. Resting all day. On duty at 7 pm in Reception rooms. Evacuation at 10.30 pm. Unloading convoys of Wounded etc. during the night.

Sat 21st Apl   In Reception Room until 7 am. Then relieved and to bed until 5 pm. On duty at 7 pm. Unloading convoys of wounded all night. Also carrying stretcher cases to be dressed. Raining slightly at 12 pm. Heavy Bombardment continues.

Sun 22nd Apl   Carrying on as usual until 7 am. Then breakfast and to bed. Tea at 4.30 pm. For walk round Saulty in evening until 7 pm. Then on duty in Reception Room.

Mon 23rd Apl   Had lie-down 12.30 am. Heavy Bombardment continues. Relieved at 7 am. Bed until 4 pm. On duty at 7 pm. Evacuation of Wounded and carrying from Ambulances all night. Our casualties rather heavy. Quite a number of Hun wounded.

Tues 24th Apl   Still receiving wounded all morning. Came off duty 7 am. Sleep during day. On duty at 7 pm. Evacuation of wounded to Red Cross train. Prisoners also sent off. On duty all night.

Wed 25th Apl   On duty in Operation Theatre 12 midnight to 4 am. (Not a pleasant task for soldiers returning to the trenches.) Off duty 7 am. Sleep and playing cards during day. On duty at 7 pm. Receiving wounded all night

Thurs 26th Apl   ...and the same until 7 am. Bed 8 am. Tea 4.30 pm. On duty 7 pm. Not much doing tonight. Playing cards,etc.

Fri 27th Apl   To sleep at 12 o'clock till 6 am. Off duty at 7 am. Asleep during day. To Saulty in evening. On duty at 7 pm. Evacuation of wounded. In Reception Room...

Sat 28th Apl   ...and until off duty at 7 am. For walk with L.Cpl sears (D) 18th Manchesters - via Saulty and Sombrin to Grand Rullecourt. (Met old friends) & Lincoln Taylor. Back at 4 pm. On duty 7 pm. Receiving wounded all night... [Tim seems to have slipped, almost unnoticed, into a new role at the Casualty Clearing Station. He makes no mention of how this came to be sanctioned, assuming (that is) that it was sanctioned. He records the monotony of his night duty as well as the horrors he sees each night as the wounded come in. That he has assisted in the operating theatre seems surprising; but his changed circumstances may be having a considerable impression on him – an impression which will affect his life after the war is over.]

Sun 29th Apl   ...until off duty at 7 am. In bed until 4 pm. On duty at 7 pm. Walking about until dark, watching 'flying' etc. Not much doing tonight – reading, etc.

Mon 30th Apl   In Y.M.C.A. with 'Manchester' 12.30 till 1.30 am. Sleep 2 till 6 am. Off duty 7 am. For walk with K.O.Y.L.I. to Pommera via Warlencourt and Mondicourt. (Lovely day) On duty at 9 pm working hard receiving sick.

Tuesday 1st May   To bed 12.30 am. Parade at 9.30 am for evacuation of convalescents by Colonel. Arrived at Warlencourt Station 2.30 pm and caught train at 10 pm arriving at Abbeville. This journey is made in trucks which are rather overcrowded.

Wed 2nd May Arrive at Y.M.C.A. Hut Abbeville at 2 am. (Laid on floor, but could not sleep.) In Y.M.C.A. Hut all day waiting for train. Concert in afternoon and evening. Attempted to 'turn in' at 9 pm, but met with no success. (Toothache is very unpleasant.)

Thurs 3rd May Left Abbeville in early morning in cattle-trucks and arrived at Bouquemaison [north of Doullens on road to Frévent and St Pol] at 6.30 am, and marched north-eastwards to Divisional Reinforcement Camp Le Souich. Giving in various particulars, etc. Am posted to 169 Company. In Le Souich evening met various old friends.

Fri 4th May Parade 9.30 am. To training area for musketry, bayonet fighting and extended order Drill. Dinner 1 pm. Parade 2.30 pm. Ammunition inspection. Also inspection by M.O. With 2nd London in evening. And a 'tres mauvais cheval'.

Sat 5th May Parade 9.30 am. March to Training Area for Physical Drill and demonstration of Attack. Dinner 1 pm. Parade 2.30 pm. Drawing various deficiencies etc. I am Orderly for day. Le Souich evening with Gluys.

Sun 6th May Church Parade at 9.30 am for reinforcements for 56th Division. Chat with Madame (next door) in afternoon. In Estaminet and various other places in evening. Meet various old Q.V.R.s during my walks in Le Souich.

Mon 7th May Parade 9 am. March to Parade Ground. Viewing an attack in new formation (French style) also Physical drill. Parade 2.30. Inspection of feet prior to Route March. In village all evening.

Tues 8th May Raining all morning. Lecture. (The use of the rifle). Parade 2.30 for route March through Bouquemaison. Whom should I meet but Lieut Farmiloe. Pay parade 6.30 (5 Francs). Yet another surprise: I meet A. Larkin from Merton Park M.G.C. and spend evening with him.

Wed. 9th May Parade 9.30 am. March to Training ground for musketry. Dismissed at 11am. Dinner 1 pm (Usual diet). Parade 2 am [pm?] - Musketry – aiming, rapid loading and sighting. (I fire 15 in 40 seconds.) (rather good). To Brévillers in evening with Yeoy (an old Q.V.R.)

Thurs 10th May Morning off. In French Cottage, etc. Dinner 11.15 am. Marched to Range 12-mid. Fired 15 rounds. Moved to No. 57 Billet in evening. Also football, etc.

Fri 11th May Parade at 5.45 am. Marched to Baths at Lucheau (4 kilos). (Rather nice walk through wood in early morning, and bath very good.) Breakfast 9.30 am. Parade 2.30. Lecture on Hygiene, and M.O. inspection. Football in evening.

Sat 12th May Parade 8.45 am. Practised an Attack, also bayonet drill. Army Corps VII Cricket Match in afternoon. 56th and 21st Div., versus 14th and 18th Div. Band also there. To concert in evening at Chateau in Le Souich. (Very good indeed.)

Sun 13th May Church Parade in field 10 am. With Larkin and his friends in afternoon. To Football Match in evening 6 pm. Officers nil, Sergeants one. Spoke to Madame at 59.

Mon 14th May Parade 8.45 am. Attack and Bayonet Fighting in morning. Parade 2.20 (Clean Fatigue). Pay and check roll call. On Quartermaster's Fatigue at 6.15 till 7.30pm. In Estaminet etc.

Tues 15th May Parade 8.45 am. Route March through Rebreuviette in morning. Parade 2.30 pm. Kit inspection and another list taken of deficiencies. Football in evening with Gluys and Cpl Hawkins. Officers 2, Sergeants 1 (good game).

Wed 16th May Parade 9 am. Marched to Training Area for Physical and Bayonet Drill. Marched to Baths at 11.30 at Lucheau (Good bath). In Estaminet. Arrived back 3 pm. Dinner 4.45 and Tea. Raining all evening. In Cottage and Billet.

Thurs 17th May   It is raining hard. We have a 'lecture' by Lieut Watson in barn. Then for a short Route March. Parade 2.30 pm. Rifle and Bayonet inspection, also Box Helmet drill. 'Back at the old game.' I am now Batman to Lieut Jones and Lieut Wilson 15th London Regiment. (Issue of Rum.)

Fri 18th May   Parade 2.30 pm. Deficiencies. Spent very easy day doing practically nothing. Paraded for Deficiencies. (I get some of them.) In Estaminet with Gluys. (We are moving off very soon.)

The last few weeks seem simply to 'happen' rather than to have any planned shape. There are delightful moments, happy times, occasional reminders of war (especially in such activities as bayonet training, and, of course, by Tim's intimate contact with vast numbers of wounded being brought in from the front line while he was technically 'convalescing'); but the entry for May 18th suggests that Tim has been involved in what could be described as 'Time out of War' and that he senses things may be about to become less easy-going. We shall see.

Sat 19th May   In Le Souich generally. Helping in Officers Mess various parts of the day. To football match in afternoon: 169 Brigade One – 168 Brigade Nil. More old Boys arrive at Reinforcement Camp. To bed 11 pm.

Sun 20th May   Parade 8.30 am. Left Le Souich 11 am in Motor Lorries, passing Frévent, Avesnes le Comte and other villages. Arrived at Duisans [WNW of Arras] (with QVR) (Yet another Officer, Mr Johnson). Walking round Camp and looking up old acquaintances in the Battalion in Evening. (They have been badly smashed.) [This last parenthesis no doubt brought a further thought to Tim that he was blest with 'luck' in that he had been very unwell, and therefore taken out of the line, at the moment when another punishing attack was about to take place.]

Mon 21st May   Messing about generally in Camp all morning. Pay in afternoon (30 Francs). Out with Howe in evening in Estaminet, etc. Gunfire heavy.

Tues 22nd May   Very miserable day (Raining). The Camp is now converted into a veritable mud-pond. I do not like this place. (We are moving soon.)

Wed 23rd May   Cleaning up in morning for Colonel's inspection. Also in village. It is fine today. To football match in evening: QVR 3 – L.R.B. nil. In Estaminets, etc, in evening. Our guns are very busy.

Thurs 24th May   Left Duisans in morning proceeding westwards, and arrived at Agnez. We are living in huts in village. Pretty busy during day fixing things up etc. To bed fairly early (and a very nice one too). (Heavy Bombardment.)

Fri 25th May   Getting acquainted with Village. Rather a nice place, and I hear that we are to be here for some time. (I hope this rumour is correct.) [Agnez is about seven kilometres WNW of the centre of Arras.] *I am acting as Caterer for Officers Mess. In Estaminet with Roe (RE Signaller) in evening.*

Sat 26th May   The 'Bow Bells' arrive. Spoke to Harry Boram (Manager of show). Heavy Bombardment on front. Weather is 'top-hole', and so am I.

Sun 27th May   Usual business in Agnez. To Football Match 5.30 pm: QVR One – 2nd Londons nil. Aeroplanes very active overhead. One Hun machine above village shelled by our anti-aircraft guns. (Another hot day) Lovely evening.

Mon 28th May   Inspection of Battalion in morning by General Hull, commanding 56th Division. Enemy aeroplanes overhead. Usual 'quiet' evening. Heard part of 'Bow Bells' Concert.

Tues 29th May   To 'Bow Bells' Concert in afternoon. (Very good show, especially revue 'Well of Course'.) Nothing doing otherwise.

Wed. 30th May   To football match in evening: QVR 2 – QWR nil. Good game. For stroll in village in evening.

Thurs 31st May   On Range in morning. Fired ten rounds. Also again in evening with Lieut Wilson. One of our Observation Balloons is fired on and has to descend.

Fri 1st Jun   Spoke to Jenny in Epicerie. Played Machine Gun Corps in evening: QVR 2 MGC 2. Usual walk in village in evening. Aeroplanes very active.

Sat 2nd Jun   Tout la méme. [Nearly !] Usual Hun aeroplanes overhead. Watching football in evening. Inter Westminster Match. Also saw finish of 2/3 Field Ambulance Concert. For stroll in village in evening.

Sun 3rd Jun   Epicerie etc in afternoon. Enemy aeroplanes drop bombs near Agnez. New Officer Mr Moss arrives for C Company. Bombs drop on C.C.S.[Casualty Clearing Station]: many killed and wounded.

Mon 4th Jun   Firing in afternoon on Range just outside village. Fired 25 rounds. To football in evening: QVR nil – MGC nil.

5th, 6th and 7th Jun Nothing doing in Agnez.

Fri 8th Jun   Rather busy day as we expect to leave for the line tomorrow. Usual aeroplane activity. Cigarettes exceedingly scarce. Had rather jolly evening with the Boys in which we indulged in 'boire et carte'. Raining during day.

Sat 9th Jun   Making preparations for departure. Left Agnez at 6 pm and marched via Dainville, Achicourt, and 'Telegraph Hill' to old trenches near Neuville Vitasse. Arrived at 9.30 pm. Made ourselves comfortable for the night in small dug-out. Huns drop a few shells.

Sun 10th Jun   In disused Hun trenches behind Wancourt [SE of Arras] during day. (Left of Neuville Vitasse). Walked to Transport at right of Beaurains to dump packs, etc. March off by Platoons via Wancourt, and relieve Bucks Regt. Our artillery is busy all night. Enemy reply very feeble. (Raining)

Mon 11th Jun   To sleep at 2 am for few hours in small dug-out. We are in chalk trench which is pretty awful. Hun artillery gets lively about mid-day. Our position is on right bank of Codeau river, with Guedmappe and Monchy slightly to left in front. Enemy shell battery slightly in rear but meet with no success. (A noisy night) [Possibly he means the Cojeul River, and Guémappe.]

Tues 12th Jun   In about trench till 2.30 am [sic] . Sleep 3 till 8 am. Guns busy on both sides. Aeroplane Hun brought down by Lewis gun. Also prisoner captured at dawn. Fritz shells village of Guémappe. Aeroplane activity overhead. I go down with Lieut Wilson. Roncourt shelled as we pass through. Ambulance at Tilloy and arrive 2/1 F.A. in Arras at 11 pm.

Wed 13th Jun   In Hôpital St Jean and Convent at Arras with Lieut Wilson. To Telegraph Hill in morning for packs, etc. In Arras most of afternoon. To 'Elegant Extracts' Division Concert Party in evening at Salle des Concerts. (A very unique Hall and finely decorated.) For walk in Arras after, and then listened to organ in Chapel attached to Convent. [Tim does not make clear precisely why he and/or Lieutenant Wilson should leave the line and go to Arras. Whatever the reason, he seems to have become almost a tourist!]

Thurs 14th Jun   Visiting various places of interest in Arras including Museums, Cathedral, Colleges, etc. All are badly smashed, but Théatre has escaped damage. Civilians are slowly returning and shops re-opening. In Hopital St Jean most of evening. A lovely building, and still occupied by Nuns.

Fri 15th Jun   *In Soldiers Club, etc. morning. Packing up, and saw Lieut Wilson off to O.R.S. in afternoon. To Théatre des Arras in evening to pictures. (A fine building containing four tiers above pit. It is partly damaged.) Quite a bit of 'Blighty' again.* [A reference to Tim's theatrical ambitions before he signed on in the Q.V.R.] *For walk afterwards, and then to Hopital St Jean. Bombardment.*

Sat 16th Jun   *Our guns are busy in front. Spent morning in Church Army Hut and in Estaminet, etc. To Théatre des Arras to pictures at 2.30 pm to 4 pm. To Salle des Concerts at 4.10 pm till 5.30. To Salle des Concerts again at 6 till 8 pm. (3rd Divisional Concert Party). Left Arras (full kit) 8.30 pm and stayed with Traffic Police for the night in old Hun line.*

Sun 17th Jun   *Arrived in Transport Lines at Telegraph Hill in morning. Living with Fred Prichard at Headquarters most of day. Huns shell Arras and round-about. Left for trenches with transport 8.30 pm. Arrived in trenches on right of Monchy 11 pm. Artillery are very busy. Hun counter-attack on left but fail to get their objectives.*

Mon 18th Jun   *Had about one hour's sleep. Huns shell trenches all day. Am living in trench – no dug-outs here. Acting as Runner to Capt Burgen. Went with him over 'No Man's Land' carrying out digging advanced posts and wiring in front of first line. Huns shell us badly, but our casualties are few. Getting men to carry stretchers 12 pm.*

Tues 19th June   *Carrying water to men holding advanced posts 1.20 am. To B Company for Verey pistol. Huns seem to expect an attack and are sending up showers of 'Flares' and also shelling at random, but I manage to dodge through. Aeroplane activity overhead around 3am. With messages during day. Capt. Burgen gets 'light-headed' and goes to Hospital. (What a relief)*

Wed 20th Jun   *Wiring parties out in No Man's Land and activity on both sides until dawn. Huns use many Minenwerfers. With messages during day to B.H.Q., etc. Communication trenches are 'straffed' by Huns and receive many direct hits. 'C'est tres mauvais pour couriers.' We are relieved by Rangers, 12th , and start back via Heninel. Ride part of way on 'Limber'.*

Thurs 21st Jun   *Arrived at our Camp in Beaurains 1.30 am. Last of Battalion arrive 6.30 am. Fritz obliges with a few shells, most of them 'dud'. Making ourselves comfortable during the day. With Lawrence, Rudkin and Yeoy* [?] *to Bow Bells and Band.*

Fri 22nd Jun   *Settling down to life under Canvas. Fritz sends over a few shells and shrapnel to let us know that the War is still on. Otherwise quite quiet. Divisional Band plays in Camp afternoon and evening. Raining most of day.*

Sat 23rd Jun   *A few shells drop round about Beaurains, but of no importance. Rather doubtful weather. Usual Camp life. Listening to Divisional Band afternoon and evening. Rather gay time in tents.* [Gay, then = merry, jolly.]

Sun 24th Jun   *Church Parade for Battalion. Usual work in Camp. Writing, etc, in afternoon. Football Match in evening: QVR 2 – MGC 2. (Draw). This match is played on our old No Man's Land amongst barbed wire and trenches and deep German dug-outs.*

Mon 25th Jun   *Number of Observation Balloons on our Front is increasing. The weather continues good. Aircraft on both sides extremely busy. Usual Tomfoolery in Tent at night.*

Tues 26th Jun   *Usual life in Camp at Beaurains. A few stray shells drop about. Our anti-aircraft guns are busy with Hun aeroplanes. Football in evening: QVR versus LRB, Lost 4-2. Heavy bombardment all night.*

Wed 27th Jun   *Enemy aeroplane overhead in morning. Huns send a few long-distance shells round Achicourt and Arras. To Arras in evening to Theatre to see Bow Bells. General Hull and all staff present. (Grand programme). Went back to Beaurains with Adams, Thomas and Simpson (D Company).*

Thurs 28th Jun   A few shells dropped round about. Bombardment is taking place in Lens direction. [Lens is about 15 km north of Arras.] *Spent quiet day writing letters and messing about generally. Old German trenches here are being filled in and barbed wire and other obstacles cleared away.*

Fri 29th Jun   Fritz sends over Shrapnel at Observation Balloon which unfortunately happens to be above us. Football Match in evening: QVR versus MGC. We won an excellent game   2-1. Usual fun in Camp.

Sat 30th Jun   Raining all day which is anything but pleasant under Canvas. Am now Batman to Lieut Cailly (very nice indeed). Usual daily strafe by Fritz. Our guns are bombarding all night towards Lens.

Sun 1st Jul   To Memorial Service in morning. Anniversary of Gommecourt last year. (Very interesting and pathetic.) Usual life in Camp. Aeroplanes are exceedingly active, and Fritz continues to shell Observation Balloon above us. With no effect. Rain, and cards.

Gommecourt had played a particularly sad part in the disastrous Somme offensive which had started precisely one year earlier, on July 1st 1916. Losses at Gommecourt were, even by the standards of that day, exceptionally heavy, yet the attack had no specific strategic significance that might be seen to justify such carnage.

General Joffre, C in C of the French Army, had proposed a joint Franco-British offensive along some 60 miles of the Somme front. (The British and French armies 'met' at the Somme.) Before this could take place, however, the entire French Tenth Army had been removed from their area of the front in order to 'beef up' the defences at Verdun, where vast French casualties had been suffered. They had been replaced by a British Army under General Rawlinson. The British C in C, Haig, realized that the Somme operation would now fall mainly on British troops. As originally planned, thirty-nine French divisions would have taken part in the initial attack, but by the time the onslaught began on July 1st 1916 only six French divisions remained in situ, so heavy were their losses at Verdun.

Haig realized that the British attack must be made on a diminished front some twelve miles in length, stretching from Serre in the north to Maricourt. South of Maricourt, five French divisions would be involved. Both Haig and Rawlinson were concerned that in the north the Germans were able to deploy flanking artillery around Gommecourt, where their position was very strongly defended. Despite the fact that Gommecourt was probably the most impregnable position on the entire front, Haig insisted that it be attacked, partly to destroy German ability to fire on the British flank, partly as a tactic to divert German attention from the main area of attack. The choice of local commander was Lieutenant- General Sir Thomas D'Oyly Snow, who reluctantly began planning his onslaught on Gommecourt, to be made by two territorial divisions: the 46th North Midland and the 56th First London. For several weeks in May and June 1916, these divisions were digging, wiring, carrying and building in preparation. Then, exhausted, they were required to go 'over the top' against the most formidable German position on the entire front.

The 56th Division alone suffered over 4,000 casualties; and during this brief and unsuccessful diversion over 2,000 British troops died. An excellent and very full account of this misguided operation is to be found in the books 'Pro Patria Mori' and 'A Lack of Offensive Spirit' by Alan MacDonald (privately published 2006-2008).

Timothy Elliott had enrolled in the 56th Division (but his part of the 169th Brigade was occupied elsewhere, at the centre of the main attack, on July 1st). Little wonder he found the Memorial Service he attended precisely one year later which commemorated Gommecourt (in his words) 'very interesting and pathetic'.

CHAPTER NINE

TIM'S SUMMER OF 1917
Hardly wine and roses

Having survived the whole year since the start of the great Battle of the Somme, Tim is soon on the move again, back to an area which he knew at an earlier stage of his deployment. He records, as is his custom, the stages of his journey:

Mon 2nd Jul   Packing up in morning. Left Beaurains and marched to Achicourt and Dainville. Then jumped on lorry and rode through Beaumetz to Monchiet. Then marched to Gouy en Artois.[About 14 km WSW of Arras.] *Billeted in Huts. Met one or two civilians whom I knew. Had rather good time in Estaminet, etc.*

The Estaminet was a form of Café found predominantly in Belgium and northern France. It was usually family-run, and served coffee, wine, spirits and beer. During the 1914-18 War almost its principal function was to provide a privately-run, informal place of relaxation for off-duty troops. It was, as Tim makes clear in his many references to it, a venue liked by the soldiery because it made no demands on them, was reasonably priced and sometimes offered the chance to meet a local girl or two. The word 'estaminet' has, perhaps unfortunately, been appropriated by a few up-market or trendy British restaurants whose prices and objectives are somewhat different from those of the 'real thing'.

Tues 3rd Jul   Left Gouy in advance of Regiment and marched through Barly Fosseau [probably Fosseux], *Sombrines* [Sombrin ?], *then lost the way and went through Warluzel arriving at Sus St Léger at 5.30 pm.*[A march of some 12 km.] *In Billet all evening, and looking after Lieut Cailly at Chateau. (Rain)*
Wed 4th Jul   We are in a fine Billet. The Lady is awfully nice and we are getting on well together. Alice is a nice little girl and runs many errands for me.
Thurs 5th Jul   I take over cooking for C. Company Mess. (Yet another occupation added to my list.) C'est la guerre. Company are practising attacks ready for ----- what is coming.
Fri 6th Jul   I have some very fine romps with Alice and Lucy aged 10 and 12 respectively. They are very pretty little girls; their mother is dead, and father is a prisoner of war.
Sat 7th Jul   In Sus St Léger.
Sun 8th Jul   Rather fine time in Estaminet.
Mon 9th Jul   The people in this village are some of the best I have met in France.
Tues 10th Jul   Quite a number of French soldiers arrive here on leave. They appear to get it regularly every three months. What a comparison with my own: one leave in 25 months.
11th, 12th, 13th   In Sus St Léger.
Sat 14th Jul   I am enjoying myself and taking advantage of this rest from the trenches. Battalion sports.
*Sun 15th Jul   *[Tim tries out his French here.] *C'est la méme toujours dans Sus St Leger mais bon pour durée de la Guerre. Encore trenchée bientout. Zut.*
Mon 16th Jul   Brigade 169 Sports commence. Q.V.R. take a good many prizes. Alice and Maria are still very amusing and we have some fun. [Has Lucy become Maria, or is there a third child present ?]

Tues 17th Jul   Brigade sports are continued today.

Wed 18th Jul   Guns bombard all night in the distance.

19th, 20th, 21st Jul   In Sus St Leger.

Sun 22nd Jul   We shall soon leave Sus St Leger. Lucy and Alice are two fine 'kids' and I shall miss them very much; but of course it is Active Service.

Mon 23rd Jul   We are making preparations to move. I have enjoyed myself greatly in Sus St Leger and I shall regret leaving it.* C'est la guerre. *Madame is awfully 'cut up'.*

Tues 24th Jul   Finished clearing up. Left Sus St Leger at 8.30 am and marched to Bouquemaison Station (6 kilos). Entrained as a Battalion. I rode on transport trucks . Passed through Frevent, St Pol, Lillers, Aires and arrive at Wizernes Station 4 pm. Marched to St Omer (tea) and then continued to Nortleulinghem 11.30 pm. (All are tired and fed up.) [Bouquemaison is north of Doullens. Wizernes is south-west of St Omer. Nortleulinghem is north-west of St Omer.]

Wed 25th Jul   Getting straight and settling down. Our quarters are not much, but it is a bad policy to grumble: the trenches are always looming ahead. I find a better billet for sleeping at other end of Village. The people are awfully good.

Thurs 26th Jul   This is a 'dead-and-alive' hole. No shops. Very few estaminets. But why complain. The trenches are much worse.

Fri 27th Jul   Marie, the girl in the estaminet next door, is engaged to a British Sergeant Instructor. Bit silly, I think.

Sat 28th Jul   I have some nice chats with lady at my Billet in evening.

Sun. 29th Jul   To St Omer in morning, walking with Saville. (14 kilos from Nort-Neulinghem.) [sic]. Spent very nice, interesting time in town. Cathedral and public buildings quite good. (Also numero katre*) [sic]. Arrived at 11 pm, very tired.

Mon 30th Jul   Company is training vigorously in all kinds of attack. Our guns bombard heavily.

Tues 31st Jul   Our bombardment continues.

The Third Battle of Ypres

Wed 1st Aug   Our Belgian attack has commenced. Our usual luck. The rain has stopped operations.

Thurs 2nd Aug   Rain all day. Everything at standstill.

Fri 3rd Aug   Another day of rain in Nort-Neulinghem [sic]. [Nort-Leulinghem is today approached by crossing (in a southwesterly direction) the E15 Autoroute about halfway from Ardres to the St Omer turn-off.]

Sat 4th Aug   Post is stopped for a while. We expect to move off at any time. More rain. Our bombardment continues to be very heavy.

Sun 5th Aug   We are now in readiness to move up at any time. Our bombardment continues. Very busy until midnight getting baggage off. Then to our excellent billet for the last time.

Mon 6th Aug   Very busy morning arranging things. We march off at 2.30 pm and entrain at Watten Station with 2nd Londons. Journey via St Omer and Hazebrouck, and arrive at Abeele 11 pm. Then march to Watteau. Much time spent finding billet and settling down. [Watten is on the River Aa NNW of St Omer; Abeele is WSW of Poperinge; Watteau is probably Watou which lies just inside the Belgian border to the west of Poperinge.]

Tues 7th Aug   To Watteau. These Belgian people are funny customers to deal with, but we are not getting on so badly with them. Fritz makes a bombing raid.

Wed 8th Aug   In Watteau. Another raid.

Thurs 9th Aug   *Our artillery bombardment continues. Another raid.*

Fri 10th Aug   *Another showery day. Many observation balloons in front of us. Enemy air-raid. Many bombs dropped all round about. Doubtless trying for aerodrome, which is 300 yards from my billet. No great damage done.*

Sat 11th Aug   *Receive sudden orders to pack up. I wait behind with kit. Battalion march off 12.30 pm and entrain at Abeele. I march with transport via Abeele, Ouderdom and Reninghelst, then via Dickebusch* [Dikkebus] *to reserve lines in Château Segard Wood. Rain nearly all night. Huns strafe wood and we receive a few casualties. Spent rotten night in mud and rain.*

Sun 12th Aug   *To Dickebusch in morning for rations, etc. Then to wood near St Eloi* [St Eloois is just south of Ypres.]. *The 'boys' leave for front line in battle order 4 pm. (I am with transport.) Hun aeroplane strafes our observation balloons and brings one down in flames. Occupants descend safely in parachutes. I return to transport lines outside Dickebusch. (My feet are awfully bad. Could not walk much farther.) But thanks to Capt. Symes I am not in trenches this time.*

Mon 13th Aug   *Great artillery activity. News of the 'boys' comes through slowly. The mud is awful. Hardly any trenches, just a mass of shell-holes. The Hun artillery is playing Hell with our line. Jack night* [Knight?] *is killed, also Lieut Caley* [previously the officer spelt Cailly, presumably] *and poor old Capt Symes, our Skipper. (I have a lot to remember him by.) Shrapnel is bursting overhead in evening: doubtless Fritz is after our balloons. He has a fearful 'wind-up' sending up all sorts of coloured lights from trenches.*

Tues 14th Aug   *Fritz makes another raid on the observation balloons above us and brings one down in flames, and compels 5 other men to descend in parachutes. (More rain and mud.) Enemy shell all round rather erratically. Reninghelst also strafed. Bombs dropped on main traffic roads. Lorries and mules put out of action. (Some War)*

Wed 15th Aug   *Casualties are continually arriving. Air fight overhead. Two of our aeroplanes compelled to descend, one falling into tent at Clearing Station. Pilot killed and Observer wounded. Two R.A.M.C. also killed. Enemy make another attack on our balloons, but it is unsuccessful. Artillery commence fearful bombardment in preparation for tomorrow. (Some sight)*

Thurs 16th Aug   *'The Boys' went over the 'top' at 5 am. and reached the objective. (Many prisoners.) One of our observation balloons gets adrift and floats over Hun lines. Our 'boys' have to retire owing to Regiments on left and right flanks failing. We take a large number of prisoners. Our casualties are heavy and not yet ascertained. Fritz makes yet another raid all round. Lorries and ammunition mules suffer badly.*

Fri 17th Aug   *Plenty of Observation Work being carried* [out]. *I see 33 balloons now, 28 of ours and 5 German. The Boys are coming out of the trenches tonight. Balloons are shelled, but without result. To cinema pictures in evening at Ouderdom (very good). Fritz makes biggest raid of all. Many searchlights follow him along. Bombs and aerial torpedoes dropped all round. (No casualties in Camp.)* [The sentence stating that Tim has been to, and appreciated, the cinema presentation, seems to sit uncomfortably with the detailed descriptions of war and carnage. But he does not even alter the handwriting!]

Sat 18th Aug   *Packing up in morning ready to move off. Left at 2 pm with transport. I rode part of way on lorry via Ouderdom and Reninghelst, then through Abeele to another part of Wattou. C.Company is 60 strong, and the whole Regiment about 500. All C.Company Officers killed except Lieut Field, who has 'shell-shock'. Fritz raids us again – bombs dropped round about.*

Sun 19th Aug   *Roll call, and sorting out missing men's kits. (The Company have plenty of parcels through men missing.) Another raid by Fritz. It seems to be a regular occurrence now and our searchlights are kept very busy.*

Mon 20th Aug   *Another glorious day. We are living in a large Belgian Farm. The people are not at all bad and sell coffee, cigarettes, etc to the soldiers. Fritz visits us once again and distributes his famous 'iron rations' all around. He is awfully generous.*

Tues 21st Aug   *Heavy bombardment is going on.   Nothing special doing in Wattou. Weather is very nice. What is the matter: Fritz has not made a raid tonight.*

Wed 22nd Aug   *Terrific bombardment going on up the line.   Weather continues fine. American aeroplane above us. We expect to move very soon. Fritz makes a raid tonight more powerful than usual: he is doubtless making up for last night.*

Thurs 23rd Aug   *The fine weather is too good to last. Showers on and off all day. Busy packing etc. Transport left at 2 pm. Oh yes, we have the usual raid. The enemy gets a direct hit on Abeele Station killing leave party and nurses. Bombs also dropped on Hun prisoners. I hope we shall be far away tomorrow night.*

Fri 24th Aug   *Preparing to move off.   Left Wattou at 3 pm and marched to Abeele Station. In Train at 5 pm, went via St Omer. Travelling all night. Curious: we pass our 2nd Battalion going to the line.*

Sat 25th Aug   *Detrained at Watten. Arrived at Serques* [NW of St Omer] *3 am. People got up and made us coffee. Then to sleep. Breakfast 9.30 am. We have a lovely Billet in a French Farm House, and the Lady and her daughter (Bertha) are awfully good to us. I am sure we shall have a fine time here.*

Sun 26th Aug   *Usual business in Serques. We have a jolly afternoon with Bertha and her four girl friends who have visited her. Yes, I think this will suit for the duration of the War. To bed at 10 pm.*

Mon 27th Aug   *Raining all day – stay in Billet in Serques. Rain – rain - rain.*

Tues 28th Aug   *Just the same. Bertha is not a pretty girl but she is very attractive and we have heaps of fun. I think she has had post-cards from every Regiment that has been here. I suppose we must keep up the reputation.*

Wed 29th Aug   *More fun with Bertha. No leave. Heaps of rain.*

Thurs 30th Aug   *Packing up ready to leave the Flanders front (Thank Heavens!) Bertha and her Mother sit up all night with us. (There are people whose kindness I shall never forget, such as these.) Of course it is raining.*

Fri 31st Aug   *Left Serques at 2.30 am. (Very dark, and steady rain). We marched via St Omer to Wizernes Station (14 kilos). Entrained at 8 am. Travelled via Lillers, St Pol, Arras and Achiet-le-Grand. Detrained at Miraumont* [west of Bapaume and well south of Arras] *5 pm. Then marched via Achiet-le-Petit and Achiet-le-Grand arriving at Bapaume very late at night. Slept in Tents.*

Sat 1st Sep   *The whole of the 169 Brigade is living here under Canvas on the outskirts of Bapaume. A fair number of 'Very* [Verey] *Lights' can be seen in the distance, but the whole front is very quiet. (Quite a change from Flanders.) Weather here is very unsettled.*

Sun 2nd Sep   *Under Canvas on outskirts of Bapaume. Rather fine day but very windy. The ground is recovering marvellously from 'Battlefield' appearance. Grass everywhere, and only ruins to show that fighting has taken place here.*

Mon 3rd Sep   *Usual business at Bapaume.*

Tues 4th Sep   *Still camping on the outskirts of Bapaume. L.R.B. and Q.W.R. move up the line. We expect to follow them tomorrow. Inspection in morning by General in charge of Army Corps.   Summer has returned at last. A glorious day.*

Wed. 5th Sep   *In Camp at Bapaume. An enemy aeroplane is overhead and is engaged by our anti-aircraft guns. Another lovely day. Left at 5.30 pm and marched via Bancourt, Frémicourt to outskirts of Lebucquière. Under canvas here. About 5 kilos behind our line.*

Thurs 6th Sep   On outskirts of Lebucquière. We are under observation from enemy balloons. Thank Goodness this is a quiet part of the line. One can hardly realize that Fritz has retired from here. Everything is as usual except for ruined villages. It is raining tonight.

Fri 7th Sep   Awfully good weather. We spend most of time building sheds and other shelters for we are miles from civilization. Guns on both sides are very quiet. Not much doing on either side.

Sat 8th Sep   In Camp on Somme. Aeroplanes rather active on both sides. Otherwise not much doing. We have relieved the 3rd Division.

Sun 9th Sep   C.Company leaves here in evening and goes to position nearer the line. I remain in charge of baggage, etc. Waiting all night for limber to take it away.

Mon 10th Sep   I arrive at transport lines 1 am. To Frémicourt in morning to Divisional Canteen. Look over old German grave-yard. Weather continues hot, though very cold at night. Aeroplane activity.

Tues 11th Sep   Ditto

Wed 12th Sep   In camp with transport between Frémicourt and Lébucquière [respectively some three and seven kilometres east of Bapaume.]

Thurs 13th Sep   Still nothing doing.

14th, 15th, 16th, 17th, 18th, 19th, 20th, 21st, 22nd, 23rd: Ditto.

Mon 24th Sep   German airman drives one of our fellows down and flying low over our camp has a narrow escape himself. I hear that I am going on leave tomorrow. (What news.)

Tues 25th Sep   Getting ready for leave. Left Camp at 7 pm in Mess cart and arrived at Bapaume Station at 9 pm. Train left at 10.15 pm. Travelling all night went through Arras.

Wed 26th Sep   Travelling in train via St Pol etc., and arrived at Boulogne 7 am. To rest Camp. Left Boulogne on the Invicta *at 10 am and arrived at Folkestone 11.45. Caught train and arrived at Victoria 3 pm., then to Wimbledon and home at 3.45 pm. Saw various friends. To Theatre in evening with Dad and Bill to see* Sweethearts and Wives.

So Tim has survived the summer and has, at last, been granted the leave which he so envied the French. His journey back (recorded in detail on 25th/26th September) is remarkable in that the trains and ships seem to be running as easily as in peace-time, and possibly even more reliably. The London Theatre was presumably his 'treat' on his safe arrival.

CHAPTER TEN

TIM ON LEAVE

At last Tim has some leave. Earlier he had commented on his discovery that French troops apparently had leave every three months, and had seen fit to record his annoyance. One appreciates, as I'm sure he did, that it was rather more difficult to arrange home leave when the English Channel (*La Manche*) was in the way; but whatever the facts of the case he was clearly overjoyed to be home for a while, and the first evening had found him at a theatre.

Sweethearts and Wives seems an appropriate title. One broadsheet of the time carried an announcement earlier in 1917 that 'A new naval play *For Sweethearts and Wives* is about to go on tour. Later it will come to town.' So that seems to be what he saw. Whether it was a production of the most popular play written by James Kenney (1780-1849) *Sweethearts and Wives* (dating from 1823), or perhaps an adaptation of it, I have not been able to discover. The Press reference to 'a naval play' hints that this might be the case, because a principal character in Kenney's work is an Admiral; but the use of the word 'new' suggests otherwise. Any information gratefully received.

1917

Thurs 27th Sep   Spent morning visiting. Saw Mr Bowman, Aunt Ellen, and others. Same in afternoon. Met Cyril in evening, and we had rather a tres bon time together.

Fri 28th Sep   Saw Audrey Rutter and others in morning. Caught 2.44 from Victoria to Maidstone, arrived 4.40 and met Mrs Reed, and also Gwen later. To pictures in evening (with Gwen). Raid by German aeroplanes, but they are driven back. A few bombs are dropped.

Sat 29th Sep   To business with Gwen in morning. Also for ride on bicycle, and in Bungalow. For walk in Cuckoo Woods with Gwen in afternoon. We try the Pictures once again, and once again the raid stops everything. Oh, it's nice to be on leave in these times.

Sun 30th Sep   To Maidstone Church in morning with Gwen and Mr and Mrs Reed. For walk round in afternoon with Gwen. Two attempts at raiding tonight at 5 pm and 8 pm. Nothing much. Rather nice time inside the Bungalow with Gwen.

Mon 1st Oct   For walk over Sand-hills in morning with Gwen, and very nice too ! Also in Maidstone. In Bungalow and in Town in afternoon. Met Dot at Station in evening, with Gwen, etc. Another air-raid, and also good time with Gwen.

Tues 2nd Oct   Caught 10.18 from Maidstone with Gwen, and arrived in Wimbledon at 1 pm in time for another raid. For walk in afternoon. Went with Cyril in evening to Restaurant etc. Then for short walk with Gwen. To bed late (as usual).

Wed 3rd Oct   For walk in John Innes Park etc in morning with Gwen. To London in afternoon with Gwen. To Advance Pay Office, Regent Street, then to Cinema. To Wimbledon Theatre in evening for A Little Bit of Fluff. For short walk afterwards and bed at 11.30pm.

Thurs 4th Oct   Raining. To Tooting in morning with Gwen, to see Fred Kibble. To Palladium in afternoon: Bransby Williams, Gus Elen, Billy Merson and other 'stars'. To King's Palace Pictures in evening (rotten) and for walk afterwards. With Gwen, of course. To bed 11.45 pm.

Fri 5th Oct   With Gwen all day in Merton Park, Wimbledon, etc. With Cyril in evening, also round to Cuckneys, Church Lane. Spent rest of evening there. Bed 11.30 pm.

Sat Oct 6th Walking round in the morning with Gwen. Over Cannon Hill, etc., in afternoon. With Gwen in evening to Kennington Theatre for 'The Yeomen of the Guard'. Met various people I knew during day. To bed late.

Sun 7th Oct Raining. To Church in morning with Gwen. For walk in afternoon; saw Mr Ballard and others. Indoors in evening with Gwen, then for short walk and afterwards had short chat with Mr Warner. To bed 11.30 pm.

Mon 8th Oct Left Wimbledon 6.30 am. Left Victoria 7.30 am. Arrived at Folkestone 9.40. In Rest Camp on beach all day. In Y.M.C.A., and then in town from 3.45 pm with London Scottish and Webb. Raining all the time. Restrictions for overseas troops are 'no bon'. To Café Oriental. Then to Picture Palace. In billets 9 pm.

Tues 9th Oct Living in specially allotted houses on beach. Parade at 7. Allowed in Folkestone from 2.30 pm till 5 pm. Walked round town, etc. To Concert in evening at Y.M.C.A. Girls of the W.A.A.D. also present. Had rather good time.

Wed 10th Oct Parade 7 am. Left Folkestone at 8.30 am: sea rather rough. Arrived at Boulogne 11 am. Then marched to 'Rest Camp' and there all night. In B.E.F. Canteen, etc.

Thurs 11th Oct Parade 9.15 am. Caught train from Boulogne 11 am. Travelling all day via Etaples, Hesdin, St Pol, Arras, arriving at Bapaume 8 pm. (Oh, these French lines.) Arrived at Transport lines Frémicourt at 10 pm. Stayed here the night.

Fri 12th Oct Raining (as usual). With Transport all day. Left with Ration limbers at 5 pm via Lebucquière and Beaumetz. Arrived at Company Headquarters 7.30. In Reserve at Dougnies. I can't say that I like 'dug-out' life after returning from leave.

Sat 13th Oct With C.Company in Reserve at Dougnies. Situation rather quiet. Looking after Capt Hadden, O.C. C.Company. Have not got over leave yet.

Sun 14th Oct In reserve dug-outs at Dougnies. [Possibly Doignies, nearly halfway from Bapaume to Cambrai.] In

Above: the Hotel de Ville at Etaples today. Tim's daughter Ann Veronica seeks entry. In 1917 the town was a most important base where troops en route to and from the front (or injured) were processed. At any one time thousands would have been there. Many still are there, buried in one of the huge local cemeteries.
Left: the fine Lutyens Memorial at the main Etaples Cemetery

sunken road. Batteries in our rear very noisy. Weather doubtful. Have had very little sleep since my return.

Mon 15th Oct   In reserve at Dougnies. Left in the evening to relieve Q.W.R. in trenches at Bougnies [sic]. Our Artillery are very noisy.

Tues 16th Oct   In dug-outs at Bougnies with A.Company. Artillery active; also aeroplanes. Otherwise quiet. Patrols out.

Wed 17th Oct   Still in line at Bougnies [possibly Beugny. Both Doignies and Beugny now have British cemeteries.] *Patrols searching No Man's Land.*

Thurs 18th Oct   In line in Boursies. [Boursies stretches along the straight line of the N30, half way between Bapaume and Cambrai.] *Huns shell village at intervals. I witness this afternoon the greatest 'air-fight' I have as yet seen. Eight German battle-planes surprised and surrounded three of ours. After fighting, two of ours withdrew, and the other fell in No Man's Land.*

Fri 19th Oct   (Rain) Rather a quiet day. Fritz shells Boursies [halfway from Bapaume to Cambrai] *round cemetery and crucifix. Our guns are busy at night.*

Sat 20th Oct   Fritz shells our positions more than usual this morning; But our reply is very good. Both sides are much noisier today. Fritz is sending 'heavy stuff' all the evening.

Sun 21st Oct   We experience quite a lively time all the morning. Fritz seems to be throwing his shells everywhere at random. Preparations are being made for Patrol of 50 men to enter German line and bomb a strongpoint. We are standing by at midnight.

Mon 22nd Oct   The raid is a failure. 'Bangalore' does not explode and the party are discovered. A few wounded, but all return safely. To sleep at 4.30 am. Guns on both sides very lively. Several shells very near quarries cause a few casualties. The 'North Staffords' are with us for instruction.

Tues 23rd Oct   Nothing much doing all day. (Raining)   We are relieved by Q.W.R. in evening. I return on Q.W.R. limber via Dougnies and Beaumetz, and arrive at Camp near Lebucquière. We are under Canvas.

Wed 24th Oct   Usual Camp life. Wind and Rain. Watching Football and Rugby, etc. We are likely to have a very rough time. Tents are pitching about in mud.

Thurs 25th Oct   Raining on and off all day. Some tents have fallen down, others are very 'wobbly'. I would sooner be in a dug-out in the trenches if this is supposed to be rest. Raining all evening.

Fri 26th Oct   In Camp near Lebucquière. Things and conditions are nothing to write home about. Mud is the chief item of interest just at present. (More rain and wind)

Sat 27th Oct   Things are much the same as yesterday. 'A' versus 'C' Company: one goal each. Fritz obliges with a few shells which fall quite near enough to make things unpleasant. Oh ! I do like 'life', I do !

Sun 28th Oct   Watching football in afternoon. C v A Company: no goals. B v D Company   1– 0. Fritz sends a few shells on Lebucquière. Most of them are 'duds'. Weather is extremely cold.

Mon 29th Oct   Busy in Camp all morning. (Rain)   Football A v C Company 0 – 1.

Tues 30th Oct   Nothing special. A few more shells.

Wed 31st Oct   On Parade at 8.30. Bomb throwing, etc. Nothing much doing.

Thurs 1st Nov   Packing up during day. Left in afternoon for trenches. Arrived at Quarries (C Company H.Q.) in evening via Lebucquière, Velu, Beaumetz. Nothing much doing in line tonight. Patrols and Working Parties, etc.

Fri 2nd Nov   Nothing of great interest to report. Usual artillery fire. We are lying on the right of Boursies and left of Demicourt. [Demicourt now has another British cemetery].

Sat 3rd Nov   The Inniskillings on our immediate right make a raid and capture 29 prisoners. Fritz replies with half an hour's bombardment on our trenches. Nothing else doing. Usual patrols.

Sun 4th Nov   A few shells are falling round about, but nothing 'to write home about'. It is cold tonight and we have heaps of wood from the Villages and naturally '*some*' fire. I expect Fritz can see it, but ... Fritz, we want to be warm and we <u>are</u>. Goodnight!!

Mon 5th Nov   Usual shelling, patrols and working parties.

Tues 6th Nov   Ditto

Wed 7th Nov   Great aeroplane activity. Fritz drops plenty of dud shells round about Quarries . Our airmen prove very annoying to Fritz. More rain. Fighting Patrols.

Thurs 8th Nov   A large flight of wild geese go over the line in complete order of single file, V shape. Both Fritz and us try to hit them with machine-gun and rifle fire, but no luck. We are relieved by Q.W.R. We arrive in reserve at Lébucquière.

Fri 9th Nov   Raining all day. Usual business in reserve. Fritz puts a few more shells on Velu. To transport lines, etc. C.Company is in reserve at Lébucquière. A miserable night.

Sat 10th Nov   Packing up. Left camp at 11 am in Mess Cart, and arrived at Bapaume Station. Train left at 2 pm via Achiet-le-Grand. We change at Candas [south-west of Doullens]. Then on to Abbeville arriving there 12 midnight. Raining all the time. Get some sleep in Officers Hut.

Sun 11th Nov   In Rest Hut and E.F.C. etc at Abbeville. Left by train 1.30 pm and arrived at Auxi-le-Chateau 3.30 pm. Captain Hadden's Billet, 9 Place de la Ville. Servants 39 Rte d'Amiens. Saw Georgette. Spent evening settling down. [Tim and Captain Hadden are now some fifty miles west of the trenches they occupied only two days previously. Tim gives no clear indication as to why he and Capt Hadden have made this journey.]

Mon 12th Nov   Parade 10.30 am. Inspection and lecture. In Billet etc. Saw Madame Vivian in afternoon. Cleaning up in evening. Then to Bordeau Estaminet speaking to Georgette.

Tues 13th Nov   Parade in morning 9 am for inspection. Also in Billet. In Auxi-le-Chateau generally. Usual cleaning up. In Estaminet.

Wed 14th Nov   Parade 8.40. On Canteen Fatigue morning. For walk round in afternoon. Are the W.A.A.C. a deficit or asset to the Army? To 6th Divisional Concert Party. In Estaminet etc in evening.

Thurs 15th Nov   P a r a d e 8.45 at Hotel de la Ville. Parade at 2 pm at R.E. Camp. Digging training trenches all afternoon. Busy cleaning up in evening, also to usual Estaminet.

Auxi-le-Chateau: 39 Rte d.Amiens today. Regrettably the street has been re-developed and re-numbered. Tim would not have been 'at home' here! And Georgette is now nowhere to be seen

Fri 16th Nov   Parade 8.45 am. Digging trenches all morning. Cleaning up afternoon. With Foster in evening at Patisserie. Fire picket 9.15 pm.

Sat 17th Nov   Parade 8.45 am for inspection. Cleaning all afternoon. In Café Bordeau in evening, and with 'Boys', also with K.O.S.B. For walk round with Still (K.O.S.B.), then to Billet.

Sun 18th Nov   Usual work in morning and for walk round. Writing letters afternoon. To Estaminet in evening, also to Pictures Cinema with Jock and Fusilier. I have seen some rotten shows, but this 'caps' all. Back to Billet 8.30 and to bed.

Mon 19th Nov   Parade 8.45 at Place de L'Hotel de Ville. Reading all afternoon. Tea at 4 pm. In Estaminet Bordeau and also to Rue d'Hesdin with Still (K.O.S.B.) and other lads. Bed 8.30, 39 Rue d'Amiens. [It seems unclear whether the correct road-name is 'Rue' or 'Route'.]

Tues 20th Nov   Parade 8.45 Hotel de Ville. In Billet, 9 Place de L'Hotel de Ville, all morning. Parade 2 pm R.E. Yard. Wiring all afternoon to 4 pm. Parade 4.30 pm to draw Rations. In Estaminet and Rue d'Hesdin with Jock and others.

Wed 21st Nov   Parade 8.45 at Place de L'Hotel de Ville. Rain. Dismissed at 9.30 am. In Skippers Billet all afternoon. To Estaminet Bordeau, then to Concert at Town Hall given by 15th Divisional Party (Jocks). Good, but want comedian.

Thurs 22nd Nov   Parade 8.45 am. The School is given a holiday on account of the success of Third Army. Advance of 5 miles. 180 [German] Officers and 8,600 men prisoners. Rain. In Estaminet with Canadian Sergeant. To Station in evening with Jean and Georgette x [sic]. Then with Boys.

Fri 23rd Nov   Parade 8.45. Dismissed 9.15 am. (Rain) In Auxi, Estaminet, etc.

Sat 24th Nov   Parade 8.45 am. 56th Division are once again in action at Cambrai. On Fire Picquet 9.15 pm.

Sun 25th Nov   With Boys in Estaminet, then to Picture Cinema. We go there of fun [?] The pictures are 'the limit'. To bed 9.15 pm.

Mon 26th Nov   Parade 8.45 am. On R.E. Fatigue all morning. In Billet and Estaminet Bordeau all afternoon. In Estaminet in evening with the Boys.

Tues 27th Nov   Parade 8.45 am. (Rain) Working with German prisoners on 'Cage'. Parade 1.45 pm. We 'strike' against working with Hun and leave off at 3 pm. In Estaminet Bordeau all evening. Concert Party at 8.30 pm. (Very good) [The idea that soldiers should 'go on strike', and that it should be tacitly overlooked, suggests that the junior officers agreed with their attitude.]

Wed 28th Nov   Parade 8.45. On R.E. Fatigue all morning. Usual cleaning up in afternoon. In Estaminet Bordeau till 8.15 pm with the Boys of the 56th Division. (I knew it would be silly to mix drinks.) Concert and to bed.

Thurs 29th Nov   Parade 8.45. In Billet all morning. Parade 1.45 pm. R.E. Fatigue. In Estaminet and then to Boxing Contest at Concert Hall. (Very interesting).

Fri 30th Nov   Parade 8.45. Taking down Boxing ring, and also on Bayonet field. Met Georgette and her friend, and for ride in the trap. In Estaminet all evening with the Boys.

Sat 1st Dec   Working on R.E. Fatigue (barbed wire). In Estaminet Bordeau. In billet afternoon (rain). To see 4th Divisional Concert Party at Hotel de Ville. (Very good, but too much 'rag' in parts.)

Sun 2nd Dec   Most of the day in Estaminet. Spoke to girls of W.A.A.C. Then to Choir Practice with two more at 8.30 pm.

Mon 3rd Dec   R.E. Fatigue all morning. In Estaminet all afternoon. Met Violet at 5.30 pm and went for walk towards Hesdin.

Tues 4th Dec   R.E. Fatigue in afternoon. I passed a girl of the W.A.A.C. whom I knew.

I was with Georgette!!! (It ended satisfactorily.) In Estaminet in evening. (I could kick Georgette.) Listening to Band. [A strange record of an encounter, with insufficient detail to explain his remarks about Georgette.]

Wed 5th Dec   R.E. Fatigue on Range all morning. In Estaminet all afternoon. Pay 5.30 pm. In Estaminet in evening, then listening to Band at No.1 Mess (With Boys).

Thurs 6th Dec   Parade 2 pm: R.E. Fatigue. Helping Mr Méjeau and Georgette. Met Violet ... W.A.A.C. at 5 pm. and went for walk to Lannoy. To Boxing at 8.30 pm: S.M. Jimmy Driscoll (World Lightweight Champion) gave exhibition spar with R.S.M. (Winner of Curragh Cup for Ireland.)

Fri 7th Dec   On Quartermaster's Fatigue. Met Violet and Louie. W.A.A.C. and '5th King's Own Liverpools' and myself went for walk with them to Bois de Justice. Tea at Madame Gayou's with the 1st Londons (Fusiliers). We met two other girls there. To Concert given by No.2 Aircraft Depôt at 6.30 pm till 9.45. (Very boring)

Sat 8th Dec   Parade 8.45. (Dismissed). In Billet all morning (working). In Estaminet and writing afternoon. Met Violet and Louie at 5 pm and went for walk towards Beauvoir Riviére. In Estaminet. Then to Concert given by 24th Divisional Party. (A very good show. The feature is the voice of the 'boy-girl'.)

Sun 9th Dec   (Rain). In Estaminet all morning. In Barbers from 2 pm to 3.45. All barbers talk. The difference is, that English talk and work at the same time, whilst French usually stop working while talking. In Estaminet all evening. Then with the Boys having a 'rag' round 'town'. Fire picquet 9.15 pm. Bed 9.30.

Mon 10th Dec   Parade 8.45. R.E. Fatigue. In Estaminet and Billet all afternoon. Met Violet and Louie 5 pm with Paterson (Argyle and Sutherland Highlanders) and went for a walk. Then to Estaminet and to Servants dance. (What a farce!)

Tues 11th Dec   Parade 8.45. Parade 2 pm. R.E. Fatigue. In Estaminet in evening with Boys. To Final of Boxing contest which was more like 'prizefighting' considering the knockout blows.

Wed 12th Dec   Parade 8.45. Parade 2.15. Acting as 1st point for Cross-Country race. With Boys in evening at Estaminet. Then to No 3 Mess listening to Band. Billet 9.15.

Thurs 13th Dec   Parade 8.45. R.E. Fatigue. Then for walk with Stacey (1st London) to Willencourt and Lannoy. Writing etc. afternoon. Parade for Rations 4.30 pm. In Estaminet with the Boys all evening. Billet 9 pm.

Fri 14th Dec   Parade 8.45. Dismissed at 9.30. In Billet rest of morning. Afternoon: preparing for departure. Parade 5.15. Met Violet and Louie 5.30 and went for walk with 'Argyle and Sutherland'. In Estaminet with Boys. Also had good time all the evening.

Sat 15th Dec   Reveillé 6 am. (Packing up). Parade 8 am and marched to Station. Train left 9.15 am and arrived at Etaples 3 pm. In Rest Camp. For walk with Boys. To Concert at 'New Cinema' in evening given by the New Zealand 'Pierrot Troupe'. Effects and Stage Machinery good but lack of talent in Artistes. In E.F.C. and other Huts. Then to bed.

Sun 16th Dec   Reveillé 5 am. On Station all morning. Train left 12.15 pm via St Pol and Aubigny, arrived at Mont St Eloi [north-west of Arras] *in evening. By lorry to 4th Corps Rest Station. Stayed there the night. Heavy Bombardment is in progress up the line. Snowing heavily all night. Awfully cold.*

Mon 17th Dec   Left Mont St Eloi 8 am by Light Railway. (Still snowing) Arrived via St Catherine and Marreul [probably Marrœuil] *at Roclincourt. Then to Transport lines 12 midday. Left for trenches 3 pm. Managed after struggle to find the way and arrived at 'Red line trench' on right of Bailluel* [sic] *at 6 pm.* [Bailleul is northwest of Arras.] *C.Company H.Q. is in deep dug-out, rather a good place, but it is all passages.*

Tues 18th Dec   In the trenches (Freezing). Fritz is shelling rather erratically round about, but nothing to write home about. The Boys are getting 'fed up' with trench life. They have been over a Month in the line. (If only the people in England knew or understood.)

Wed 19th Dec   Usual trench life. Fritz carries on serious bombardment from 3 am to 5 am. I draw the rum issue for the Boys and upset it. (Nuff said !) Gilfillen arrives. He has taken a commission.

Thurs 20th Dec   (Still freezing) Left red line trench at 2.30 and moved to more advanced position in the front line. Quite a good dug-out but too near the Hun. Trenches are very near – anything from 50 yards.

Fri 21st Dec   Up until 2.30 am. Usual business in trench all day. Water is very scarce. Heavy bombardment of left. Most of Company sleep in deep dug-out. 16 hours 'stand-to'.

Sat 22nd Dec   Fritz gives us rather a good supply of Mortars and Grennenwerfers, and we reply with our Mortars and Artillery. Our position is near Gavrille [E.N.E. of Arras], *and on the right of Vimy Ridge. Sapping is in progress.*

Sun 23rd Dec   To sleep 2 am. Still freezing hard. Our guns commence and keep up a heavy bombardment on the right Sector in the evening. Cannot make out line yet.

Mon 24th Dec   Hurrah ! We expect to be relieved tonight. Packing up ready. We leave trenches at 3 pm and arrive at Aubrey Camp near Roclincourt and St. Catherine at 6 pm. It is a drafty [draughty] *rotten hole, but still we mustn't expect too much.*

Tues 25th Dec   Freezing hard. Very busy all morning. To Arras in afternoon with Robinson and Hutchinson. Heavy snow storm. We have the best of time possible under such miserable conditions. (Cheer-oh Mr [or 'the'] *Raven!)*

Wed 26th Dec   In Aubrey Camp near St. Catherine. Freezing hard and snowing occasionally. It is all Work here and I shall be glad when we get out of it. The Companies have their Christmas Dinner tonight. It is nothing to shout about.

Thurs 27th Dec   More snow and freezing hard. It is fearfully cold and our shelter is scanty. I shall be glad when we go up the line again for one can get warm in the deep dug-outs.

Fri 28th Dec   Reveillé 5 am. Company move off at 7 am. Colonel Follett makes a farewell speech. We leave at 9 am and reach the trenches in reserve at 12 midday. Aeroplane fight above us. Fritz is using poisonous gas shells. Mr Tabero joins us.

Sat 29th Dec   Usual trench warfare. Nothing special to 'shout about'. Spend lots of time writing to a little girl who goes by the name of 'Gwen'. It is still freezing, and the snow lies crisp and deep like the proverbial Carol.

Sun 30th Dec   It is a good War today. Not much doing, and we are in a deep dug-out. This is certainly better than being out 'on rest'. Capt Hadden is going on leave so I go to transport lines with him. I ride in limber via St Nicholas and St Catherine. Sleep in Blanket Store.

Mon 31st Dec   Packing up Capt Hadden's kit in morning. Freezing hard and cold wind: too awful for words. With Giblett all afternoon to Canteen, and speaking to Oram, Boram and other 'Bow Bellistes'. To Bow Bell Concert in evening. Rather good as far as Cinderella goes, but great lack of imagination. Harry Brandon and others do not get a chance to distinguish themselves. Back to our 'Blanket Store', and we get between a good few of them. It is far too cold to see the New Year in. May it be the last of the War.

Tim then carefully completes, in a neat hand, a summary of where he was on each day of the year, with a further abridged summary month by month. He utilises pages in his Agenda intended for *recettes* and *dépenses*, with the last page (the abridged summary) headed RECAPITULATION. See examples below:

Janvier 26	Laventie	Avril	Arras Trenches
Juillet	Sus St Leger, Resting	Aout 31	Travelling

CHAPTER ELEVEN

1918

Tim's 1918 diary was British, unlike his 1917 *agenda* which was French. The 'Onoto' Diary was published by Thomas De La Rue and came with 'An Accident Insurance Coupon for £1000'. Did that, one asks, cover injuries sustained in the trenches? There is one improvement over his previous diaries in that this one has eight spaces on each double-page, so it is laid out starting each 'top-left' position with Sunday, and filling the bottom right space (after Saturday) with an entry for 'Week-end'. Tim utilises this additional space to expand his entries when he wishes to do so. Inside the back cover is a pocket which will accommodate a small photograph; and Tim's 1918 diary still has here a picture of a bald soldier who looks German. Will this be referred to in the entries? Tim also saved a touching picture of a German mother and two handsome sons. This he retrieved from a captured German trench, and marked the reverse accordingly. In my wish to preserve it I put it in some very safe place, and can no longer locate it. Such is life.

Tues Jan 1st   To Arras in morning with Giblett. To Reserve trenches in 'Red line' afternoon. On side of Gavrille Rd.

Wed 2nd Jan   Usual exchange of 'Shells'. We are in a deep dug-out. The frost still 'holds out'. The Battalion is wiring at night for the Army Corps.

Thurs 3rd Jan   Heavy shelling on right. Our dug-out catches fire. Aerial activity.

Fri 4th Jan   Battery of 4.5 guns in front of us makes themselves conspicuous.

Sat 5th Jan   Left trenches. Guns active. Arrived transport lines. The frost continues.

Sun 6th Jan   In Transport lines all day. To Arras in evening with Surtees. Freezing.

Mon 7th Jan   To Arras with Lieut Taberra's kit.

Tues 8th Jan   Transport lines. To Arras.

Wed 9th Jan   Ditto. Snow and frost.

Thurs 10th Jan   Left St Catherine with Surtees via Etrun, Maroeuil and Aubigny. Arrived at Cambligneul [NW of Arras] *in afternoon. In Estaminet etc.*

Fri 11th Jan   In Cambligneul. Living at No.3 Billet. Still with Lieut Tabberran [sic]. *In Estaminets etc.* [This was Tim's 23rd birthday, but it passes without comment.]

Sat 12th Jan   Nothing special.

Sun 13th Jan   This is a very small village but better than the line. There is now a Battalion Mess for Officers.

Mon 14th Jan   We (Batmen) are messing at French Madame's House. She is very good.

Tues 15th Jan   Her daughters Madeline and Lucienne are very attractive girls ages 14 and 12 respectively.

Wed 16th Jan   We have some very good times here with Madame and her family. Madeline is very interesting.

Thurs 17th Jan   Our Mess is going along famously, thanks to Madame.

Fri 18th Jan   C'est la méme nouvelles.

Sat 19th Jan   To 'Bow Bells' Concert Party at Camblain Abbé in evening with Tom Wilson, Neville and Marshall. Monsieur (Madame's husband) has arrived for the week-end. A very fine fellow, and also lucky for he is at Arras.

Sun 20th Jan　　　Toujours the méme. *In House all evening. Monsieur gives us a bottle of red wine.*
　Tues 22nd Jan　　　*With Tom and Houston to Estaminet.*
　Wed 23rd Jan　　　*We have had our orders to move tomorrow morning to the line. Hurrah,* they are cancelled.

　Thurs 24th Jan　　*Things as usual in Cambligneul. Great rumours are now floating re amalgamation.*
　Fri 25th Jan　　　C'est rien. *Tom Wilson, James and Dawson have good time in Estaminet.*
　Sat 26th Jan　　　*We are amalgamating with our 2nd Battalion very shortly. (Men are scarce.)* Madame Doubet at No.5 invited me to dinner 6 pm. Very nice, so far as French meals go.

　Sun 27th Jan　　　*To Aubigny in afternoon with Tom. (Not a great place.) Monsieur is here.*
　Mon 28th Jan　　　*We are near the last days of the old Battalion. With Madeline and* Lucien[ne].

　Tues 29th Jan　　　*The 'breaking up' has commenced. A lot have to join the Kensingtons.* 'C'est la guerre !'

　Wed 30th Jan　　　*Packing up. We (the remnants of the 1st Battalion) move off as a draft to* join the 2nd Battn. We entrain at Tincques. [East of St Pol and WNW of Arras.]

　Thurs 31st Jan　　*Arrived at Villers Brettone* [sic] *2 am. Then with Officers to Corbie by* Lorry. To bed 5 am. Billeted in La Neuville [East of Amiens on the River Somme.]

　Fri 1st Feb　　　*Living at 17 Rue Francis with Capt Hadden. We have not settled down yet.*
　Sat 2nd Feb　　　*I am now living with Capt Hadden at Rue de Panchelet, La Neuville. It is* an excellent billet. The amalgamation with the 2nd Battalion is now complete, and we are now known as the 9th Battalion London Regiment. There is a little friction between 1st and 2nd.

　Sun 3rd Feb　　　*In Corbie most of the day with George and Tom. Tom and I had little fun* in evening with French man.

　Mon 4th Feb　　　*In billet all day with Madame. To 'The Goods' in the evening: rather a* good knockabout.

　Tues 5th Feb　　　*In bed all morning very queer. Spent very quiet day in Corbie and with Madame.*
　Wed 6th Feb　　　*Packing up. Moved off and entrained 11 am Corbie, via Longneuil,* [Longnueau?], *Montdidier, Moreuil, Compiègne, Noyon, and detrained at Appilly* [On the River Oise between Noyon and Chauny]. *Slept the night Marest Dampcourt.* [Just north of the Oise, WSW of Chauny.]

　Thurs 7th Feb　　　*Left Marest-Dampcourt by lorry and went through Chauny, Villequier-* Aumant and Rouez. Living in Camp (French) in Bois de Genlis.

　Fri 8th Feb　　　*(Rain) We have taken the line over from the French. To Villequier-* Aumant in afternoon with Nankiville.

　Sat 9th Feb　　　*We leave Bois de Genlis and go into the line at Mennissis. We are living* in shelters amid the ruined village. Madame at Dampcourt was awfully nice. It is the first time she has seen British troops having been 32 months in German hands until they retired. [Mennessis is on the Canal de St Quentin, north of Chauny and Tergnier.]

　Sun 10th Feb　　　*In Mennessis as usual. Spend day among the ruins. Front very quiet.* Weather fine.

　Mon 11th Feb　　*Fritz bombs all round in evening and thus relieves the monotony.*
　Tues 12th Feb　　*Usual working parties. Spend time reading and writing.*
　Wed 13th Feb　　*Nothing special to report.*
　Thurs 14th Feb　　*Lawson , Pratt and I go for a walk to next village. Everything ruined but* the church.

　Fri 15th Feb　　　*Packing up. Left Mennessis and arrive at Liez, taking over R.E. places.* Fritz bombs round about.

Sat 16th Feb   Liez [north of Tergnier]. *The bombing raids each night by Fritz are quite a nuisance. The Huns cut down every tree here before retiring. The R.G.A. are billetted in a church at* [gap]. *I notice all the Saints and other statues have had their faces blackened. (Hun work)*

Sun 17th Feb   Great Aerial Activity all day. Liez shelled 5.9. Our Observation Balloon brought down in flames. Also one Hun plane.

Mon 18th Feb   Aerial Activity. To Villequin in afternoon via [gap]. *On bicycle. Usual raids and bombs.*

Tues 19th Feb   Up goes another O.B. I wonder how long it will stop there. Aerial Activity.

Wed 20th Feb   Guns continue to arrive and consolidate in various part. The tables are turned. We are now on the defensive.

Thurs 21st Feb   Liez Port shelled. Also Working party on posts. Once again Fritz flies over and sends Observation Balloon down in flames. Then they shell 6" Howitzer Battery 100 yards in front of us.

Fri 22nd Feb   Change in weather. Cold. Usual Aerial Activity. Fritz is also very liberal with Shrapnel. No more O.B. have appeared so far.

Sat 23rd Feb   Shelling round about. I like the Aisne district immensely. It is the best part of France that I have as yet seen. The German airmen certainly show their superiority in this Sector. Two Observation Balloons in one week and continual raids. The vaults in Liez Churchyard have been burst open.

Sun 24th Feb   Left Liez and marched to Butte de Rouz. for the night I went to Villequier-Amount. [Reproduced as handwritten.]

Mon 25th Feb   Relieved 8th East Surreys. Left Rouz with John Lawson and via Viry. Spent an hour in Chauny. Then to Cinseny for the night.

Tues 26th Feb   Preparing to leave Cinseny. Went with Capt Hadden via Buttes de Rouy [sic]. *To Amigny-Rouy. We are support Company to left sector.*

Wed 27th Feb   A few shells are flying. La Marins is on our left. Foret Servais on our right. Servais in front on No Mans Land. We are a long way from Fritz owing to the Marshes.

Thurs 28th Feb   The Higher Command are expecting Fritz to take the Offensive. Great Aerial Battle. We are digging positions and blocking roads. All available men are in their positions.

Fri 1st March   We are still waiting all through the night. Patrols are out. No sign yet. The Hun is strangely quiet in front. Heavy bombardment on our left and right.

Sat 2nd Mar   Stand to Arms 3 am. Then again at 5.30 am. Both end up with no Infantry assault. (Snow) The weather decides (no action). Chauny is full of great factories, all completely smashed. The suspense of waiting for an attack is awful and very little sleep soon 'knocks one up'. Snow has set in – rather favourable to us.

Sun 3rd Mar   The expected offensive has not happened and things seem more calmer. I explore Village and find it very interesting.

Mon 4th Mar   Rather miserable day. Snow has turned to rain. Apples are lying about in thousands. Wild boar are numerous in the forests.

Tues 5th Mar   We leave Amigny, Rouy and go up to the front line Posts in Faye de Servais: this is a huge wood. Fritz spots our relief and shells day and night.

Wed 6th Mar   Great Aerial Activity all day. Hun planes attack one of ours. He brings one Hun down and unfortunately falls himself. (Clements). Both dead. Artillery very active.

Thurs 7th Mar   Still holding posts in Faye de Servais. Activity by enemy Artillery continues in Wood. One of the Huns Observation Balloons drifts over our lines. Brought down in flames.

Fri 8th Mar   Usual Aerial Activity.. He shells the Wood at two special points most of the day, and at night drops four 8" shells very close to our position.

Sat 9th Mar   Weather continues fine. Usual Aerial and Artillery Activity. This Wood is getting decidedly uncomfortable. Usual nightly activity. Another point in the Hun Kultur:- Directly our plane crashed to earth the enemy immediately shelled the spot for over three hours to prevent us from assisting the Airman even if aid was any use.

Sun 10th Mar   We are relieved by the 10th London in afternoon, and we go to reserve position in sunken road on outskirts of Amigny. Awful place.

Mon 11th Mar   There is a Battery 100 yards on our left, and what with that and movement he seems to have discovered our position. Shells and some sort of Werfers burst nearby.

Tues 12th Mar   The line in this case is much preferable. I spend the day building a dugout. Usual amount of shells etc., also bombing at night.

Wed 13th Mar   The weather continues lovely. Usual shelling but no direct hits. Our guns are rather active today. I put more work into my dugout. Fritz sends a few shells at night about every hour.

Thurs 14th Mar   Enemy artillery very quiet all day. Still in the same position. We have to man 'Battle Positions' in evening. (Wind up)

Fri 15th Mar   Things are normal. Aeroplane activity, especially at night when Fritz drops bombs on villages behind us.

Sat 16th Mar   To 175th Brigade H.Q. with Capt Hadden. Then back to Amigny Sunken Rd. Returned to Brigade H.Q. at Sinceny at night on limber with baggage. Captain Hadden has been appointed Asst. Staff Captain at Brigade H.Q. I accompany him. I think this is too good to last. Artillery activity increases.

Sun 17th Mar   At 175th Brigade Headquarters, Sinceny. Bomb drops 200 yds away. To Transport Lines in afternoon. Hun troops are reported to be massing at Servais.

Mon 18th Mar   Capt Hadden to report to Battn: as 2nd in Command. Leave Brigade H.Q. at 3pm and go to Transport lines. Proceed with convoy to Battn H.Q. in Amigny-Rouy.

Tues 19th Mar   Lively Activity on both sides with Artillery. We move to the Northern end of Amigny-Rouz [sic]. (Rain)

Wed 20th Mar   To Chauny and Transport lines in morning. Rumours! Rumours! We are on the eve of the Hun offensive. (Rain)   Artillery and Infantry are standing-by awaiting orders. What will happen!

The Germans advance

During the past year the Germans had been preparing strong positions in what had become known as the Hindenburg Line. They had decided to abandon their trenches in the area that had seen the bloodiest fighting, pulling back and leaving such strategic towns as Bapaume (virtually in ruins) to be occupied by the British. In March 1918 German troops left their Hindenburg positions and attacked on a wide front, with alarming success. Operation Michael was intended to win the war on the Western Front before the arriving American troops could prove decisive. In the East, the Russians had signed the Treaty of Brest-Litovsk, effectively ending their part in the war and ceding much territory to Germany and Austria. (See picture on page 100.)

Now seventy German divisions attacked thirty-five British divisions, scoring such immediate successes as the re-capture of Bapaume on March 24th. Tim is well aware that something big is under way, and for a week or so it seems likely that he will either be taken prisoner or killed.

A sad picture by the distinguished Russian artist Wladimiroff, who was commissioned by the 'Graphic' to act as resident artist on the Russian front. It depicts an accompanied German officer riding by an abandoned Russian howitzer battery in deep snow

Thurs 21st Mar   5 am.   The enemy Offensive has commenced at last.   Bombarding is taking place all round.   18th Division on our left is compelled to retire some distance.   We hold our original positions.

Fri 22nd Mar   We are in danger of being cut off in the rear if Enemy advance any more. The canal and Oise on our left is at all events a good protection. Seven prisoners (deserters) arrive.

Sat 23rd Mar   He shells our position at Amigny horribly causing casualties.   We expect to retire at any moment or be cut off owing to his advance on left.   Bombarding is terrific. Situation precarious. French division has arrived to support our left flank.   75 mm guns are strongly in evidence.   Enemy has burst dam of canal and flooded marshes on our immediate left.   Enemy massing in front.

Sun 24th Mar   Our guns have withdrawn owing to position and shellfire.   Many are lost. We retire about a mile at dusk.   Gas is awful.

Mon 25th Mar   In Butte de Rouy.   I take party to old H.Q. to recover stuff left behind last night.   We are caught by machine-gun fire.   Enemy patrol.

Tues 26th Mar   Enemy artillery are behind us on left flank and shell our position from rear. Sgt Neale and No. One Platoon go out on Patrol and are taken prisoners.   We are nearly surrounded.

Tim is not alone in finding his position precarious.   In five days the German offensive had proved remarkably effective.   What might with justification be called a 'panic' conference was arranged at Doullens on March 26th with the aim of better co-ordinating British and French military operations.   On the 23rd Tim had noted that a 'French division has arrived to support our left flank', but such close co-operation was by no means the rule. And furthermore General Sir Hubert Gough's Fifth Army had been so overwhelmed that a total German breakthrough seemed likely. In mid-March 1916 Tim had briefly stayed in Doullens; now the meeting taking place there two years later might well decide his fate. To demonstrate the imperative need for closer co-ordination it was noted that Sir Douglas Haig had already arranged to meet his own commanders there *without* ensuring the involvement of the French, who were belatedly invited. And the Germans were threatening that very town! Nonetheless the 'big guns' turned up: General Pétain, French President Poincaré, French Premier Clémenceau, General Foch, General Weygand, Lord Alfred Milner, Field Marshal Haig and General Wilson. Foch declared, in terms that may have inspired Churchill's 'We shall fight them on the beaches' speech, 'I shall

An equestrian statue of Foch on the hill at Cassel

fight without a break. I shall fight *in front of* Amiens. I shall fight *in* Amiens. I shall fight *behind* Amiens. I shall never surrender'. Unsurprisingly within hours he had been appointed Supreme Allied Commander. Haig would, in future, accept his orders.

Wed 27th Mar   Enemy gets some accurate hits on the Buttes. Enemy planes are very daring and fly low thinking we have retired. We work hard loading bombs, grenades etc to be sent back. Fritz brings transport up all day.

Thurs 28th Mar   He is still advancing but keeps on left bank of Oise. All our bridges we have blown up, but if he succeeds in crossing river we must be cut off. He has advanced 40 Kilos in places.

Fri 29th Mar   French, after heavy bombardment, attack on our left flank. We have checked German advance and are holding him up all along. The 10th London Regt relieve us. Capt Hadden and I go to Autreville.

It is observed by Tim that it is a *French* attack on their left flank that finally makes it possible for the Tenth Londons to bring relief. Tim now finds himself 'attached to the Sixth French Army', and very doubtful about the eventual outcome of the conflict. Significantly the French General Foch had swiftly assumed supreme command of all the allied armies, which had become his remit recently at Doullens.

Doullens today is a charming, peaceful place on the River Authie. It seems largely to

have forgotten its wartime past: the magnificent Citadelle is so badly signposted that it eludes the casual tourist.

Sat 30th Mar   In   Autreville.   Our 60-pounders here keep up a harassing fire all day. We are now attached to the 6th French Army, being over 30 miles from British troops.   To bed at 5.30 am. German Prisoners captured say it is impossible for us to win the War. Well, judging from their present position and their doings of the past few days I think they have every reason for holding their present views.

Sun 31st Mar   Huns cross river at Chauny by means of Pontoon Bridge.   The bridge is blown down in our barrage and about 100 Bosch are cut off. Autreville shelled.

Mon 1st Apl   I go to Communion in little hut. [Yesterday was Easter Sunday.] *It is a glorious day. Oh! Why is the War on? I celebrate today by washing clothes. The Bosch will persist in shelling Autreville. Usual patrols and stand-to-arms.*

Tues 2nd Apl   Packing up. I go to Praast [south of Chauny on the Soissons road] *to look over officers' quarters for tonight. Then return to Autreville. Had chat with French soldiers of 343 Infantry Regiment who relieved us here. I return to Praast.* [His view of the French military organisation had long been one of admiration; and now he had been a beneficiary.]

Wed 3rd Apl   To sleep 2 am. Breakfast 10 am. Enemy keep up continuous shelling on side of Praast. Casualties inflicted. I start with Nankival at 5.30 pm via Trossly [Trosly-Loire, perhaps] *and St Aubin, and arrive at La Meslin* [possibly Le Mesnil] *at 8 pm. Only two old women remain here.*

Thurs 4th Apl   Raining all day. We march from Le Meslin 9 am via Vic-sur-Aisne, Morsein, Cauvres, to Gutry. We are soaked and billets are few. It is the first time they have seen British troops.

Fri 5th Apl   We are near Soissons and Rheims. Q.M.S. Taylor, Nankivall and I leave at 9 am, go via Soucy to Villers-Cotterêts [SW of Soissons]. *We have a fine time there with French soldiers, etc, and lose the train. Catch one at 8 pm.* [Close Anglo-French co-operation continues even outside the battle lines, apparently.]

Sat 6th Apl   Travelling till 6 am. Arrive at Longueau [just SE of Amiens]. *(Gas shells are falling). Go to position in wood near Blangy* [on the Somme just east of Amiens]. *Move up at 2 pm to position on left of Gentelles* [ESE of Amiens] *and relieve Australians. No shelter and shells are falling around. The time spent in the Aisne and Oise has greatly improved my opinion of the French organization. Their ways and methods are better than ours. The French 75* [?mm] *barrage is excellent. They have guns here with which I think we can hold Fritz now. He will not get Amiens.*

And in that prediction, Tim proved right. Gradually the allied defence was able to grind down the German advance; and the rapid movement of troops from one part of the front to another (described from his point of view in Tim's diaries) enabled potential gaps to be plugged before the historic cathedral city could fall into enemy hands. (That would have to wait until the 1940s!)

Sun 7th Apl   Mud, shells and rain. I go to Transport lines to get Capt Hadden's revolver. Am glad to get out of my hole. Transport lines are on the left of Amiens, which is being shelled.

Mon 8th Apl   Go up line with Transport to little trench in front of Villers-Bretonneux. We relieve the Australians who have just captured Villers-Bretonneux. They are good fellows. Heaps of French colonial troops are here. The Colonel told Capt Hadden that 'we had lost the war'. I will not state my own opinion. We are standing in mud and water 200 yards from the Hun. Raining all day. I want sleep badly. Am sent out at dusk to look over Chateau 100 yards behind line. (Scrounging)

Tues 9th Apl   Looking over Chateau etc. Heaps of things have been left; but we cannot carry them away. Needless to remark, we live like Lords for the time being. Heavy bombardment is going on. Men are nearly 'done'.

Wed 10th Apl   We are relieved by 10th Londons at 1 am. I lead C.H.Q Platoon to Boves [just SE of Amiens] *after a long and tedious journey. Arrived at 5.30 am. Various jobs till 8 am. Then breakfast 9 am. To bed at 8 pm. (Shells in village)*

Thurs 11th Apl   Boves. More shells in village. We are warned that we are to make an attack tomorrow at Villers-Bretonneux. 'Surplus personal' [personnel] *are sent down. The cooks and ourselves have merry evening.*

Fri 12th Apl   Waiting to move off. The attack is postponed until the next day. Fritz shells the village strongly, causing many casualties, mostly Australians. Another good night.

Sat 13th Apl   The Hun has attacked and spoilt our plans, so we await further orders. Boves is again heavily shelled. We move off eastwards at 3 pm. Skirting Gentelles we arrive in the trenches behind Cachy.

Sun 14th Apl   Rain. Trenches. To Cachy in morning with Giblet looking for souvenirs. There is one of our old aerodromes 300 yards in front. Hun shells heavily.

Mon 15th Apl   Usual trench life. Wind is awfully cold, and we are only 3 feet in the earth. Shelling on both sides continues, especially at B.H.Q. (Casualties) We are relieved by 53rd Australian Regiment at 7 pm. Back to Blangy Tronville with Captain. [On the Somme east of Amiens.]

Tues 16th Apl   We are in reserve, ready to move off at an hour's notice. The village is shelled at intervals. A few civilians remain here. We get a big roaring fire going in an old-fashioned open fireplace.

*Wed 17th Apl   Hun shells the village rather badly. (Many casualties) Bad news from the North. Fritz has captured Baillieul and other villages. What is our position now? What can we do? Our organisation is simply ***, but we may muddle through.*

Thurs 18th Apl   Blangy-Tronville. Raining all day. Preparing for departure. Left at 6 pm, went to position in reserve between Hangard and Gentelles. Digging a shelter all night.

Fri 19th Apl   Still digging till 2 am. Raining and snowing at intervals. Artillery starts and develops into fierce bombardment. Great aeroplane activity. (Something is in the wind.)

Sat 20th Apl   Trenches badly shelled. (Casualties.) Artillery on both sides continue hammering; meanwhile aeroplanes are busy observing. Raids at night: many bombs dropped. (The artillery activity has reached a high state. The French and Colonials are holding the line at Hangard, and we are on the left. I think the Hun will make another attempt for Amiens.)

Sun 21st Apl   Fierce bombardment going on, which slackens a trifle at dawn, especially on right flank. All day the Hun keep up continuous long-distance shelling. (Some war!)

Mon 22nd Apl   Bombardment still develops to great intensity. Our planes are causing Fritz some annoyance, flying in parties of 30. H.Q. are badly gassed.

Tues 23rd Apl   Everything continues as before. Something must happen very soon. Will he get through? I think we can hold him. We shall see.

Wed 24th Apl   The bombardment is Hell, and the gas is awful. (All helmets on.) Fritz attacks and gets through a few hundred yards. All communications cut. R.F. take over. We move up to support in Quarry. Made counter-attack 10pm, and after steady fight took the German front line. We had received only fifty minutes warning that we were to attack. We reached our objective, but have no real knowledge of our position.

Thurs 25th Apl   No sleep. Consolidating ourselves in narrow chalk trench. We scarcely know our position, and we are being severely shelled. Capt Hadden is missing. Huns attack at 5 pm on our right and left. It has been an awful day without shelter or rations. We are in danger.

Fri 26th Apl   We retire to a depth of 500 yards at 1 am. Our left flank is open to the enemy. Shelling is cruel, and casualties awful. The French relieve us at 3 am. We straggle back to a wood and sleep for four hours. General Rawlinson speaks to us on our way from the line and congratulates the Regiment. We then march to Pont de Metz.[Just WSW of Amiens]

Sat 27th Apl   Parade 9.30 am. Left Pont de Metz and marched via Ferrieres, Fourdrihoy, Cavillon, and arrived at Riencourt 4.30 pm. Spent the night in various houses with Tom Wilson, and had very good time with the people.

Sun 28th Apl   Parade at 9 am. Left Riencourt. Marched north via Le Mesge, Soues, Hangist-sur-Somme, Condé-Folie. Halt for dinner at Longpré, then via Long to Ailly-le-Haut-Clocher [East of Abbeville on the Amiens road]. *On duty in the evening.*

Mon 29th Apl   Cleaning up and preparing for inspections. Also on duty. Visited various old friends who recognized me after two years. [In later years Tim always said that you should judge yourself by whether people from your past recognize and welcome you. He clearly already had the knack of getting-on with people even then, and in a foreign country.]

Tues 30th Apl   Raining. Gas helmet inspection. On duty, then with Tom in various Estaminets and for walk round village.

Wed 1st May   On duty all morning. Pay in afternoon. With Tom in evening to various estaminets, and visit friends.

The Abbeville Conference

Five weeks after the Doullens Conference, which had made Foch Supreme Commander of the French and British forces, it had become evident that, despite the far closer collaboration, the Allies were facing a grave shortage of men. The Germans had similarly suffered huge losses, but their offensive was proving difficult to contain, and they retained the initiative.

Envious eyes were cast at the huge American forces which were well on the way to becoming battle-ready. At a conference in Beauvais on April 3rd, U.S. General Tasker Bliss had spoken in support of Foch's appointment as supreme commander, but that was far from saying that U.S. troops could now move swiftly into the line.

In order to make decisions regarding the manpower shortage, a remarkable Conference was arranged in Abbeville on May 1st and 2nd. Abbeville is a strategically sited town on the Somme. The principal aim of the British and French representatives was to secure immediate American commitment to deploy their troops before the German offensive had become decisive. Some 120,000 U.S. troops were arriving each month; but by April they had not seen combat. Despite the pleading of Clémenceau, Lloyd George and Foch, American General Pershing insisted that his troops were not to be seen as available simply to plug British and French deficiencies, and certainly were not to be placed under Foch's command.

On May 2nd Pershing proposed a compromise whereby 130,000 of his troops would join the allied lines immediately, as would another 150,000 due to arrive by the end of June. This represented about one third of those available, and he insisted that the remainder would not be committed until they were fully trained and organized, which he estimated would be around one year later than this Abbeville meeting . He could not at that point have foreseen the reality in which (by the time of the Armistice in November 1918) more than 2,000,000 U.S. troops would have served on the Western Front, and that some 50,000 would have been killed.

Tim, though usually well-informed, knew nothing about the extraordinary meeting that was taking place in Abbeville (a town he had often visited). The simple memorial (right) to it was, in May 1968, affixed to a modern building just off the almost entirely rebuilt shopping-centre.

Emplacement de l ancienne Chambre des Notaires où eut lieu les 1 et 2 Mai 1918, la conférence d'organisation du commandement unique de toutes les Armées alliées par le

général FOCH

sous la présidence de

Georges CLEMENCEAU

en présence de M.M. les premiers ministres
LLOYD GEORGE pour le Royaume uni,
ORLANDO, pour l'Italie
de Lord MILNER ministre britannique de la Guerre;
de M.M.les Commandants des Armées alliées:

FOCH, WEYGAND, PÉTAIN,

de l'amiral de BON pour la France,
du Maréchal DOUGLAS-HAIG,
des généraux WILSON, SACKEVILLE-WEST
de l'Amiral WIMMIS pour la Grande Bretagne,
des généraux PERSHING et BLIS pour les Etats Unis
et du général de ROBILANT pour l'Italie.

8 MAI 1968

(Abbeville's town centre was virtually destroyed following the German WW2 occupation and the Normandy landings in 1944.) The security in 1918 must have been intense; and the decisions taken there probably fashioned the ultimate defeat of Germany. The location of this notice is far from easy to find; but it is well worth the effort.

Thurs 2nd May   Parade 8.30 am. Rifle inspection. Musketry and firing on range. Resting all afternoon. With Tom in evening visiting friends and Estaminet, etc.

Fri 3rd May   Parade 8.30. With Observers map reading and compass work. Margaret, the girl at A.H.Q., is not unlike Audrey R. Had chat with Ernescille also.

Sat 4th May   *Parade 8.30 am. Same as Friday (some mike!) Madame at our Billet is awfully nice. On duty at A.H.Q. evening (officers dinners). Chatting with Madame 10.30 pm. Fighting still goes on heavily at Villers-Bretonneux. I think we shall soon be called on again. Am now a Runner. Perhaps risky, but preferable.*

Sun 5th May   *Raining. On duty in morning at A.H.Q. Tom and I are to report to B.H.Q. as Battalion Runners. (For the 'Stunt'.) Surplus personnel leave us. Farewell visit to several friends.*

Mon 6th May   *9 am left Ailly-le Haut-Clocher in buses with H.Q. via Flexecourt, Villers-Bocage* [North of Amiens], *Moulyn* [Moulliens?]*-au-Bois; left buses at Contay. Marched to position in Wood near Baizieux* [West of Albert]. *Raining.*

Tues 7th May   *Spent awful time in Wood. No shelters and raining. Soaked through. To all Companies at 3.30 am with orders to relieve West Kents 17th and 19th Londons, 47th Division. To Brigade HQ. Moved up to Baizieux 6 pm. To A Company in evening* [This entry is reproduced as written.]

Wed 8th May   *with various messages. We are under canvas at Baizieux. Front fairly quiet. We are in reserve. To Warlen in evening with Vokes. Fierce artillery bombardment all night. Am just recovering from the soaking of the previous day. The weather is fine.* [The last entry seems to follow on from the previous. Despite the intolerable conditions and the movements, Tim's entries are made clearly with a pen, and no ink has run.]

Thurs 9th May   *Weather fine. Rifle inspection 11 am. Great artillery and aerial activity. To A Company with message. Sports in evening. (Won prize from Colonel Powell.)*

Fri 10th May   *Rifle and gas-helmet inspection 10 am. Huns shell Baizieux in afternoon. Football match 6 pm. Signallers and Runners v. Rest of HQ. (Won 3-1) Linesman. Baths 9.30 pm.*

Sat 11th May   *Weather doubtful. On duty at Orderly Room, morning. To Transport Lines on bike in afternoon. Football 6 pm. HQ v. RE. We lost 2-1. Tom and I slept at Orderly Room, on Duty.   The 47th Division lost a trench this week, but regained it the next day. An attack is expected; but our defence is good. 18th Division is also here. Cavalry stand by all the time and tanks are also in readiness, both Light and Heavies. More machine-guns are also brought in readiness.*

Sun 12th May   *Rainy. Rifle and Ammunition Inspection 10 am. Took new draft to A. Coy: Had near 'shave' with them. Fritz straffed the 'Cross Roads'. Usual bombing by Fritz in evening.*

Mon 13th May   *Raining all day. A few shells fall round about. To A Coy in afternoon with Fred Drew (Signaller). We are in awful mess inside our tent. 14 Runners and heaps of mud. I sleep in Orderly Room with four others.*

Tues 14th May   *Orderly for the day. Hun aeroplane attacks our observation balloon and brings it down in flames. He is brought down by our planes. Football: HQ 1 v B Coy Rangers 0. To A Coy with orders. Hun planes drop bombs round about during night. Heavy artillery 'strafe'.*

Wed 15th May   *On duty at Orderly Room 9.30 am to 10.30. Fritz shells outskirts of village. Great aerial activity. Matches I saw:- 'Buffs' in afternoon. B v C Company 6 pm one goal each. 7.30 pm Sussex 1 v R.E. 1. Fritz does lot of bombing all round. Slept in Orderly Room with Hursea and Wiltshire.*

Thurs 16th May   *Foot and gas-helmet inspection 8.30 am. Looking for 'Stragglers Post' (on bike). On duty O.R. 2.30 – 3.30 pm. To Brigade H.Q. 175th and T.L. Left Baizieux 9 pm via Henincourt, and in line at 11.30 pm (Battalion H.Q.) Trenches.*

Fri 17th May   *With Dorkings 2 am to front line B and D Companies. (Made a dash to reach B.H.Q. by dawn.) Great aerial activity all day. Our artillery catch tanks in Albert. With Capt. Nichols round front line 11 pm. (To Well)*

Sat 18th May   Heavy bombardment on both sides all night until dawn. (Two runners are lost.) Usual artillery duel all day. Terribly hot, and water is scarce. Great aerial observation on both sides. On R.E. Fatigues (deep dug-outs). Our line is immediately in front of Albert. We shell Albert so badly that he can hardly occupy it. Aerial craft excellent in this part. We are waiting for 'him' to attack on this front. He is using Minenwerfers on front and support lines but we retaliate with trench Mortars.

Sun 19th May   Terrific gunfire on our immediate right which spreads across our front. 3 am we retire into deep dug-out. Casualties bad. We shift our position. 300 prisoners taken on our right. To D Company front line with Tom.

Mon 20th May   Usual strafe by artillery until dawn. Many casualties. Heat is terrible. Took orders to B Company: with Bartlett, and showed 'Rangers' the way. We are relieved by 12th London at midnight. We go to Brigade Reserve.

Tues 21st May   Carrying ammunition, etc., 3 am. The bombardment continues till dawn. Sleep 4.30 am to 9.30 am. To C Company with orders. On duty 4 pm to 6 pm. Heat is awful. Aerial activity on our part. Usual gunfire after dusk. He also gasses B.H.Q.

Wed 22nd May   I am an ass. Double issue of rum and gas. Sleep 3 till 9 am. Shell falls outside Runners' shelter. Wiltshire, Potter and three others wounded. My luck is marvellous. To transport lines with orders re relief.   Came back with Transport.   We move in Divisional reserve on right of Senlis, and occupy shelters.   He gasses us again.   Usual Bombing and Artillery 'strafe'.

Thurs 23rd May   To A, B, C and D Companies with orders. Very strong wind today. Writing letters and reading. Not much Artillery during day, but Bombardment at night. Usual Bombing.

Fri 24th May   Rain and terrific wind all day. Front rather quiet. Surplus personnel leave. To A Company and Transport Lines with orders, with Britten. Am now a permanent Battalion Runner. (Wet through.)

Sat 25th May   Not much doing. On duty 3.15 to 4.15 pm. Artillery have usual bursts. Great aerial activity.   We bring one enemy plane down.   Usual bombing at night. We are shelling Albert horribly. Tom Wilson goes to hospital. Has Fritz given up his offensive or not? We are shelling twice as much as he. Is he storing something up for us? It is a question of wait and see. We appear to be very confident.

Sun 26th May   Fine day. Aerial activity. We reconnoitre our H.Q. in the line in afternoon with Chitty [altered and hard to read] *and others. Bombing at night. Attack on left which lasts throughout night.*

Mon 27th May   Gas shells at 2.30 am. Helmets on. To A, C and D Companies with orders. To line with Major Renton and Captain Nichols. H.Q. on right of Albert. We occupy deep dug-out. Usual artillery fire.

Tues 28th May   All round front line with C.O. Col. Causton 10.30 am till 1.30 pm. To front line A and C Co's with officer and party of R.E. Heavy bombardment some distance away on our right flank.

Wed 29th May   Great aerial activity. Our planes show superiority. Round front line with Maj. Renton. Fritz is busy with Minenwerfers. Our artillery keeps up the usual harrassing fire. Usual bombing by planes on both sides. Huge Flare seen in enemy line.

Thurs 30th May   British plane crashes down (through a shell).   Round front line with Major Renton. Usual strafe in the evening, but I get down the dug-out.

Fri 31st May   In dug-out most of the morning. Went round the front line with Major Renton in afternoon. Front rather quiet.   We are relieved by 7th Queens, 18 Division. Strafe develops in evening.

Sat 1st June   *Arrived at Wood in front of Béhencourt 3.30 am. Slept till 11.30 am. (Am feeling very queer indeed.) Lying down most of day. I think I have had too much gas. Fritz has attacked and met with success at Chemin des Dames, driving us back to the Aisne. So far this has not affected this front. The bombing at night is now the limit.*

Sun 2nd June   *In Wood. Am still feeling queer. To Baths in morning at Béhencourt. Football: H.Q. v 10th H.Q.: we lose 3-1. Slept in Orderly Room. Usual bombing at night.*

Mon 3rd June   *Parade 9.45 am: Rifle Inspection. To Transport lines on bike. Fritz shells village on our right. C Company beats Australians at cricket (very exciting). To all Companies with messages.*

Tues 4th June   *On duty in Orderly Room 8 to 9.30 am. Various messages to all companies. Listening to Divisional Band. To cricket, etc., in evening, and to all companies with orders. Usual bombing. Intense artillery duel all night.*

Wed 5th June   *Taking down tents, etc., in the morning. To 175 Brigade H.Q. Bavelincourt on bike via Béhencourt. Resting in Wood all afternoon. Tea 4.30 pm. Moved off westwards at 6pm, H.Q. leading, via Béhencourt, Montigny, and arrived in large Wood near Molliens.*

Thurs 6th June   *Lovely weather, and Molliens Wood is an ideal spot. I am Orderly. To Brigade in morning. Took C.O. in afternoon. For ride in evening with Shirtcliffe to Molliens-au-Bois. Usual bombing at night.*

Fri 7th June   *Breakfast 7.30 am. (Guns noisy.) Throat still bad. Not much doing in Wood. Usual Company stunts, and waiting orders.*

Sat 8th June   *Weather continues fine. To open-air performance of 'The Goods' in evening. Not bad, but have seen better. Fritz has launched another attack south of us between Soissons and Rheims. He has met with success, and has crossed the Marne. We are expecting to be ordered into it every day. Air-raids are becoming a pest.* [A rapid advance by the Germans had indeed reached the Marne, and from there had turned to threaten Paris. The population of that city was so concerned that more than 1,000,000 inhabitants left.]

Sun 9th June   *With orders to Q.M. Bombardment in line lasts throughout the day. Usual aeroplane work at night.*

Mon 10th June   *Reveille 4 am. Walker and I left at 6.30 am via Molliens au Bois and Villers Bocage. At 8 am Brigade mounted busses, rode west via Flesselles, Vignacourt, Picquigny, and de-bussed at Cavillon. Marched via* [gap]*, and arrived at Bougainville* [west of Amiens]*. To Brigade H.Q. at Oissy, rode via Mollien-Vidame with Dorkins.*

Tues 11th June   *For walk. Helped cooks. Britton and I dodge parade. Usual messages during day. Careering round village on bicycles in evening with Rowan and Combly.*

Wed 12th June   *To Picquigny in morning on bicycle (25 km). Not much there. Then via Oissy, Fourinoy, Cavillons. With boys in Estaminet. Dinner at 8 pm at Madames. Had excellent time with boys, etc., and 'girls'. (Champagne also good.)*

Thurs 13th June   *Parade 8.10 am with B Company. Despatch cyclists for attack on Cavillon. Dinner in field 1 am.* [pm?] *Arrived back at Bougainville 4 pm. In Estaminets in evening with Rowan and others. Also good time.*

Fri 14th June   *On duty till midday. Usual business. Went with Renée to milk cows etc midday. With Harry Ballard all evening in Estaminets, etc., and watching football. Then in Madame's house.*

Sat 15th June   *Usual games with Renée; Amié; Aundrie at the house. In Estaminet in evening with the Boys. Playing French Cannons. Rather good time. I think this is too good to last. We expect 'marching orders' soon. The German attack still in progress. Usual raids on all fine nights.*

Sun 16th June   Stormy. Played football in afternoon: Runners v. Buglers. We won 3-0. On duty 5 till 10 pm. Usual games in evening.

Mon 17th June   On duty all day. Messages to all companies. In Estaminet playing French Cannons with Bert Hursee and Ballard. Dinner in evening at Madame's house with Bert, Darby, Smith, Dorkins, Collins, etc.

Tues 18th June   Packing up in morning. (I am on Surplus Personnel with Rowan and others.) Parade 1 pm. Marched via Floxicourt to Briquemesnil. By bus via Amiens etc to Molliens au Bois. Marched to Mirvaux. Round billets with Lieut. Hall .

Wed 19th June   Kit inspection by Col. Powell 11 am. In billet all day. Rain. To 2/10 Officer, and various other messages. (This is an awful village. Only a few civilians, no Estaminets, and it is impossible to buy anything except milk and eggs.)

Thurs 20th June On duty at 175 Brigade Orderly Room. Also parade at 8.30 under Mr Holloway for Map and Compass Reading. Had good time in Rubempré in evening with Seaman, Rowan and Combly.

Fri. 21st June   Duty all day at 175 Orderly Room. To Rubempré in afternoon for papers. Divisional Band plays in evening. (What a quiet life!)

Sat. 22nd June   To Baths at 9 am in Beaucourt. Duty at Orderly Room. With Runners in evening to 18 Division Concert Party (Vin blancs) (Fair). Then for walk in Molliens au Bois. The Line is comparatively quiet. Heaps of American troops are now arriving in Villages round-about. The feeling between us is much better than I anticipated. Weather is changeable: sun, wet, oh what a mixture.

Sun 23rd June   On duty at Divisional Signal School Orderly Room, and 175 Brigade Orderly Room. To Rubempré in afternoon. Evening in Billet.

Mon 24th June   Reveille 6 am. Breakfast 6.30. Parade 7.15, and marched to Molliens au Bois. By bus to Baizeux. Then in Battle positions. Shells are dropping a few hundred yards away. Saw Boys. Went back to Mirvaux via Contay and Beaucourt.

Tues 25th June   To Bavlincourt in morning (Bicycle). To Rubempré in afternoon. Sitting in house most of evening talking to Mart (little French girl of 3 or 4).

Wed 26th June   To Rubempré in morning for newspapers, but managed to get vin blanc and bicycle as well. Sleep afternoon. To Molliens au Bois and Pierigot [?] with Boys. Bombs all around at night, and on Molliens au Bois.

Thurs 27th June   To Villers-Bocage in morning via Pieregot [?] and Septomville.   With Rowan in evening to Rubempré to 17 Division. Brigade Concert Party 'The Gaspers'. Quite a good all round show.

Fri 28th June   In Mart's house most of morning.   To Rubempré for papers. Billet afternoon. Listening to Divisional Band in evening. Bombing as usual. Serious.

Sat 29th June   On duty in morning at Orderly Room. To Rubempré for papers. In Billet afternoon and evening. Bombing at night is becoming quite serious. Casualties all round. We have an epidemic of P.U.O. everywhere. [This may be Pyrexia of Unknown Origin, a serious fever which is sometimes related to influenza.] *Cases are going to hospital rapidly. Fritz is strangely quiet. Has he something similar? Our guns are now keeping up a heavy harrassing fire, especially at night.*

Sun 30th June   Mirvaux. To Bavlincourt in morning. Writing in house afternoon. Spent quiet evening also. Usual bombing at night.

Mon. 1st Jul   Killing time in Billet, and packing up. Artillery bombardment. 18 Division take two lines of trenches. Fritz counter-attacks, but fails. By bus to line via Contay and Franvillers. Join Boys in support.

Tues 2nd Jul   Fritz makes another counter-attack for trenches just on our left, but fails. We move up to front line and relieve 10th Londons. Fritz makes another attack after dark and captures trenches back.

Wed 3rd Jul   Fritz is registering on ridge 100 yards below us. Duty Orderly Room 11.30 to 1pm. To 12th London Rangers with message. Round the front line with Capt Nichols at 11 pm. Trench is badly minenwerfered. We wander round and lose our way. (I know why!!)

Thurs 4th Jul   We arrive back at B.H.Q. 2 am. At 3 pm we commence attack on our right. Australians capture two lines of trenches at dawn and 600 prisoners. Fritz's barrage causes us many casualties. He attacks at 7 pm, but our artillery stops it.

Fri 5th Jul   Our Artillery keep up harassing gunfire on Fritz's lines. To all Companies in morning with Harry, and Bert Grace. We send off the latest gas projectiles accompanied by heavy artillery bombardment for an hour.

Sat 6th Jul   Fritz attempts another counter-attack at dawn on his lost positions. But fails. To Transport Lines Bavlincourt in evening. Then to Borgeux [?] We take over 2/3 London Billets. Americans are mixed with British troops for obtaining insight of trench warfare. Our attacks and German counter-attacks have been many this week. Our artillery is good, but some ammunition faulty.

Sun 7th Jul   Bed 3.30 am. To 2/2 Londons 11 am and 12th Londons in line via Laviéville and Bresle. Runners beat H.Q. Company cricket. The[n] had a 'rag' with Signallers: smashed their house.

Mon 8th Jul   Pay morning. Bombs dropped all round. Duty as usual. Another 'rag' on Signallers. Troops man battle positions. Very heavy gunfire all night.

Tues 9th Jul   To bed 2 am. (A night of incidents.) Not much doing all day. Playing various games, etc. Usual harassing fire all night.

Wed 10th Jul   Enemy aeroplane attacks two observation balloons and brings them down. To Mervaux and Rubempré in evening with Dorkins via Conty and Beaucourt. Back at Baizeux midnight.

Thurs 11th Jul   In Baizeux all morning. Artillery still assume an active part. Various rumours are floating round. Usual time in evening at house.

Fri 12th Jul   Resting all morning. Heavy bombardment in progress near Hangard. Australians take a village. To line 3 am and relieve 7th Londons on Albert Road.

Sat 13th Jul   To A Company with Rowan. Usual shelling on each side. Aeroplane activity. Wiring on 'No Man's Land' is very poor. (We'll do it!!) We have eight Americans attached to us for observation and patrols. The artillery is unusually restless here: it is believed to be German naval division. We prepare various 'stunts', but they all come to nothing.

Sun 14th Jul   Usual duty at Orderly Room. Enemy shelling is getting dangerous. Led 'B' Company Surplus to their trench. Shelling continues.

Mon 15th Jul   This sector Laviéville is about the worst on the Brigade front. Trenches are shallow and under Minenwerfer fire. Duty as usual. Aeroplane activity. One of our balloons is set on fire.

Tues 16th Jul   Rain. Duty in morning. To B Company and 2/10 H.Q. afternoon. One enemy balloon brought down. Harassing fire each side. Enemy planes drop bombs round H.Q.

Wed 17th Jul   Usual shelling round about. Rain sets in. To Brigade with message. This front is getting decidedly unpleasant: shells, minenwerfers, mortars, gas and bombs are all the rage. Trenches are now blown about badly.

Thurs 18th Jul   A patrol of Australians arrives – 8th Brigade. Also company of Americans. Enemy balloon is fired. The whole Battalion front is badly shelled (casualties). To 3rd Londons with message. Gas is bad in evening (I like it not). Owing to great movement on top we are shelled continuously. French advance 10 kilos at Soissons, capturing 1,500 men and 200 guns.

Fri 19th Jul   *More casualties through enemy shelling. Generals can be seen riding on horses, but naturally they are gone when the shelling starts, and we have to suffer.*

Sat 20th Jul   *Sleep 4 am. till 8 am.   To Transport with 'Operation Orders' 11.30 at Bavlincourt. Arrived line again 7.30 pm. We are being relieved by 10th Londons. Shelling not so bad.*

Sun 21st Jul   *Waiitng for relief to complete. Dawkins and I arrive at line between Millencourt and Laviéville 3 am.* [Just west of Albert.]   *Sleep till 8 am. With orders to all Companies. Bombing as usual.*

Mon 22nd Jul   *Irregular shelling all day. We bring down enemy Observation Balloon. Round to all Bays with Capt Nichols. Nothing of great importance at the moment.*

Tues 23rd Jul   *Raining. On duty in Orderly Room. Our relief is doubtful. Our guns continue their destructive work on Albert.*

Wed 24th Jul   *47th Division makes a raid at dawn. (Just as I thought, we do not get relieved.) V.O.s capture 27 prisoners and 4 machine-guns but with 80 casualties. These daylight raids are usually very disastrous to us. I later hear the casualty figure is 130.*

Thurs 25th Jul   *P.O. Raid is at 10 am today. We put up a fine barrage, but Fritz also has a lot to say in the matter. The weather is doubtful. I sleep in Orderly Room.*

Fri 26th Jul   *With Mr Keeson to 6th Londons: Fritz is shelling all round with 5.9s and keeps it up all afternoon. Raining heavily, causing me and a bike to 'fall out'. We are relieved by 24th Londons and 6th. I pass through Laviéville and arrive at Baizeux weary, wet and muddy. Waiting for Johnny and Charlie. To bed 8 am.*

Sat 27th Jul   *Up again at 9.30 am (splendid, isn't it?). I am Orderly for the day. (Oh, a soldier's life is full of strife). Fritz obliges again with hot iron. We have many cases of men partially blind through gas. I have seen the largest bomb-hole as yet, just in front of Laviéville: over 30 feet across and 20 feet deep. And officially the left-hand salute is from now onwards abolished.*

Sun 28th Jul   *Weather very bad. To Baths at Bois Robert 8.30 am. I am now Mess President for Runners' Section, and I fulfil my duty accordingly. We play Old Transport Section at Cricket (draw).*

Mon 29th Jul   *Runners go to view 'tank' demonstration. With various messages in afternoon. We (H.Q. Company) play 2nd Life Guards Cricket, and beat them by three runs: 46-43. Usual raid at night.*

Tues 30th Jul   *Weather fine. Fritz shells round about Baizeux. Preparing to depart. We leave at 10 pm, and arrive in support to 'Yanks' on Albert Road. Usual shelling.*

Wed. 31st Jul   *Not much doing all day. On duty 6-7 pm. Fritz sends shrapnel over B.H.Q. in evening. Quite an exciting night. Fritz sends relays of planes over, and bombs are dropped uncomfortably near, about forty in all. Shelling.*

Thurs 1st Aug   *Usual shelling round about. Duty at Orderly Room 11.30 – 12.30. To C company with West Kent Officer. We lose four Observation Balloons. We are in support to the Americans in this position.*

Fri 2nd Aug   *Fritz is again busy with shrapnel. He has left his front and second lines owing to bad weather. Raining all day. (Relief tomorrow.)*

The intense fighting that resulted from the rapid German advance was every bit as desperate as had been the First Battle of the Somme; but, since the defenders generally suffered fewer casualties than the attackers, the British, French and Americans slowly wore down the enemy while making plans for a final offensive themselves. On August 8th 1918, with Foch in overall command of the two longstanding allies, and General Pershing (later, significantly, to give his name to a tank) in charge of the Americans, what proved to be the decisive assault was launched. Nowhere could the Germans hold the line, and they were soon in full retreat. Tim, however, had a few more days of doubt and anxiety to get through before all this happened:

Sat 3rd Aug   Fritz gets very nasty with shrapnel, and puts a few gas shells on main Albert Road. To Northampton H.Q. We are relieved by 6th West Kents (12 Division) by midnight. On bicycle to Béhencourt. Fritz has commenced a retirement which has every sign of developing . We are shifting up our 6" Howitzers. Roads are simply blocked with ammunition. Things seem to be looking brisk.

Sun 4th Aug   Left Béhencourt by bus 4.30 am, via Contay, Hérissart, Rubempré, Villers-Bocage to Vignacourt [NW of Amiens] *arriving 7 am. Found place and had meal, then sleep. Out in evening.*

Mon 5th Aug   On duty 9 am to 3 pm. Various runs etc. In Café afternoon with Boys. (Speaking to Charlotte.) Out with Boys again in evening: quite a good time (et tout bien).

Tues 6th Aug-Wed 7th Aug   Rumours. Bad rumours. Rifle inspection. Yes, we move tonight at dusk by bus for the line. Enemy is retiring. Spend day having final drinks and feeds. Then left by bike via Flesselles, Villers-Bocage and (after struggle in mud) Raineville, then on to St Gratien and Querrieu. Bombs dropped all round here. Arrived in Wood by La Houssouge [?] *Am sent to find and guide   Transport home. Heavy ammunition limber runs over my   bike. (I dump it.) Sleep 5 to 10 am.*

It has been a harrowing and very confused few weeks. Tim has repeatedly mentioned the strength of the enemy's position: German aircraft, minenwerfers, and so on. But now he has noted that the tide seems to be turning ('Enemy is retiring'). He is finding the French rather better organised than the British, and twice probably owed his life to their being able to reach his positions when hope of relief by the British seemed gone. The Americans had arrived, and were steadily building up their forces and equipment. Tim's 'luck' has held; but his entry for August 7th 1918 shows him losing perhaps his most treasured possession, his bicycle. And not by enemy action!

Tim carried this battered photo of a German prisoner in his 1918 diary (see page 96)

CHAPTER TWELVE

THE SECOND BATTLE OF THE SOMME
Successful allied attack near Amiens

Tim, as in the first Battle of the Somme, was involved in the initial massive assault, which was launched by British, French and (this time) American forces on August 8th 1918. Although on this occasion the overall operation was to prove successful, that fact was not known at the time, and nothing really made life any less perplexing for the foot soldiers leading the charge, as Tim's diary entry for that day shows:

1918

Thurs Aug 8th   We attacked this morning at dawn. Nearly all objectives gained. We move up via Bonnay in reserve to 18 Division 53rd Brigade. I go to meet Transport and reconnoitre roads. Eventually lead them via Sailly-le-Sec and Sailly-Lauriette. [On Somme, halfway from Amiens to Péronne]

Fri 9th Aug   We find the Battalion has advanced. Captain Filbrick and I go ahead and find them. I lead mules to H.Q. at 3 am., and guide Pioneers to H.Q. too. We are in a valley left of Chippilly, and under terrible 5.9 fire. We go to valley K51 CC-1 [?]   We attack at 5 pm with the Americans and advance 1,000 yards.

*Sat 10th Aug   I guide mules to H.Q. by map reference after difficult and unenviable task 2am. *[sic]*. We are now left of Malade Bois. We attack again at 1 pm and advance 1,000 yards towards Bray. H.Q. moves to old front line N.W. of Morlancourt. Smith and I get through enemy barrage with orders to attack again at 6 pm. We advance another 500 yards. There is now a gap between our Division and the 12th. I take up three Companies of Berkshire Regiment to fill same. Get in Hun barrage and are spotted by enemy as dawn is breaking. Many casualties.*

Sun 11th Aug   I get back to H.Q. with marvellous luck. Take messages to all Companies. Enemy attack Australians on our left, and gain small part of front line. I guide up 100 R.E., but Gas overcomes us in the Valley and we are forced back.

Mon 12th Aug   I have searched for Rangers H.Q. before dawn. Our captures are now 2,400 men and 1,000 guns, and heaps of machine-guns. To D Company with advance relief. Hodge and I start off at 9.30 pm. Relieved by 47th 22nd London. We go to old line north of Morlancourt.

Tues 13th Aug   Waiting for rest of Regiment to roll in. Last turn up at 6 am. We are now south of Morlancourt. Bert Grace and I swim in the Somme at Vaux. We move off at 4.30 pm to old Wood. Hodge and I ride to Brigade at Fréchencourt [which lies about one third of the way from Amiens to Albert] *– 14 kilos. Bombs at night.*

Wed 14th Aug   In Wood in front of Le Houssoye. Advance continues slowly. To Bonnay in afternoon for swim in River Ancre. Usual bombing at night. One enemy Gotha brought down. Crew of seven men. One bomb dropped.

Thurs 15th Aug   To Transport in morning. Swim in River Ancre in afternoon. Various inspections, etc. Usual enemy raids at night.

Fri 16th Aug   Parade for Map Reading. Swim in Somme lakes in afternoon.   To 'Rangers' Concert in evening (fair). Usual bombing by Fritz at night.

Sat 17th Aug   To Transport and all Companies. Cycle to Mirvaux in afternoon via Le Houssoye, Fréchencourt, Béhencourt and Beaucourt. Bombing at night. 58 Division captures

1,800 men and 175 officers. We had difficult task at Chippilly but eventually win through. This is how my bike arrived back: piece of shrapnel in front of bike, 2 pieces in saddle, 1 piece in mug, another in haversack; emergency ration blown to pieces; blanket and waterproof sheet torn. [One can well imagine that after an experience like that Tim might come to the conclusion that 'someone was watching over him'. He often refers to his 'Luck'.]

Sun 18th Aug   H.Q. beat A Company by four runs. Parade for inspection by Brigadier, then Church service and more drill (which I dodged). Swim in lake between Bonnay and Vaux in afternoon.

Mon 19th Aug   On duty all day. Runs to all Companies. We are still in Bois Escardonneuse. H.Q. beat C Company at cricket by 23 runs. We also pull off several events in swimming.

Tues 20th Aug   Parade with A Company. Then with H.Q. for 'Map Reading'. Orderly in afternoon, also boating and swimming in the Somme lakes. Bombing at night has not happened lately. What is the matter?

Wed 21st Aug   Searching for cigarettes in morning for 'Boys'. Went to Pont Noyelles, Querrieu, St Gratien and Molliens au Bois (500 cigarettes). Swimming and boating in lakes in afternoon with Signallers. On duty in evening. New advance commences at dawn tomorrow, and we are ready to move up.

Thurs 22nd Aug   We move off at 4 am via Bonnay, Mericourt-l'Abbé and Treux to a position behind Morlancourt. We are spotted on ridge by Hun balloon, and shelled. With message to Brigade and then to Companies. Attack goes well, but we lose 500 yards on our front.

Fri 23rd Aug   Orders to move at 2 am. I take Hodge with me to locate new Brigade H.Q., and join Regiment again at Bois Sailles. We are attached to 47th Division who lost a Brigade in yesterday's counter-attacks by Fritz. I go to Transport lines to guide up rations to 'Boys'.

Sat 24th Aug   We move up and attack at 1 am. We advance 2,000 yards, capturing 'Happy Valley'. Prisoners amount to three figures. I reconnoitre with Lieut Johnson, and we get caught in Hun barrage at dawn. Hun counter-attack fails. But enemy fire with 8" shells is simply hell. We are blown from one position to another. (My God, if a cat has nine lives, then I am a cat.) I get across valley to guide up mules with ammunition, but they cannot get through and go back. We spend every spare moment digging, but we cannot do much through lack of sleep. Our casualties are heavy, but our advance good.

Sun 25th Aug   Our artillery open barrage, and we attack at 3 am in heavy mist, and go forward three kilos in front of Bronfay Farm. (60 percent casualties through our own shells.) I take disposition report to Brigade, and bring up Brigadier to B.H.Q. on Bray-Fricourt road. Advance continues. (Rain) In ravine all night installing Companies.

Mon 26th Aug   Advance continues. 173 Brigade goes through us. We are in reserve. I get three hours sleep in old dug-out. H.Q. moves to ravine north of Bray. We occupy old Hun shaft. There is no relief for 4th Army (We must carry on and smile). Our total strength is 230 men left.

Clearly this assault was far more fluid than during the First Somme battles. The diary records much rapid movement, noticeable advances, enemy counter-attacks, and (always) danger and discomfort. Somehow, among all this, Tim has found a niche for himself, trusted to act as a guide for example, and he finds time for swimming in the rivers and lakes thereabouts. (He never lost his love of swimming as an activity that refreshes body and mind.)

Tues 27th Aug   Advance continues. We move to position south of Carnoy. (More rain) Heavy artillery is rapidly moving up, and what is today enemy territory is tomorrow occupied by our guns. Tanks seem completely out of it. Have not seen one for a week. Why is it ?

Wed 28th Aug   Fritz is still retiring, and we follow him up. In the evening we move to a position north-west of Maricourt. We get caught in his strafe, and sustain casualties. His machine-gun fire is severe. We are now in the old 1916 line. I take Transport to the new line.

On the next page, Tim has re-numbered the printed dates. The transcript below shows his corrected dates, which were inscribed out of strict chronological order. Presumably he was aware of space problems, and wanted to get everything down. (For whom?, we ask.) His new arrangement of just that double-page 'spread' enabled him to use the eighth space, printed as 'Weekend', to write rather more than usual about Thursday 29th. To make the story intelligible, I have re-arranged his material so that the dates appear in the correct order.

29th Aug Thurs   Fritz has retired in front of us, and cavalry are operating in advance. I go to Companies with Orders. It is strange to see our artillery going forward in front of our first line troops. Roads are black with heavy guns and lorries, yet Fritz's gun does not get many direct hits. Aeroplanes supply us with ammunition dropped by parachute. We move forward with bikes. The Boys have been in the line for too long, and they are just about beaten. Oh, to take ones boots off.

30th Aug Fri   We are now in Valley south of Maurepas, and four kilos to the right of Combles. Orders to move up, and we go 3 kilos through heavy Hun barrage. A bicycle is the limit under these conditions. Our position is just behind Marrière Bois, and we are under TM [trench mortar] *and MG* [machine-gun] *fire. I reconnoitre route to bring up Transport.*

31st Aug   We withdraw slightly to allow 174 Brigade to advance through us at dawn. We gain another 3 kilos, and capture many prisoners. News of Relief! Cheers!! 18-pounders take over our place, and after a dash through Hun barrage by bike we manage to get back.

Sun 1st Sep   (Rain) We ride skirting Maurepas to position in Valley east of Vaux, north of Curlu. [Tim's geography is not quite logical at this point, but places him some 10 km west-nor'-west of Péronne.] *Enemy is still sending over heavy-velocity shells. Prisoners continue to pass on their way down, and German retirement continues. Bapaume is ours. At last I can take off my boots.*

Mon 2nd Sep   (Rainy) Fritz is still going back. Peronne and Bapaume are ours. 74 Division (who relieved us) lose a Brigade. Great quantity of smoke rising on horizon (probably dumps). Fritz bombs as usual at night.

Tues 3rd Sep   Observation Balloon has gone forward since last night. Advance still goes favourably (also leave) [The significance of those two words is not made clear. Possibly by 'leave' he means 'periods of rest out of the line'.] *Dumps continue to go up. Fritz also obliges with a few high-velocity shells. Usual bombing.*

Wed 4th Sep   On duty at Orderly Room all day. Messages to all Companies, etc. Weather much better. Good news still comes through of the advance. (Court of Enquiry at O.R.) Why do I get no letters? It is now nearly a week since I heard.

Thurs 5th Sep   Not much doing so far. Weather is terribly hot today. I think our rest has nearly ended. Usual bombings from aerial planes at night. We get heavy storm in evening. Artillery very heavy.

Fri 6th Sep   On duty and assisting on Orderly Room duties. We get orders to move, and leave by bus at 4.30 pm. via Curlu, Clery, Bouchavesnes, Moislains [north of Peronne]. *Left buses and went along Peronne – Cambrai Road, through Eplincourt and Gurlu Woods to Aizecourt, arriving at midnigh*t.

Sat 7th Sep   In Aizecourt-le-Bas [9km north-east of Péronne]. *We start our advance at 8 am. Shellfire heavy, and we encounter heavy machine-gun resistance in Jean Copse after passing Longavesnes and Liéramont. Enemy Observation Balloons a nuisance, but our planes bring them down in flames. We capture Jean Copse and press forward in front of Saulecourt, Villers Faucon and St Emelie. Casualties* [gap]. *B.H.Q. is now in bank E16 c 8-5. Enemy shelling all round. All objectives gained, we have advanced 5 kilos by 12 midday. I am sent to Brigade on Péronne Road to reconnoitre best roads for Transport and Rations. I bring them up via Saulcourt and Lièramont. Riding Capt Filbrick's* [Killred's ?] *horse.*

Sun 8th Sep   Mist and rain. Observation very difficult. I go in advance to a position north of Guyencourt to prepare positions for Battalion with Mr Hall. Intermittent shelling in progress all day. Weather rough. Spent night getting D Company into position.

Mon 9th Sep   I go to find 175 Brigade at 1 am with Rowan, via Liéramont to Aizecourt-le-Bas. (Rotten job: Fritz is bombing and shelling.) Leave Aizecourt 3.45. 12" shell gets direct hit on ammunition twenty yards in front of us. Our move is postponed. Two hours sleep in afternoon. Shelling continues.

Tues 10th Sep   Present weather very bad. Situation is obscure. Advanced posts are fixed in front of Battalion for emergency. Heavy bombs dropped, to say nothing of shells. Three attempts have been made to take Epéhy, but all failed. Fritz means to 'hold on'.

Wed 11th Sep   Usual shelling all round. Harry, Theisty and I reconnoitre new B.H.Q. I go up in evening with C Company (the usual game: guides lose way). We relieve Rangers in front line, and they go on our left. Spending the night roaming round the country and dodging 'pieces of iron'. We are immediately behind Epéhy and right of Heudicourt.

Thurs 12th Sep   Reach B.H.Q. 2 am. Get few hours sleep. (We send off gas.) Hellish fire on our left. Fritz makes a surprise attack and captures a 'post' and fifty yards of line in depth, and takes prisoners. Fire from our guns and Newtons on Epéhy very heavy. We have casualties.

Fri 13th Sep   Round front line and Companies with Major Renton visiting line. I take up one Platoon of 2/24 Londons to relieve one of D Company. I carry out relief and bring platoon back. Get caught in strafe, but get through. We carry on, and eventually arrive near B.H.Q. at 1.30 am.

Sat 14th Sep   Our guns bring down two aeroplanes. Fritz masses behind Epéhy for attack, but our guns smash it up. I lead up the Platoon again to D Company's front line. We send over gas. We are now practically on our old line of March 20th. When will this Division be relieved? It has been in during the whole advance. Heavy battle still in progress near Cambrai. (I often wonder what would happen sometimes if there were no runners [rumours?]. *Some officers are the limit!!!!)*

Sun 15th Sep   Usual artillery fire. Very fine day. To C and D Companies with orders of relief. One of our Observation Balloons down. Fritz strafes the Sunken Road as usual. We leave at 11 pm (relieved by 8th London), passing through Guyencourt, Templeux-la-Fosse and Aizecourt. Artillery are shelled heavily. We arrive at Quarry near Bois Eppeviette [?] *and* ---[illegible] *early in morning.*

Mon 16th Sep   Weather windy. Quiet all day. I go to find Transport Lines in evening, ride to Moislains, then towards Peronne, and find them.

Tues 17th Sep   Return from Transport Lines. Terrific thunderstorm breaks out at 1.30 am. Tents and bivouacs blown away. (This is the worst I have ever experenced.) To T.L. at mid-day. We are evidently moving up again tomorrow. Shall we ever get out of the line? Bombs! Bombs!

Wed 18th Sep   New attack starts at dawn. We move up to Guyencourt at 7 am. Standing by for orders. (I lead regiment up.) Attack goes favourably, although great opposition is met in Epéhy. Heaps of prisoners. One of our Observation Balloons brought down in flames. Shelling all round. We open another barrage at dusk and continue attack. Advance goes well. Weather doubtful.

Thurs 19th Sep   Divisions in front are reported all in touch: 74th, 18th, 12th . 'Mopping up' now on. Five doctors among the many prisoners. One Fritz plane down. Epéhy is now in our hands, also line of posts 800 yards in front. Heavy attack goes on in Flavincourt sector.

Fri 20th Sep and Sat 21st   Orders to move. I go to all Companies with messages. We move off at 8 pm and relieve 173 Brigade. We go skirting Epéhy and Peizières, and make B.H.Q. in railway cutting on St Quentin – Cambrai line. 10th and 12th Londons make an attack, but it turns out a failure. Position is very obscure. Attacks still continue on left and right. (Raining) There is no relief in sight. We have the Alpine Corps in front of us (Jägers), the 2nd German Guards Division on our right, and 101 Division on our left.

Am now expecting 'leave' at any time. Don't like the present position at all. We live in hopes !!

Sun 22nd Sep   Heavy bombardment in progress until dawn, with sudden bursts all day. (Rain) I go to cross roads in Peizières at 9 pm. to guide up rations to new B.H.Q. two kilos east of Epéhy. Q.V.R. with Suffolks and others attack at 9.30 pm. Barrage causes great inconvenience.

Mon 23rd Sep   Heavy fire continues. A party of enemy Guards makes a dashing raid into part of our line, but they are repulsed after casualties on both sides. Enemy machine-guns active. I go round to all boys with Pergram and advance relief. We are relieved by 9th Fusiliers at night.

Tues 24th Sep   We are the last to leave H.Q. at 1 am, and proceed to Villers-Faucon via Epéhy. (At last the Division is going out.) We embus at dawn and go north to camp between Trones Wood and Bernafay. Oh !! Memories !! I pass monuments in Trones Wood.

Wed 25th Sep   We are living in huts and dug-outs between Trones Wood and Bernafay Wood. I go to Brigade H.Q. with message. Also to Companies. How quiet it is here now, and oh what recollections this place has for me. I remember the 2nd West Kents, and others.

Thurs 26th Sep   We move off at 8 am. I march via Mametz [WNW of Peronne], Maulte, and entrain just outside Dernancourt [SSW of Albert] at 11 am. Then via Corbie, Amiens, Vignacourt [NNW of Amiens]. We are travelling all night in very uncomfortable trucks.

Fri 27th Sep   Arrive at Aubigny 1 am [WNW of Arras]. Then by bike to Comblain Lillié [?]. To Cambligneul with other runners to have a feed in an Estaminet. Concert by 2nd Canadian Division Party in evening. (Excellent)

Sat 28th Sep   To Baths (Corps 8th) in morning, and in the village with Harry, Denis and Sharpe. (Pommes de terre frites.) In hut all afternoon. To Cambligneul in evening to see Madeline and Lucy, etc. Then dinner at Principal Estaminet.

Good news from all fronts. We have now got Boulon Wood, and are 3 kilos from Cambrai. Apparently things are rather quiet on this sector (Lens). Great numbers of our planes return from bombing each night.

Sun 29th Sep   Orderly for day. To all Companies. To Aubigny in morning (bicycle). Cleaning up in afternoon. Cambligneul in evening. Heavy rain.

Mon 30th Sep   Packing up. Final drink in Estaminet. Left Camblain l'Abbé at 3 pm by bus, going NNE via Ablain St Nazaire and Souchez. Then by bike to outskirt of Liévin, passing through Angres. Regiment holding front-line posts in Lens at 7 pm, after relieving Sussex Regiment. B.H.Q. is in Liévin.

Tues Oct 1st   Roaming about most of the day, reconnoitering the country. To Transport Lines at Bully-Grenay via Calonne in evening. This part of the line is terribly difficult to negotiate. It is a city of ruins.

Wed Oct 2nd   Not much doing. To Brigade in morning, and searching for Canteen in Angres, Liévin, and around Lens. We send out patrols. Huns are preparing to evacuate.

Thurs 3rd Oct   To Brigade in the morning. Then obtained Warrant and went to Transport Lines at Aix Noulette. To Bully Grenay, and then left Transport Lines at 2 pm via Bouvingny, Servins, etc., and caught R.A.F. car to Aubigny. In Town and Y.M.C.A. in evening.

Fri 4th Oct   Left Aubigny 12 midday via St Pol, Frévent, etc. Arrived at Boulogne 11 pm. Had dinner, etc. Air-raid warning given, but no results.

The surprising aspect of the last couple of entries is that Tim never actually mentioned that the Warrant he had obtained was his permission to go on leave. The reader could easily overlook what's implied, until Tim tells us of his arrival at Boulogne. Nor is there any evidence of the excitement that the prospect of home leave evoked on the previous occasion. It is as if his entire existence is now geared to responding to immediate problems, such as locating a canteen in a largely destroyed environment, or getting about and understanding the geography of the area. However, leave it certainly is; and we know what Tim did not know at the time, namely that the War will end in about five weeks.

CHAPTER THIRTEEN

LEAVE – BACK TO FRANCE – ARMISTICE

1918

Sat Oct 5th   Left Boulogne at midday. Sea awfully rough, so we arrived at Folkestone at 2.45. *Reached Victoria at 4.45 pm, and arrived home at 6.30. Raining. Went round Wimbledon in the evening. The place is very quiet. It is impossible to describe ones feelings on reaching England again. How delicious it is after France. The ordinary civilian's idea of the war is very vague.*

Sun Oct 6th   To Harvest Festival at Church in the morning. Saw various friends. To Mrs Bartlett in the afternoon, and Mrs Rigby in the evening. With Annie, Madge, etc.

Mon Oct 7th   Visiting friends in morning. Mr Warner shows me round the Notable Electric Light Company. Blowed organ for wedding at 2 pm. Interview with Mr Jaegger. Round Wimbedon in evening, and for walk.

Tues Oct 8th   Mrs Bartlett's in morning. For walk afternoon and evening.

Wed Oct 9th   Caught 10.50 from Waterloo and arrived Exeter 2.30 pm. Met Gwen and visited Mrs Eastling. Caught 4.15 from St David's Exeter, changed at Newton Abbott, then to Moreton Hampstead, and by bus to Chagford. With Gwen's people.

Thurs Oct 10th   Living at Teign View, Chagford. For walk with Gwen round Valley of Teign River in morning. Also at factory with Mr Reed. In hills with Gwen afternoon and evening.

Fri Oct 11th   On Milden Hill in morning – awfully pretty place. To Merchendon in afternoon with Gwen and Lewise's Tea etc. [as written]. *Chagford again at 8.30 pm.*

Sat Oct 12th   Left by bus usual route. Walk round Newton Abbott. Arrived Torquay 11 am. For walk, then theatre in afternoon, Carrying On *(rot).* ['Rot' or not, this stage play, if play it was, seems to have disappeared without trace.] *We lost train and went by car, arriving at Chagford 9 pm.*

Devon is indeed a glorious county. Have had lovely walks round here. Teign Valley and the high hills form excellent scenery. There is no War here.

Sun Oct 13th   Church in morning, and walk with Gwen in Teign Valley afternoon and evening. It is glorious.

Mon Oct 14th   Walk in morning. Tea at Ingleside in afternoon. To Hale [Hole?] *Farm in evening with Gwen and Mrs Lewis. A typical Devonshire farm. Home midnight.*

Tues Oct 15th   In Lewis's all morning. For walk in afternoon with two Miss Reeds – Teign Valley. Party at Lewis's in evening. Short walk with Gwen.

Wed Oct 16th   Gwen and I left Chagford 9.30 am. To Newton Abbott, and arrived at Exeter 12.20. Walk round etc. Gwen caught train at 4.15, and I left at 4.22. Tea on train. Arrived Waterloo 9.45. Reached home 10.30 pm. Very cold.

Thurs Oct 17th   For walk in morning. To theatre with Lionel Hutchinson afternoon: Seven Days Leave. *To Miss Carey's in evening for supper, etc. Home at 11.15 pm.*

Fri Oct 18th   To Mrs Bartlett morning. With Mr Reed in afternoon to Victoria, then met Cyril 'Pall Mall' 5.30. Had 'some' night in Town: met various people, Capt Mason, etc. We roll home at 1.30 am.

Sat Oct 19th   For walk in morning (saw Ethel), then up to Town with Cyril. Tea at Mrs Bartlett's. To dance at Church Room. Saw various girls home, and so ends my leave!!!

Oh, what a night of dreams and imagination:- I am in Devon – walking with friends – I go over the 'top' at Lille – shells all around me – Where am I ? – Who is sleeping beside me? - I am in the West End – Ma calls: it is 6 am.

Tim's last wartime leave appropriately ends with a vivid description of his dreams before being woken by his mother in time for an early departure – back to France Dreams are said by psychologists to combine our wishes and our fears: Tim's night-time excursions certainly demonstrate the classic responses to the situation he is in: perched, as it were, between an idyllic leave and a return to – who knows what in France.

Sun Oct 20th   *Left home 6.45 am, and Victoria 8.15. Arrived at Thorncliffe 10.30, and No.3 Rest Camp Folkestone 11.30. Left by boat at 4 pm. Rough passage. Arrived Boulogne 8 pm. To Camp in Boulogne for meal and sleep. (Rain)*

Mon Oct 21st   *Continuation of journey. Reveille 5.30 am. Marched through Boulogne (flags flying). Train left 9.30 am via Hesdin, St Pol, and de-trained at Mont St Eloi 5 pm. (In Rest Hut). In St Eloi all evening; Estaminet with the old 'Eggs and Chips'.*

Tues Oct 22nd   *We continue. Left Mont St Eloi 9.30. Marched via Acq, Camblain Abbé, Servins. Had meal here, and an hour's rest. Then through Bouvigny and Aix Noulette, arriving at Bully-Grenay 4.30 pm. In town, etc., with Reggie Sharpe.*

Wed Oct 23rd   *Slept at Estaminet in Bully-Grenay. Marched off at 10 am., skirting Aix-Noulette, and through Calonne and Liévin, arriving at Cité St Pierre 12.30 pm. Many civilians are walking about here, visiting their old homes. We stay here the night.*

Thurs Oct 24th   *Breakfast 7.30 am, and draw biscuits, etc. Left Cité St Pierre 9.30 am. Marched via Lens, Sallaumines, Billy Montigny, Flévin, Liétard, Courcelles and Douges. Stayed the night at Le Forest [east of Lens]. Spoke to civilians who are living in their wrecked homes.*

Fri Oct 25th   *Continued march through Moncheaux, where we stayed for two hours. Spoke to Mademoiselle who had just returned home from German lines. Then we went through Mons en Pévèle, Bersée, Cappy, Orchies, and stayed the night at Nomain.*

Sat Oct 26th   *Continued through Mouchin, Aix, and reached transport lines at Rumegies [near the Belgian border south of Tournai]. We are now on the Belgian Frontier. With civilians in the evening, who were very kind. I sleep the night with them. I shall not forget the sights I have seen during the past week. The wanton and ruthless destruction by the Hun is terrible and disgusting. All the sympathy I ever had for him has vanished.*

Sun Oct 27th   *In Rumegies all morning. Went to other part of Rumegies in the evening and met the boys from the line. Enemy sends a few shells into the village at intervals during the night. Civilians are killed.*

Mon Oct 28th   *To Transport Lines in Hamleaux Belanges [?] Also to all Companies. More shells in the village. Civilians are buried. Found a room in the village to sleep. Had dinner in evening.*

Tues Oct 29th   *To Transport Lines and C Company. Enemy aeroplanes very low over the village. A dozen shells from Fritz. We have our usual Sectional Dinner at night. (Scrounged goods.)*

Wed Oct 30th   *Parade 8.30 am. Inspection and Arms Drill. On duty at Orderly Room. To 'Goods' Concert in afternoon (not much). Enemy planes active. A few shells in the evening.*

Thurs Oct 31st   *Parade at 8.30 am for Rifle Inspection and a little drill. Duty in Orderly Room. To Concert in evening at 'Communal Magasin'. (A huge success.)*

Fri Nov 1st   *Usual runs. I spend most of the time in the billet, chatting to Madame, etc. The usual shells greet us in the evening from Fritz; otherwise very quiet.*

Sat Nov 2nd   *Parade for Brigadier's Inspection, and Brigade Drill in morning. (Rain). In billet afternoon and evening, and a few runs.. Fritz obliges with a few more shells. The news is good this week. Turkey has thrown in the 'sponge', and Austria has just about finished. Madame has given me quite a good bed: she prefers the cellar. Of course, I don't mind!!*

Sun Nov 3rd   *Dodged parade and stayed in billet. Madame à la maison elle est vraiment trop bon. Nous boire du café toujours. Good news from Lille. Withdrawal expected.*

Mon Nov 4th   *Usual daily doings in the village. Playing chess, etc. Artillery are very active, and Huns still send a few shells round about our area.*

Tues Nov 5th   *Parade cancelled (Rain). Usual time in billets in Rumegies. Various runs to all Companies. We are expecting great news any day.*

Wed Nov 6th   *Parade 8.20. Rifle inspection. Raining all day. To Concert in evening at Magasin Rumegies: 10th Band and Q.V.R. Turns. Excellent show. Very heavy artillery fire on Valenciennes front and here.*

Thurs Nov 7th   *Parade 8.30. Rifle inspection. Duty 12.30 to 4.30. German Delegates leave Germany for Peace Conference. Fritz has retired. We march from Rumegies through Rongy and Flecelles, and stop at Maulde.*

Fri Nov 8th   *I am attached to Forward Company A as cyclist. We go through Mortagne, Flines, Legis, Rouillon, Wiers (a great welcome here). I stop some hours with various people, then go through La Garrone and reach Péruwelz at 10 pm.*

Sat Nov 9th   *The people are too excited for words. They cannot do enough for us, and would give us anything. 'Vive les Anglais' is always the cry. I have many interesting chats with them, and never sleep in barns, etc. They always have a room ready. Four years under German rule has been simply terrible for them, and their joy at being released is obvious.*

Sun Nov 10th   *In Orderly Room all night with Capt Filbrick. Left Péruwelz 9 am. We are welcomed everywhere as we march past. Café, wines, etc given to us. We go through Quévaucamps and Basècles, and stay the night at Ecacheries. A good time.*

Mon Nov 11th   **To Stambruges at 9 am to find Supply Convoy. Have lunch with Madame at Chateau, and return to Ecacheries at 2 pm.**

Hurrah ! The War is over. We have a good dinner.

I have taken the liberty of highlighting Tim's elegantly simple record of Armistice Day. I have, additionally, made one small change: he refers to having had dinner with Madame at the Chateau, when he clearly meant lunch. He had reverted to his pre-war habit of calling the meal served at mid-day 'dinner', even though he had learnt to call it 'lunch' while in France. He actually wrote 'dinner' twice, one with Madame, one in the evening at an unspecified location.

I seriously considered ending at this point my task of transcribing his diaries ; but since I have looked in some detail into what follows I have come to the conclusion that the War had made more changes to Tim's life than even he then perhaps realized. Before the War, as we read his journal, we encountered a young man who was passionately interested in the stage, the theatre, and the craft of performing. Everything pointed to the likelihood that he would set out to make his career proceed either as actor or producer, and perhaps even as playwright. In the event, however, although his immediate reaction to 'peace' was to get back into show-business, that was not to be where his long-term future lay; and it is intriguing to see a change of career beginning to overtake him. So – it's back to my magnifying glass (some of the books he writes in are still tiny), to see what Tim's continued attention to his diary-keeping reveals. Knowing, as I do, that in later life he was for some time actually to live in Eton College and Kensington Palace, I have little doubt that the changes in his intentions during the immediate post-war situation were the catalyst for a future that was to be very, very different.

Tim presumably received this 14" by 10" cardboard example of contemporary design through the post. He kept it in its envelope. Possibly the ink-blob obscuring part of the presenting rifle (and in the distance the Tower of London) discouraged him from framing and displaying it. Three soldiers from the County of London Regiment (brothers all, to judge from their profiles) climb the steps to receive a congratulatory wreath from a "Votes for Women" campaigner who wears fancy dress for the occasion. Her wingèd partner waits to greet the ghosts of dead companions. The dates remind us that the soldiery was not disbanded once the war ended but graciously continued serving into 1919. Sundry laurels tell us that these lantern-jawed carriers of fixed bayonets were rendering their services not only in France, but in Palestine, Africa, Gallipoli (wisely obscured by the lady's head: the campaign there had been a disaster), Belgium, Salonica and Italy. On the pillars we see Mesopotamia, India and Egypt. A British lion fiercely defends the world from the assaults of foreigners one and all. The citation is signed by the President of the Territorial Force Assocn (bit cramped there) of the County of London, and T.G.Elliott's name appears down right as a Member of that Territorial Force. Outlines of St Paul's and the Tower Bridge remind the viewer that we are in London. The artwork is credited to" Bernhard Hugh 1919" (Bernard would then have been a safer choice, surely) and the printer who made this dream reality is named just under Tim's scroll (Truscotts London).

CHAPTER FOURTEEN

THE WAR'S LEGACY
Back to the stage?   or – Is Tim a changed man?

Following the Armistice, even though he was not to be released from the army for some time, Tim immediately swung into 'peace' mode. He seemed confident that his exemplary army record gave him the right to determine much of his day-to-day activity; and (while he never rebelled against the discipline) he gives the impression of one who is now going to take charge of his future life. With his extraordinary skill at getting on with people of all ranks and classes, he immediately set out to put his confidence to good use, finding better billets for his friends rather than accepting anything offered, for example. At an even more practical level, we observe that he had come to love his bicycle in the way a great violinist loves his Strad, and that he can now make use of it without anyone trying to kill him as he dodges and weaves through what had been No Man's Land. We have seen his account of how well the Belgians had received him and his comrades. With that reception in mind, he sets off to explore his environment in greater depth. He also, very swiftly, decides to taste again the pleasures of being onstage: pleasures he had denied himself throughout his wartime service.

1918
Tues 12th Nov   Spent the morning repairing bike. For walk in afternoon with John and Phillip to Beloeil, and went again in the evening. (Had good time.) Then an excellent dinner at No.20 with the Boys. To Companies with orders, and on duty.

Wed 13th Nov   Left Ecacheries at 10 am and cycled to Stambruges before the Regiment arrived. Found billets for the boys, and met old acquaintances. Found an excellent billet for myself and Gibbs in a small Chateau. It is a good war here, and just like being at home.

Thurs 14th Nov   Church Parade in morning which I did <u>not</u> attend. On duty all afternoon. Had excellent meal in opposite house. Then to bed.

Fri 15th Nov   On duty and 'runs' all morning. Spent afternoon playing with Irène (a pretty little girl aged eight), and talking to Madame. Spent the evening with Irène and her frère.

Sat 16th Nov   For walk round with John in the morning. Spent an interesting afternoon with C.Dufour (Gamekeeper to Prince de Ligne) catching rabbits in the wood. (Bag six rabbits and one pheasant.) On duty in evening, and to all Companies. (Also had a good time.) [This phrase 'a good time' could mean anything. Was it a code for drink, sex, or simply merriment?]

I am living with Madame [gap]. *Her husband is in the Belgian Congo. There are two children. The people here are simply the very best. This is quite a lovely part of Belgium, and I can enjoy myself for the French language is spoken.*

Sun 17th Nov   Special Parade with civilians 10am. Marched round the town, then to a Service of 'Liberation' and thanksgiving to the British at the Catholic Church. Duty 1 to 6pm. Had dinner at Madame Nemesie's (very good) with Harry, John, Gibbs and Lerise[?]

Mon 18th Nov   On duty 8 am till 1 pm. In billet all afternoon. Playing chess in the evening with Gibbs, and afterwards had a chat with Madame. Then to bed.

Tues 19th Nov   Parade 9 am. Route March through Beloeil, Chateau and Ecacheries, then to Harchies via Grandglise in the afternoon. (Visited coal-mine) Spent evening with Madame at No.21.

Wed 20th Nov   Left Stambruge at 9 am with orders to meet a draft at Basècles at midday. Went through Quercamps with Shirty and Phil to Péruwelz, and saw old friends.   Then to Basècles, sent the draft along, and arrived at Stambruges 4.30 pm.   With Madame in the evening, and had supper with Harry, etc.

Thurs 21st Nov   To Harchies in the morning.   Made enquiries about coal at the mine. Went over again at 1.30 pm and returned to Stambruges at 4.30 with a ton of coal. [Was it really a ton? How did he transport it? Not, surely, on his trusty bike !] *Had supper with Harry and Dawkins, and spent rest of evening with Madame.*

Fri 22nd Nov   To Harchies again with the limber for one-and-a-half tons of coal.   Cost 60.50 Francs.   Rifle inspection at 9.30 am.   In billet all afternoon.   On duty 6 pm to 9.   Supper with Madame at Guard Room.   Then to billet and bed. [The last two days' entries are difficult to interpret, but are printed as written.]

Sat 23rd Nov   Managed to dodge parade.   To Harchies in afternoon to buy coal at mine.   Had café with Madame.   On duty till 6 pm, then supper with Madame, and soup.   Usual chat evening. Belgian soldiers are now coming on five- to ten-day leave every day. The village band always turns out, and plays the same old tune.   There are also the usual town cries.   I have altered my opinion of Belgium (or rather of this part). [Tim spoke highly of Belgium earlier on, so are we to suppose that he likes this area less? More likely he is simply repeating his liking for 'this part of Belgium'. But what is he doing with all that coal?]

Sun 24th Nov   We all (Bath Chair Section) have our photograph taken in the afternoon. With Gibbs and Dawkins in evening having a 'round-about-town' game.

Mon 25th Nov   Parade cancelled. Rain. To Brigade Armourer for tyres. Repairing bike all morning.   Baths afternoon at Brasserie.   Duty evening to 8 pm., and early to bed. [This is the point at which we can deduce that his cycle is 'official'; and it is fascinating to see

This photograph of what was described as the 'Bath Chair Section' of QVR was taken on Sunday November 24th 1918. Tim is right in the middle, making sure he is well seen: no shrinking violet he!   His lightish-coloured belt clearly identifies him

No-one seems to have taken a picture of the King passing through Stambruges (see entry for 5th Dec), but this photograph shows King George V visiting the town of Montreuil (Haig's Headquarters) at about the same time, possibly on the same tour. Sir Douglas Haig hovers in the background

that tyres for it are held by the Brigade Armourer.]

Tues 26th Nov   Rifle   inspection 9.15 am. Then spent morning cleaning bicycle. On duty 1pm to 6. Billet in evening.   Supper with Harry and Dawkins. Then chat with Blanche, etc.

Wed 27th Nov   Miserable   day. Parade cancelled. Orderly Room duty all morning. Am feeling very queer. Hope it is not 'Flu'. Perhaps it is the Belgian suppers. I go to bed at 5.30 pm and get a good night's sleep.   Rain.

Thurs 28th Nov   Am better today, but off duty. I visit the Ecole on business. To Concert in evening at Salle de Fète Stambruges by 1st Corps Party. 'Very Lights' (very good). Had a rough house getting in with a stove and soot.

Fri 29th Nov   Off duty all day, cleaning bike and messing about generally. Writing in evening. Usual chat with Madame, and wander round village.

Sat 30th Nov   On duty 8 till 1. Football match in afternoon. QVR v Rangers, Draw 1-1. To concert in evening with the Section given by Battalion Concert Party. (Good but stiff). Sports and Concerts are now getting up steam. Dances to which civilians are invited are also frequent. I do <u>not</u> attend these. Am thinking of trying my hand as a 'girl' again.

Tim had a knack of spotting opportunities; and there seems little doubt he calculated that not too many all-male soldiers would be looking for exposure dressed as a girl. By putting himself forward as willing to dress up as a female he could achieve two objectives: he would be more likely to be chosen; and onstage (if chosen) he would stand out. His diary entry for December 3rd shows how swiftly his calculations came to pass.

Sun 1st Dec   In Mess all morning. To meeting of 175 Brigade Concert Party at midday. Afternoon in billet. On duty 6-8 pm, then with Madame and her friend in the evening.

Mon 2nd Dec   Inspection of 58 Division in the morning by 1st Army Commander, General Horne. (I was not there.) On duty 1 till 5. With Harry and various others in the evening.

Tues 3rd Dec   Am chosen to be the girl for Battalion Concert Party, and attend rehearsal at theatre. Usual duty and on Ration Fatigue. Am now excused all parades and put in the Concert Party.

Wed 4th Dec   To rehearsal in morning at Salle de Fetes Theatre. In Madame's house for the afternoon. To see Concert in evening by our 'Party'. (Not too bad.) Then with Harry, Gibbs, etc, and home to billet.

Thurs 5th Dec   Rehearsal at Salle de Fetes till 11 am. The King with Prince of Wales and Prince Albert pass through Stambruges at 11.45, and stay until 12.15. He has grand reception. Swotting in evening.

Fri 6th Dec   *Rehearsal at Zigomar Café in the morning, and to a meeting of the Christmas Dinner Committee. Swotting in the afternoon. To billet in evening, writing and passing time.*

Sat 7th Dec   *Rehearsal in morning at Zigomar. Tried song with Reggie Hughes there in afternoon. Football QVR v Brigade H.Q. We won 6-0. Rangers Concert in evening. Mme Louise Filsaux, Rue de Quaucamps is making my Pierette Costume for the Concert Party, which is being called 'The Quavers'. Things are progressing very well.* ['Quavers' is clearly drawn from the initials QVR, Queen Victoria's Rifles.]

Sun 8th Dec   *Service at Theatre in morning. Then to No.19 billet. Football match in afternoon: QVR v ASC. We won 2-0.*

Mon 9th Dec   *Getting measured for costumes, and then Rehearsal in morning. To Zigomar and then to No.19 for practising songs. In billet in evening, and tried the Cogniac* [Cognac ?] *of Stambruges.*

Tues 10th Dec   *Rehearsal at L'Alhambra in morning. (Rain) Not much doing rest of day. With Vokes most of the evening.*

This photograph shows Tim working with the Bow Bells Troupe. He is not, perhaps, immediately recognizable. He is in the centre, wearing a fetching female wig with long pigtails, a charming dress, and high-heeled shoes. If one of his objectives in playing the 'girl' was to stand out from the crowd, he certainly seems to have achieved it

Wed 11th Dec   *Rehearsal at L'Alhambra. With Reggie Hughes in afternoon. To Fancy Dress Ball in evening at the Theatre.*

Thurs 12th Dec   *Rehearsal at L'Alhambra in morning. Practised with Reggie Hughes at Zigomar in afternoon. To Cinema show in evening at L'Alhambra. (Not too good.)*

Fri 13th Dec   *Parade 9.15 for Battalion Drill. (Thank Goodness the rain stops it at 10.30.) To Boxing contest in afternoon at L'Alhambra. Saw Major Nicholls at 9.30.*

Sat 14th Dec   *Rehearsal 9.30 at L'Alhambra. Rehearsed with Major Nicholls at Theatre morning and afternoon, and in evening played Madame Acquatais* [?] *with him at Brigade Concert. This was my first appearance as a girl, and rather difficult as I only had on a bathing costume. It was a great success. The Concert for Christmas is also going on very well.*

Sun 15th Dec   *Church parade in morning. To Grandglise in afternoon with Boys. Football Q.V.R. v D.A.C. We lost 3-1. To Pictures in evening at Theatre. Huge crowd there.*

Mon 16th Dec   *9.30 rehearsal at L'Alhambra. I am getting Soubrette Crinoline costume in afternoon for Gymkhana.*

Tues 17th   *To Jeffries in afternoon. Madame dressed me as a girl for Gymkhana in evening, and it was quite a success.*

Wed 18th Dec   *Rehearsal in morning. Making various arrangements about costumes during the day. In Billet most of evening, making preparations for departure.*

Thurs 19th Dec   *Rehearsal in morning at L'Alhambra. Boxing contest in afternoon. Then practised duets with Mr Locksley. Had a good time with people in the Estaminet.*

Fri 20th Dec   *Pouring with rain as we leave Stambruges at 8.40 am. We march via Quevacamps and Basècles 16 KM to Leuze. I find billet in a farm on outskirts of town.*

Sat 21st Dec   *Rehearsal at Theatre in College, Rue Martin in the morning and afternoon. Visiting various places in town, and also arranging another, nearer, billet. I find one in Rue Basse Restaurant Economique with Madame Delaunoy and her two daughters, Marguerite and Maria (14 and 16 years old) and Joseph. I like this place very much.* [As well he might. The attractive French towns of Douai and Valenciennes border the southern edge of what is now a National Park, and if one crosses into Belgium one finds that Tournai, Leuze and Péruwelz are more or less on the northern border of the same Park. Tim was there well before European motorways cut swathes through the area.]

Sun 22nd Dec   *From Leuze I bike to Tournai, 23 Kilos. To Hospitals and C.C.S. for Harry Ballard. Left Tournai 3 pm and reached Leuze at 5.30, soaked to the skin.*

Mon 23rd Dec   *Rehearsal morning and afternoon at Theatre, Rue St Martin. Spent evening in house Rue Pont Martin, with Angelic, Gabrielle and Yvonne.*

Tues 24th Dec   *Rehearsal in morning at Concert Hall, Rue Martin. (Raining) We give our first 'Performance' to Labour Company. Not a great attendance, but we break the ice.*

Wed 25th Dec   *Christmas Day. Went round Town in morning with Surtees and Joe Reeys* [?]. *Had dinner* [probably lunch] *with Mme Dalaunoy, and games with Marguerite and Maria. Dinner with H.Q. Company at 5 pm, then to billet.*

Thurs 26th Dec   *Rehearsal in the morning at the 'Theatre'. Section dinner at 4 pm, and then to* [give our] *concert at 'Theatre'. The Brigadier is present. We score a huge success. Then to dinner again with the boys.*

Fri 27th Dec   *Usual rehearsal morning and afternoon. We give another 'Show' in the evening at 'Theatre'. The hall is simply packed.*

Sat 28th Dec   *Rehearsal morning and afternoon. I spend the evening in my billet settling up dinner accounts, which cost 450 Francs. We do not 'show' tonight. The Quavers Q.V.R. concert party commenced showing this week and made a great 'Hit'. I have the fortune to be playing the Girl and like this pastime very much indeed.*

Sun 29th Dec I spend a very lazy morning in my billet and have dinner [lunch] *with Madame. Usual games with Maria and Marguerite in afternoon and evening.*

Mon 30th Dec Rehearsals all day. Concert in evening. Good show, but light very bad; otherwise everything well.

Tues 31st Dec Rehearsing all day. We show to Rangers in the evening. Then for walk with Maria and others to see Tattoo.

1919

Tim is still in the army, and seems bent on an acting career.

Wed 1st Jan   *Rehearsals as usual. Spend rest of day with Madame, etc., and visiting friends. (Belgian fête). We show to civilians in the evening.*

Thurs 2nd Jan   Rehearsals all day. Last night of present programme. We show to the 10th London, then to Signaller dinner – in costume. A merry evening.

Fri 3rd Jan   Rehearsing hard all day. We commence new show which we present to Labour Corps at 6.30 pm. A success.

Sat 4th Jan   Rehearsing hard with Mr Dixon (10th London) as Producer. We give show at 6pm and score a 'bumper' evening. The Quavers Concert Party is now reckoned by everyone to be a first-rate show, and easily defeats the Divisional Party. We go on tour soon.

Although we are into 1919, the last four days' entries appear near the end of the 1918 diary. But not quite *at* the end, because this small booklet has several pages for notes at the back, and Tim at some stage has therein inscribed three short Essays (if that's the right word for what he writes). Is this, perhaps, the sort of thing he was doing on the occasions when he has earlier made an entry saying something along the lines of 'Writing all evening' ? Each essay reflects upon aspects of his experience in the Army; and they are all reproduced here, precisely in his words, and at the spot where they appear chronologically. To the best of my knowledge he never made any attempt to send them anywhere for publication. The first uses as its title a phrase familiar to old soldiers : 'Wind-up'. It refers to fear, and is pronounced with a short 'i': not to be confused with the similarly-spelt phrase with a long 'i', as in 'I felt he was trying to wind me up.'

Wind-up

It is the indefinite and shadowy that is apt to cause fear (otherwise wind-up). Waiting and suspense and not knowing what is likely to happen next will make the coldest and coolest man more or less unnerved. Fear occurs when the will has no longer the power to control and master the body. A brave man may control himself in the presence of a danger that is definite; but the vague, indefinite danger is disquieting and treacherous to the nerves. There is nothing to see. Nothing to confront. Something is going to happen; but what ? It is impossible to formulate a plan against a thing that is unknown. Something may or may not happen. Perhaps the danger may pass; but it is there, and the will cannot direct the body against the unknown and unseen. From experience I find that in nine cases out of ten a man has the 'wind-up' from thoughts of what might be. Yet whilst in danger he has no fear at all.

The surprising ending –the last sentence- goes far to explain how Tim managed to survive the dangers and the horrors of the Western Front. Had he been killed, we should not have been privy to his opinion: he speaks with profound authority. To one such as I who has not seen actual wartime combat his conclusion is astonishing. I would have assumed that as one charged forward, one would be paralysed by fear – terror, even. Yet it seems that in Tim's personal experience, the fear is felt *before* the charge, and cvaporates *during* it. Is he accurate in suggesting that this was the majority experience at that time? And what about the ten percent whom he implies were different? Was it some of the members of this one-tenth who were shot for cowardice in the face of the enemy? Were there great variations in response? How I wish Tim were here to answer these questions.

Army Gambling

For gamblers in civil life I hold no brief; but on behalf of those on Active Service I must write a few words.

Most men are not born gamblers, but they love excitement in any shape or form, and when

128

the opportunity occurs partake of it greedily. There is no truth in the common statement that vice is bred of idleness; the really idle man is a poor creature incapable of strong sins. It is far more often the man with superior gifts, with faculties overwrought and nerves strained above concert pitch by expressive mental exertion, who turns to vicious excitement for the sake of rest, as a duller man falls asleep. (I grant exceptions of course.)

Men whose minds and lives are spent amidst the vicissitudes, surprises, disappointments and terrible trials of this War are assuredly less idle than the ordinary gentleman, consequently it cannot be wondered at that the soldier seeks relaxation in excitement whether innocent or the reverse instead of in sleep. The soldiers in the line whose nerves are the more severely strained are those who seek strong emotions in their daily leisure and who are the more inclined to extend that leisure at the expense of bodily rest. The soldier's day in the trenches is a long one and the mental strain though not of the most intellectual order is incomparably more severe than that required in normal life. The civilian has everything to turn to if he needs relaxation; but the soldier only his own excitement.

Thus vice begins when opportunity occurs, and let he who protests first undergo the indescribable ordeal of a trench soldier's life. It is wrong, yes; but then the whole War is wrong, and when the latter ends so will most of the former.

Honours

One of the evils which the War has brought with it is the perfect epidemic of honours. Some get them through pure merit; but the vast majority through Heaven alone knows. It would be far more reasonable to give out **dishonours** rather than honours: that would at any rate buck the slackers up a bit. The worker who works for love or duty doesn't really need honour at all, for knowing that he has done his utmost is sufficient satisfaction for him. But those who work for these rewards only are not worth considering either as workers or patriots.

It would be far better to give out **dishonours** to those who are doing nothing at all. Half honours to those who might do more, and to have no honour at all bestowed upon them would be the greatest honour to those who have done all in their power.

I know heaps of instances where medals have been bestowed in a manner absolutely scandalous, and they are a most delightful joke to those who **really** did the work and received no recognition at all. This then is the point. If nobody were thus singled out there would be no injustice done. Medals focus attention on certain individuals, and they focus it upon them to the exclusion of all others concerned, many of whom are far more worthy than the one singled out to stand in the National lime-light.

Honours then are manifestly wrong, they are a mistake. Every man has a duty to perform in this War, something to accomplish according to his means and capabilities, and to fulfil that duty is his honour. If then you honour some in preference to others you slight those who have done as much and in many cases more. Leave rewards out of it altogether, for men are always left out who for nobility and sacrifice cannot be equalled. To place one man in a higher grade than the rest is wrong. We are all equal after a battle, and we share the honour and glory together. Therefore medals are unfair.

There are phrases here that suggest Tim wrote this while the conflict was still in progress: 'has a duty to perform in this War', for instance, rather than 'had a duty to perform in the War'. Regrettably he neither dates the 'essays' nor mentions names.

The 1919 Diary

Tim had two diaries for 1919. One, 'The Soldiers Own Diary', is full of useful information:

there are definitions of such words as 'Platoon', hints on First Aid, names of rifles used by the fighting powers, and much, much more, including a large section on looking after horses. Possibly Tim was given this diary, and found it useful for reference. He used it mainly as an address book, and it is perhaps interesting to note that the first entry is: 'Mme V. Delaunoy, 11 Rue Basse, Leuze, Hainant, Belgique'. Another entry is: 'Cpl H.W.Elliott, 6316, A.S.C., No. 4 Canteen, Rouen, France', who might, or might not, have been Tim's brother Harry.

But the diary he actually used for his 1919 entries was a small, leather bound volume with pockets front and rear, and a rather clever metal device for locking it shut so that it could not gape open if, for example, it was stuffed hurriedly into a kit-bag. In the front pocket is a magnificently generous £1000 Insurance document provided by T.J. & J. Smith, marked 'This insurance does not include any war risk'. Tim never completed the application form ! This tiny black volume is called 'Smith's Automatic Self-Registering Diary', and unless the sliding metal rod is intended to slide into the page you last completed (in which case the diary would always gape open) there is no indication as to what the title implies.

Tim has helpfully completed several pages at the front of the diary by entering, day by day, a note of his whereabouts. He presumably did this so that he could later more easily locate other detailed entries within the body of the diary. One can get the idea by looking at an entry in this 'quick-reference' section:

23rd Jan   Leuze   Concert   ＊

The asterisk implies that an 'important' event occurred on that date, as will become evident when the reader reaches that date in the main body of the diary.

It is my belief that he sat down after his other (main) entries had reached the end of December for a long session writing these useful entries in the 'Contents' pages, because they are all clearly done without any change of pen or ink, and done with unaccustomed neatness. As he reaches mid-August, he seems to run out of ink: the last five entries, i.e. up to Aug 25th , get progressively fainter, and then stop. He never bothered to complete the list on some other occasion, presumably because by then he was well-ensconced in a new life in Leicestershire, training to be a male nurse. His entries by then have become less interesting to the lay reader, except insofar as they demonstrate his extraordinary ability to use his off-duty time to catch-up on the shortage of English female company he experienced during his four-year stint in the army. This aspect of his life will not escape my attention!

Sun 5th Jan   Gave concert to civilians and soldiers at 6 pm. Then with Maria.
Mon 6th Jan   Rehearsal in morning at Rue St Martin. To bed in the afternoon. Madame invited three of us to dinner in the evening. The party broke up at midnight. (Good)
Tues 7th Jan   Not much doing. Spent the evening in the billet playing with Maria.
Wed 8th Jan   Rehearsal in morning. Forty winks and then to see football: first round of Divisional Championship. To farm in evening with girls.
Thurs 9th Jan   (Rain) Rehearsing in morning. Spent evening with Madame and the girls.
Fri 10th Jan   Gave concert in evening to 10th and 12th Londons. We are going on tour very soon.
Sat 11th Jan   My birthday. I am 24 today. Gave concert in the evening to troops at the Theatre. (Harry Ballard and Rowen have returned.)
Sun 12th Jan   Gave a concert in the evening, then had my birthday dinner. A huge success. [The dinner, or the concert? Both, perhaps. It has been some years since his birthday could be celebrated.]
Mon 13th Jan   Packing up in the morning. Left Leuze 2 pm in the lorry, and arrived

130

The triumphant tour continues. In his fetching female attire, Tim is clearly the centre of attention, onstage at least

Quevaucamps. Gave concert to A.S.C. at Quevaucamps 6pm, and then went on to Stambruges.
   Tues 14th Jan   Rehearsal at Zigomar in the morning, and then visiting various friends.

Tim continues the tour, giving concerts with great success, reaching a climax on the 23rd.

Thurs 23rd Jan   Gave Command Show at 5pm to Corps Commander 1st Corps, Lieutenant General Sir [gap] Holland, the Divisional General, etc. Supper after.
   Tues 28th Jan   We give Command Show at 5 pm at 'Victoria Palace' to Major General Ramsay. Supper in Sergeants Mess.
   Thurs 30th Jan   I hear wonderful news!!! I am to be demobilized on account of long service. My feelings are indescribable.
   Fri 31st Jan   Making arrangements for departure all day. See dress rehearsal by Quavers, and bid them Goodbye. Then a final supper with Madame.

It is interesting to observe that despite Tim's conspicuous success in the Concert Party tours (success in which he shows great pride) he has not the slightest hesitation in opting for immediate repatriation and discharge from the army. This decisiveness was a feature of his psychological make-up which helped to carry him through life both in and out of uniform. Once he had analyzed a situation he could make a swift decision, and usually proved that decision, whatever it was, to have been correct. At the same time, he seems to have had a well-developed social awareness: as shown by the fact that he attended a final dress rehearsal in order to 'bid them Goodbye'.   In later years he was always proud of the fact that whenever he revisited previous friends and colleagues he was welcomed; and he would state that one way of judging success in life was to ask yourself if old contacts *did* so welcome you.

Sat 1st Feb   Goodbye. Au revoir. Leave Leuze at 9.30 am by lorry after many farewells. Arrive Tournai. Then in town all day. To 'Very Lights' at Music Hall with Reg, Harold and Tom.
   Sun 2nd Feb   Standing by all day in hospital at Tournai. Left by train at 6.30 pm., travelling via Lille, Béthune, and St Pol.

Mon 3rd Feb   *Freezing cold, and still travelling. We reach Boulogne at 2 pm, then march to St Martin's Camp. Have meal and sit in hut all evening with the Boys.*

Tues 4th Feb   *Baths at Camp, and minute inspection (for which the Army ought to be 'sat on'). Then marched to Wireless Camp. Spend night in Salvation, YMCA huts, etc.*

Wed 5th Feb   *Parade 3 pm for Roll Call. Then went into Boulogne with the Boys, where we spent enjoyable evening. Went to the Cinema, then to Huts in the snow.*

Thurs 6th Feb   *We parade at 6.30 am and march to the boat 'Invicta'. Left at 10.30 am, arriving at Folkestone mid-day. Then to Shorncliffe [Thorncliffe?], and home at 11.15 pm.*

Fri 7th Feb   ***I am now a discharged man.***

This is the point at which Tim's War ended; and it is tempting to end the story here. Possibly alone among surviving Riflemen, Tim had kept his diary virtually every single day, come rain or shine, mud, or snow and ice, attack or retreat, danger or relative safety. His entries paint the most accurate picture we have of a soldier's life in the Great-War-to-End-Wars. Because he managed to retain a simple, almost telegraphic style, giving us facts rather than comment (except where comment was necessary to highlight some fact), we are in a better position than hitherto to understand what that war was like for the unpromoted soldier. This is documentary history at its amazing best: to the point, detailed, and remarkably unemotional. There are elsewhere many descriptions made as memoirs years after the events, and if one wants adjective-led accounts of charges and slaughter one can find them in such memoirs. But if we are honest with ourselves we must admit that the passing of time brings changes in perceptions and memories. The 40 year-old ex-Major, setting down on paper his battles of ten years previously, will certainly put a particular gloss on his experiences. Tim's measured tones act as a counter-balance to all that we have come to believe about life in the trenches. To read what he wrote (so carefully, briefly and probably secretly night after night, in the line and out, in hospital, spotting the girls in his time off, watching football, and later -after the Armistice- taking part in female attire in the shows put on to entertain those who had survived and were awaiting discharge) is to experience not only each day of Tim's war, but the overall sweep of four remarkable years in his life.

However! In a sense Tim's War was by no means over. No man is the same at 24 as he was at 19; and if one has survived the battles of the Somme along the way it's pretty certain that the War will have left its legacy. One thing did *not* change as far as Tim was concerned: he continued to keep a diary, day after day after day. Although I see little point in reproducing every single entry (as I have felt to be essential where his military service was concerned) I have little doubt that Tim's story is incomplete unless we highlight some of the areas where his life thereafter was affected by his experience from 1914-1919. For that reason I shall set out in the next chapter a number of entries that give insight into his altered psyche, and shall attempt some linking commentary based on (but not printing in full) the many entries I shall omit.

Furthermore! Tim was to survive the next war as well. 1939-1945 still found him making entries in his journals; and though he never again had occasion to charge against the Hun his comments on what we now call World War Two provide a remarkable insight into the views of a 'WW1 Veteran' faced with new perils and inconveniences. By then he was a family man with a career, a wife and three children. His choice of wife, and his views on English life, on German militarism, on his career, all stem directly or indirectly from his military experiences. He left remarkable accounts of his search for a wife, and these I shall attempt to summarise. He watched the aftermath of Dunkirk, and wrote about it. He was forced to move house and to live away from his family for a while during the second War, and he wrote about that. Later, after the Allies were again victorious, he recorded details of his life at such venues as Eton College and Kensington Palace; but that's material for quite a different book. For now, back to 1919, and another chapter.

CHAPTER FIFTEEN

A CIVILIAN AGAIN

Tim's time in uniform may have ended on February 7th, 1919, but it was to be nearly three more years before the changes wrought by his war service worked themselves out. Initially, back in Merton, he tried to carry on as if nothing had happened; but he was not, in many vital ways, the same young man who suddenly enlisted in 1914. Ultimately, two strands emerge from his continued diary entries after discharge: his change of direction as far as a career was concerned; and his search for a wife.

Before the war Tim was captivated by the theatre; and every indication was that he would make a career on the stage. As a young man he had acted, written and produced, and had accompanied a number of semi-retired 'pros' to outlying stages where he was able to learn his craft. Though after the war he went on visiting the theatre, and commenting on it, he made no serious attempt to enter that particular profession. And, just as his decision to enlist in the army had come 'out of the blue', so his decision to train as a Male Nurse appears in his diaries with very little explanation of his reasons. There are several references to his visiting 'The Ministry', and these seem to tie in with his relatively sudden move to Leicester to take up a trainee position in a mental hospital:

Fri. May 9th, 1919   Very busy.   Left for St Pancras and caught the 12.15 to Leicester, arriving at 2.40.   Then to the Mental Hospital at Humberstone to start my duties as Attendant.

Until then the love of his life had been Gwen Reed, with whom he had spent some idyllic days during his brief and infrequent leaves. In Leicester he not only entered into the demands of hospital life, but set about a determined, and often amorous, examination of the female population of Leicester. He records in detail the day-to-day happenings at the hospital, leaving a valuable document for future students of the treatments and attitudes that obtained then in a mental ward. And he names many 'young ladies' with whom he spent his spare time. Within two months we have been introduced to Evie Smith, Dorothy Cole, Jean, Alice, Gertrude Toms, Mabel, May, Nellie Smith, Ada Browne, Gladys Higgs, Lucy Westcott and Connie Gilbert. His secret system of assessment (consisting of an asterisk for 'something special') suggests

Tim ready to start a new career in Medicine. Never one to underrate his own abilities, he dresses in the style one might expect from a young doctor at the time (in rather the same way as after joining the army as a Rifleman he had been photographed giving a good imitation of a cane-carrying commissioned officer)

that Lucy was well ahead of the field by the end of July 1919. Nonetheless, we meet Dorothy many more times. August has three entries that sum up his activities and feelings at that stage:

Aug 1st, 1919   *Bought a Waterman pen.*
Aug 8th   *In afternoon to first Psychological lecture by Dr Lucas.*
Aug. 12th   *Sat on the grass in Spring Hill Park - fed up !*

A year passes, and Tim's search for a soul-mate is still producing a number of competing entries:

Sep 5th 1920   *I went for a walk to Abbey Park. (Have I met <u>the</u> girl at last?)*
Sep 17th   *I met rather a fascinating girl, Kathleen, at 9 pm.*

Quite why Gwen, his 'special' when he was enjoying one of his rare leaves from the army, dropped out of his diary for so long is not indicated. One suspects that she had found other interests, perhaps at work, perhaps of an amorous nature. Fidelity was a rare virtue in such times of separation. In November 1920, however, he writes:

Nov 13th   *Gwen has written to me after nearly two years, prompted by the unveiling of the Cenotaph a couple of days ago. I can hardly grasp it yet. Is it a bolt from the blue, or will it lead to other things? We shall see!! Met May Waite and for walk near Western Park. (Dull)* [Poor May. How could she compete with Gwen's letter? It would take someone very special to do that. A couple of weeks later Fate came knocking on the door] :
    Nov 29th   *Tom and I met two girls in Winns and Millers, Market Street: Alma and Dorothy. Went to the pictures at King's Hall:* The Case of Lady Camber. *Then I went for a walk with Alma to Humberstone.*
    Tues 30th Nov   *Met Alma Faraday again at 3 pm. Tea at Winn's Turkey, and for walk to Humberstone. (She is a replica of Gwen.)*
    Sat 1st Jan 1921   *Home in Merton I met Lulu at 6 pm.*
    4th Jan   *Caught 4.25 Underground to Mansion House and met Gwen Reed at Gracechurch Street. We went to Clapham and had dinner at the Crichton, then to cinema for* Earthward Bound. *Left Gwen at 9.30. (She is a dear girl and just the same as two years ago.) I enjoyed myself.*
    5th Jan   *Met Lulu at 7.10 pm and went to her house, where we had a song rehearsal and played about generally.*
    8th Jan   *To Mary's party at 6.30. Spent very good time with Lulu. I sang and flirted, especially the latter.*
    11th Jan   [Tim's 26th birthday, though he makes no mention of it.] *To Faraday Road. Lulu and I went to Kingston by car. For walk by river, then tea at Lyons' Café. To Kingston Empire 6 pm* Aladdin. *Very good for two houses. Home by train, and stayed at Faraday Road till 11 pm.*
    15th Jan   *Train to Bank and met Gwen at 12.15. Lunch at Lyons, Whitehall, then caught 3.15 to Leicester. On duty in Ward Three at 7 pm.*
    My holiday was really a great success, and I felt awfully fed-up on my return to Leicester. I spent an interesting and enjoyable time with Lulu Le Brun, and I like her. I also had a real good time with Gwen Reed, and also like her. Now I am with Alma Faraday!!! Oh, how will it all end?

A picture of Alma Faraday, taken in Leicester around the time Tim first met her. Although it was to be many months before she became his chosen one, from this point onwards Tim spent a disproportionate amount of his free time with her. The only real competition came from the girls back home, in Merton, or wherever Gwen Reed was to be found

One gets the impression that Tim is finding it extremely difficult to sort out his feelings for these three 'treasures'. Another brief trip to London enables him to meet Lulu and Gwen again, after which he wrote:

I cannot but admit that, after my last visit to London, Gwen still impresses me far more than any girl I have yet known. It is now nearly seven years since we first met; she is my oldest girl 'pal', and to my present way of thinking <u>she</u> is the person who means everything to me.

Alma, however, had youth on her side. At this point she was only eighteen. Tim's 1921 Diary had a somewhat larger and more useful format than those he had used hitherto. Closed it measured 14.5.cm high and 8.5 cm wide. Each double-page spread had eight equal spaces, with Monday, Tuesday, Wednesday and Thursday on the left, and with Friday, Saturday, Sunday and a space marked Memo on the right. Tim's entries bottom-right contain useful insights into his thinking and feelings:

Following March 6th, 1921 I write to Lulu and I write to Gwen, and I still see a lot of Alma: in fact we have hung on together very well. The question is how long can I keep up a 'blue-beard' business of three girls.
Following March 13th   Some time ago I mentioned the <u>disadvantages</u> of this work; now I will name its advantages. (Labour is terrible in England just at present. Strikes, etc.) We are always sure of our week's wages. We have fairly decent quarters and our next meal is always forthcoming.
Following March 20th   Alma sails for Vancouver, Canada on the 22nd April. I hardly know whether I am sorry or indifferent, but I rather fancy I shall miss her company when it is too late. It is hard to know what to do for the best.

On Saturday March 26th, Tim went back home to Merton to act as Best Man for his brother's wedding to Edie. While there he met Gwen again.

Memo following March 27th So Harry has beat me in the Marriage Market. Well, good luck to him. Gwen and I had quite a day of romance on Easter Sunday. Love in the train, then under a rhododendron bush at Kew, and then by the river at Richmond.

Following 3rd April   Because of a hitch with regard to berths on the boat, Alma does not now sail on the 22nd. I fancy if I tried I could induce her to remain for good. Shall I? Oh, I cannot decide!

His indecision had increased a week later:

Following Sun 10th Apl   A very pretty nurse (always in brown) who resides near the Terminus in Humberstone, and who I know by sight, came to me in great distress saying she had shut the door of the house and could not get in again, everyone being out. After brief conversation I climbed up to her bedroom window, got in, and opened the door for her. (We now hope to be on good terms shortly.)

And then the need for economy struck him:

Memo following Apl 17th   I am now trying hard to be economical in many respects. Teas in town must be strictly moderated. Many other useless expenses must also be dropped. My average expenditure of £1-15-0 per week is much too heavy.

Following May 1st   The far reaching claws of the Coal menace have now directly affected me. All coal for fires at night has been stopped, and I now sit with blanket wrapped round me each night like an old lady waiting up for her husband.

And then, news of the pretty nurse in brown:

I heard just recently that the nurse in brown, previously mentioned, left her situation suddenly a day or so after my impromptu experience. (I fancy that this is at the bottom of it.) She does not know my address. I do not know her new one. Result, matters are at a 'deadlock'.

Tim suddenly comes to a decision:

Events have moved rapidly this week. Lulu tells me I write more coldly, and Alma is at present the one, for I bought her an engagement ring, and presented it to her on the last day of May. Is it an inspiration of the moment ? [Tim's accounts show the ring cost him £7.10s.0d.]

On June 9th, he writes:

Met Alma at 3 pm for tea at Turkey Café, and then for a walk to fields at Garden City. Alma is mine. [And then a very significant asterisk].

Three days later, however, he is writing:

This week it is Gwen and nothing but Gwen. She has awakened all my old interests in her by first sending a telegram asking me to meet her, and then a letter containing two lovely photos of herself. Oh, what is one to do? I feel I simply cannot resist her at this moment. Poor little Alma.

136

The start of July, however, brought significant progress in Tim's relationship with Alma, because they went to stay at his Aunt Polly's house in Bingham, Notts.

My romance progresses. Alma and I are spending a week with my Aunt and Uncle. It is a lovely spot here, ten miles from Nottingham. The house contains seven rooms, with garden all round the house. It is ideal!!

Tues Jul 5th   Alma and I spent the morning like two butterflies in the garden, wandering about and not settling anywhere very long.

Thurs Jul 7th   Alma and I made good resolutions in the shadows of the apple trees.

Memo. Everything went to make our week in Bingham simply glorious. The weather was perfect, the conditions admirable. We only wanted each other and cared nothing for the future or what it held in store. We lived only in the present. I could picture a honeymoon like this.

A week back home in Merton gave him the opportunity to see again both Lulu and Gwen. His comment afterwards was significant:

This week has been good and indifferent:. With Lulu it was always the latter; but Gwen and I had some ripping times together and went back to our madcap days of Hindhead and Devon. She is not exactly in love, neither am I, so two pals go mad.

Sun Jul 24th   Once again installed in Leicester, and incidentally back with Alma. Sometimes we are serious, sometimes comic, and sometimes a little offish; but on the whole we agree and really jog along quite well together. I hope we shall.

Sat 13th Aug   I have received a letter from Lulu Le Brun. It is evident that she has at last convinced herself that I only <u>like</u> her, and <u>that</u> very little. I think my reply will have to endorse her suspicions for it is useless (and also a nuisance) to carry on. Alma is still 'top dog' and we are happy.

Early in September, Tim shows signs of being concerned for Alma's welfare:

After consideration I am convinced that Alma is in the wrong environment for a girl of her age. Apart from the general behaviour of neighbours her own relatives leave a deal to be desired. Language is a secondary consideration even in the presence of young children, and their whole system of life is entirely erroneous. I have yet to see the family sit down together for a meal. On the three occasions I have been to tea it has been with Alma only at the table. Public houses form their chief attraction, and Alma is a minor concern. On one occasion she waited in the street until 1.30 am before they returned to let her in. (This girl of 19!!) [In fact she was still a couple of months short of her 19th birthday; and an outsider might have added that she was at risk from an older man. But Tim's occasional intimacies were, one might say, justified by his serious intentions.]

Sun Oct 2nd   I think Alma has taken a decided move for the better in removing her residence from Earl Street to 53 Willowbrook Road. Many times her uncle and aunt have hinted that her room is preferable to her company. It is the old tale of 'familiarity breeds contempt', so perhaps she will be much better off with strangers. We'll see.

Sun Oct 16th   I have now visited Mr and Mrs Hickling at Alma's new abode and am very pleased with my first impressions of them both. They seem a homely sensible couple jogging comfortably along, and I am of the opinion that Alma is now very comfortable.

Memo after Nov 6th   Alma is now making rapid headway in the matrimonial stakes. She is <u>the</u> girl now, and I have an idea that at last my reckless days are nearing the end and I must take the 'big chance' as others have done before. Some are successful, others not. How will it be with me?

After Nov 13th   The preparations and propositions of 'Two who are about to take the fatal plunge' now form the topic of all conversations. Alma has already succeeded where I failed in regard to 'rooms'. I hope she will be as successful in all other matters relating to our future.

After Nov 20th   Time moves on, and the New Year will dawn with Alma and me in a very new and strange relationship to each other. What will it bring forth? - that is the question of the hour. I hope oh so very much that it will be successful.

After Nov 27th   The time has now arrived for me to concoct a letter to Alma's father, who is a tailor in Hull and also in rather a good way. [rather well off financially] *Of course I want to be on the right side of him, but if he is disinclined we shall have to do without a Parental Blessing.*

Tues Nov 29th   Alma and I went to the Verger of St Barnabas, Mr Bailey and gave him our names for the Banns to be published. I paid 5/-, this being the first deposit.

Here Alma gave me a surprise. Her name is not Faraday but Freitag, and she is of German descent. Her father was born in London, but his brother is German. Ah me! I spend five years in France fighting them and then come back again and marry one. Such is the World.

On Dec. 13th he bought the ring for £1-15-0 having 'hovered around a jewellers like a moth round a candle'. His soon-to-be father-in-law came south to Leicester for Christmas, and Tim packed his own things ready to take them to Willowbrook Road where he and Alma planned to reside, albeit temporarily. On the last day of 1921, December 31st., they were married at 11 o'clock. After photographs they went briefly to No.53, then caught the 2.30 to London. At 4.45 brother Harry met them at Wimbledon Station, after which there was a party 'at home'. Their first child, a girl whom they named Joan, was born on July 4th, 1922, back in Leicester. Tim wrote:

I am now the father of a little baby girl, and Alma is going on well in Westcote Nursing Home. My bébé *is ever so pretty, and as she lies asleep with her tiny face puckered up, giving occasional little grunts of contentment, it seems too wonderful that this little darling is all mine.*

On July 29th, 1922 Tim heard that he had passed the final examination of the Medico Psychological Society: *Oh what a relief. My Certificate* [left] *is the highest award given at present for proficiency in mental nursing, and it carries with it a rise of 4/- a week.*

This was the point in Tim's life when it could be said that his Great War experiences are firmly in the past. He has made a happy marriage; he has qualified in his chosen profession; he has become a father. If there were any remaining psychological traumas resulting from those harrowing days in the trenches, then he knew now how to overcome then. He was ready for a new, a peaceful life.

CHAPTER SIXTEEN

THE INTER-WAR YEARS

Tim Elliott continued to keep a regular diary; but his day-to-day peace-time existence is not the concern of this book. He was to have two more children after Joan (who was born in July 1922): a son, Royce born in 1924; and another daughter, Ann Veronica (named after the heroine of H.G.Wells's novel) in 1933. In the main he left the war behind, but occasionally it recurred in an entry clearly inspired by his army experiences. A few of these entries are worth quoting on the grounds that they have a wartime resonance; and a few others are necessary simply to keep the real man in focus as World War II approaches.

1925 found him qualified as a mental nurse, and perhaps the most significant entries report his progress in giving-up smoking ('That will help pay for Royce's operation') and in becoming a regular tennis player. 1930, however, found him acquiring a decidedly more literary approach to diary-keeping, and the distance from the Great War finds him wonderfully evoking the sort of nostalgic reminiscence that may have been characteristic of so many veterans. By now he has a nursing assignment with 'an irritable old reprobate' in Warminster:

Jan 5th 1930   Took a walk through Bishopstrow to Sutton Veny, both small and uninteresting villages, the latter being three miles from Warminster. I came to the church, in front of which stood a monument of stone which appeared to be very old. On reaching the monument I found, greatly to my surprise, that it was actually the Great War Memorial to the village fallen. I could not but stare in amazement, struck by its aged appearance. A hundred years might have elapsed since this structure was erected, for the growth of moss, and its worn, weathered, neglected look, gave it an 'almost forgotten' tone. Yet it is only ten years since it was consecrated. How swiftly time leaves its signs and tracks behind, and how swiftly we pass from one phase of life to another before we fully understand how and when the passing was.

He spent much of his time attending the London offices of the agency through which he, and other nurses, obtained private work. Having time to kill in the capital he re-visited the headquarters of the Queen Victoria's Rifles (9th London), where he came upon an old acquaintance:

Feb 8th 1930   There was only one other person present this evening whom I could in any way associate with my life in the Army. He was Regimental Sergeant Major Thompson, formerly Company Sergeant Major of C.Company to which I was attached for some time. His present occupation seems also to be R.S.M. (Respectfully Serving Mixtures), for he is now behind the bar counter. I ordered a drink, and while consuming it I stood a little in the background and surveyed him intently. He caused my mind to jump back fifteen years, and I saw him again as the strictly regimental regular S.M., typical in every respect of the over-caricatured, fierce-looking, awe-inspiring terror of recruits and curse of the old 'uns. A very devil was he at times, making us shake in our boots when he barked out an order or merely looked at one; yet withal a cheerful, rough though kindly disposition often loomed to the surface in spite of his seeming harshness, and I think he had a warm spot in the hearts of all his Company. As I stand here now I yet see that merry twinkle in his eyes, and I can with pleasure place the following words behind his name: 'He was a good sort and meant well'.

Two days later finds Tim at Grantbourne, a nursing-home for neurasthenic cases at Chobham in Surrey:

My patient is Lieut. Colonel D.C. Phillott, late of the 24th Punjab Regiment and retired Professor of Philosophy at Cambridge. He speaks nine oriental languages and has quite a charming disposition, appreciating all that is done for him, which is in contrast to the average Army Officer. In consequence of a stroke the articulation of speech is badly affected and he is unsteady in his movements. A 64 year-old bachelor, he hates women in general (so he says), and was brought yesterday by his nephew and niece, Sir Basil Blackett and Mrs Hartnell.

Early in this book I put forward a few thoughts concerning Tim's reasons for such meticulous wartime diary-keeping, and on February 25th 1930, after quoting from the writings of Andrew Soutar, he addresses this issue himself. Soutar (1879-41) was a novelist and film-writer:

I agree with Soutar that it is exceedingly difficult to confide to a friend the various emotions that occupy our minds at times. We imagine the friend may ridicule us; or perhaps the atmosphere or place goes against relating our innermost idealizations. In consequence an exceedingly pleasant experience is repressed into the mind, hidden and in time forgotten. However, I shall not lose my little musings, nor need I relegate them to the 'hidden cupboard of my heart' as Andrew Soutar accurately suggests often happens. No! My little book, this little book, shall be my cupboard and also my friend, to whom I can communicate, though perhaps very crudely, just a few of life's impressions as they appear to me; and then no matter what happens to my little companion (this book) we have at least spent many hours of pleasant and absorbing interest together, and I also have the knowledge that the thoughts are not lost. Perhaps even a stranger may take up this book, and though I cannot hope that he will approve of me from a grammatical point of view, yet if he will overlook that weakness then I may hope that he will glean a few crumbs from my little musings.

Tim underrates his talent, surely. His legacy to history is considerable.

The 1914-1918 diaries make specific mention of long marches; and on March 15th 1930 Tim was again to experience the fatiguing experience of a very long walk. He had travelled from Chobham, his place of work, to Kingsclere where Alma, Royce and Joan now lived in rented accommodation. His late arrival meant that only two hours after arriving he had to start back:

The 8.30 bus from Kingsclere, though 15 minutes late, enabled me to catch the 9.25 from Newbury to Reading, where I arrived a few minutes too late to catch the last train to Sunningdale. A short talk with a Railway Inspector elicited the disconcerting news that the nearest I could get to my destination tonight was Wokingham, which is about 17 miles from Chobham. With many mutterings of a pessimistic character I clambered into the 10.45 and eventually stepped on to the platform at Wokingham shortly after 11 pm. A porter confirmed the ill news given by the inspector, so I strolled into the town debating my next move. I knew nothing of Wokingham. The streets were empty, and all the houses and shops in darkness. What should I do ? I searched for a phone box, and rang Greatbourne 21 to acquaint the night nurse of my whereabouts. Then, while endeavouring to find some shelter for the night , I hit on the first piece of good fortune that day. I encountered a motor coach, empty but for the driver who was busy at one of the wheels. He informed me that he was bound for London, and that the nearest place he would touch so far as benefited me would be Ascot. This news put me in a much easier frame of mind for it meant a lift of ten miles and raised my hopes of reaching Chobham after all, for a walk of seven miles was nothing out of the ordinary, excepting that I should have to traverse strange ground and endeavour to find my own way, there being little or no prospect of encountering anyone so late. Off we went, and immediately after passing Ascot race-course I alighted from the coach after tipping the good fellow. (It was well worth the shilling.) I struck off the main road and found a route to Sunningdale. Although it was dark, lonely and strange I walked along with a good heart, for was not each step a little nearer to Chobham ? I was fortunate eventually to reach Sunningdale without loss of time or direction........... After crossing the main London-Portsmouth road I came upon open country over which the moon cast its reflection into countless pools left by the recent rain, giving them a silvery aspect as they glistened among the gorse and grass and clumps of bushes on Chobham Common.

Although I was now becoming tired and the journey tedious, the countryside to right and left gave me much food for thought on account of its rugged beauty under the moon's pale light. At times, broken clouds, dark and foreboding, obscured my guiding light making progress heavy and true direction difficult to maintain. Yet, unfamiliar as I was with this particular district, I knew sufficient to warn me that once off the beaten track it would be impossible to proceed without encountering bogs, marshland and hidden pits, for all around was long, innocent-looking grass which, when trodden on, gave way to the feet like a sponge, so treacherously waterlogged was it.

On I went, the squelch, squelch of my shoes sounding strangely in the silence. Then an object loomed up on my left about 100 yards from the roadway, and as I drew nearer it took the shape of a massive stone cross standing on a rise, similar to Hill 60 at Ypres. On this spot, now commemorated with the cross, stood the great Queen Victoria when she reviewed her troops in 18?? What a splendid and picturesque array it must have been: the long lines of infantry, guns and accoutrements, and the rattle of weapons as they manoeuvred around. I could not but contrast the scene with its present aspect, the look of desolation, and the uncanny silence as I strode along. The moon threw down its pale and silvery light on the now-neglected waste, and the cross stood out aloof, grim, cold and weather-beaten, appearing to stare unceasingly at a phantom army disguised as stunted growths and gorse, an army in ambush awaiting the trumpet call to infuse it with life and activity once again. The fast-moving leaden clouds denote the rapid passage of time: whence came they and where go they? Like we poor mortals they suddenly appear on the horizon, loom for a brief moment and then disappear silently and are forgotten. But the cross remains, ever vigilant and watchful, always performing faithfuly its allotted task...........

Presently a small wood of pines and firs appears, and as I entered under their shadows the profound silence is broken by owls and other night birds calling one another................A flock of water-fowl on a nearby pond glistening in the moonlight evidently resented my intrusion near their domain and set up a continual clucking as I passed; but this subsided as they saw I meant them no harm.

The end of March found Tim writing 'I have hoped long since for a "Case" at home'. Clearly he loved home life with Alma and the two children, Joan and Royce, whom he nicknamed 'The Twins'; and now he saw an opportunity to put his wishes into action. Accordingly Col. Phillott (who has already figured in his discourse) moved into the Kingsclere house so that he could more continuously enjoy Tim's medical care; and Alma readied herself to cater for the increased 'family'. A few driving lessons from the local garage sufficed in those days to prepare one for going solo at the wheel of a car; and by April 17th permission had been received from Mrs Hartnoll (the colonel's niece) for the purchase of a vehicle:

Hambly [the garage owner who had taught Tim the little he knew about driving] *and I set off for Basingstoke where, after viewing cars at Messrs Webbers, we selected a Morris Oxford saloon 1926 model for a trial run and afterwards closed the bargain for £90. I drove home through Basingstoke in semi-darkness and piercing rain accompanied by claps of thunder and lightning. How I went through strange streets on to the Kingsclere Road will always be a mystery to me; but happy to relate we arrived home safely.*

Tim with the (not really) 'Twins', Joan and Royce

On Good Friday the following day, Tim spent *the morning going round the car, touching this and that, raising the bonnet and closing it, and generally pretending to exhibit a great knowledge of all engines and matters appertaining to cars. Alma finds odd moments to rub various parts with a duster, and the 'Twins' are jumping in and out greatly excited and asking questions which prove most embarrassing to me. The afternoon sees me, the family and the Colonel on the high road hooting through Whitchurch, Hurstbourne Prior and Longparish.*

1930 was an important year for Tim. He was now 35, married with two children, and he was a driver. He is getting interesting private cases but there is a snag:

Sun May 4th 1930   Alma and I have decided that Kingsclere is no place for us. Seven miles to Newbury, eight miles to Basingstoke, a poor bus service. Moreover the house we now occupy is damp, over 200 years old and unfit for occupation. There is no bathroom or indoor convenience, general dilapidation and draughts, for which we pay 16/- a week. So today sees us setting off to start house-hunting seriously. I see in the Reading Gazette that there is a house in Tilehurst with car thrown in at a reasonable price, so off we go to inspect it.

What seems surprising to our ears is the speed at which, in 1930, one could take to the road at the wheel of a car. Similarly it seems one could purchase a house very swiftly. After viewing several in Tilehurst ('on the Sabbath') Tim and Alma are attracted by 'The Den', 10 Beechwood Avenue. The opinion of a local worthy known to them, a retired solicitor- now-farmer called Barnett, is sought:

A man of means, well connected, bluff and to the point. Many people would not get on with him at all, but I like him and it is always my principle to take a man as I find him. I admire his temperament and in some ways his outlook on life. He told me that Haddock the builder was sound and reliable, that the houses in question were the best value he had ever seen, but (there's always a 'but') 'In my opinion there is not room to swing a cat in them.' I bore in mind that he was over six feet tall and weighed about 20 stone, so he and the cat would not leave much room; so later I clinched the deal with Hedges the estate agent and made arrangements for a solicitor.

Brain and Brain were instructed, the manager of the Abbey Road Building Society was consulted, and a week later everything was in place. On Saturday May 24th the removal van collected the contents of their Kingsclere home, and *then with Colonel Phillott, Alma, Joan, Royce and the cat in the car I drove off. After arriving at 'The Den' we had to wait four hours before the furniture turned up, so we passed the time by having a meal on the floor of the empty room. Mrs Grant, our next-door neighbour, kindly handed us over a tray of tea.* [This house, purchased and occupied within three weeks of viewing, was to feature throughout the rest of Tim's life, and indeed beyond, not least because all the diaries he kept were discovered in the loft many years after his death.]

1931 may be seen as a sort of halfway point between the Great War of 1914-18 and the World War of 1939-45. Mathematically it came <u>after</u> the mid position; and in any case historians are sometimes now inclined not to refer to two wars but to describe a <u>single</u> conflict that reflected German expansionism extending from 1914 to 1945. At the time of the Armistice, American General Pershing is thought to have dissented from the idea of granting a peace treaty to a beaten Germany on the grounds that they would, unless pursued right to the gates of Berlin, re-open hostilities as soon as they felt a recovery of strength. How right he proved to be! And interestingly Tim's diary for 1931 tentatively seems to agree with that position. We find him still occasionally pondering the war in which he fought, and hinting that he feels something 'nasty' in the air.

On April 1st 1931 he revealed some aspects of his innermost thoughts which, obliquely, give us, his readers, a hint of how he survived four years of horror with mind intact and was able to carve out a new profession. While living away from home on a 'case' he copies out the following section from a book called 'The Pilgrim of a Smile' by Norman Davey, published in 1921 in the USA:

'When, on the ending of the War, the Army no longer needed me, I returned to my pre-war avocation, only to find the minor posts that I had held and detested so sought after as to be outside my reach... By good luck I got this billet (Private Medical Attendant to a case of delusional insanity)...'

One can see why this character in the novel, Dr Andrew Hall, caught Tim's eye. Hall describes in detail the dangers inherent in having medical supervision of the mentally ill. In a finely written passage he suggests that one may find oneself taking on the deficiencies of one's patients:

'If you live for some time with somebody who stutters, you will readily acquire the impediment'; 'I once had charge of a lunatic who was afraid of the moonlight, and I have had to exercise the utmost will-power to restrain myself from pulling down the blind over my bed'; 'I have often, alone in my room, filled in certificates of lunacy with my name in both places – just to see how it looked', and so on.

Tim will have none of this, and his prose rises to similar heights to refute the assumptions expressed by Davey through the mouth his character, Dr Hall:

I said to myself, 'Who is this Norman Davey? What experience and knowledge of psychology does he possess? On what grounds does he make such sweeping statements? I have lived for a period of thirteen years amongst all types of insanity, in public institutions, in private hospitals and private houses, and treated them according to their peculiarities, yet I refuse to add my name to Norman Davey's 'countless legions who have gone mad'. What is more, I have not the slightest fear of impending madness... I refuse to believe that a specialist in phthisis is liable to consumption, or that a professional dancer must be 'jigging' all day. Nor have I yet met the milk-maid who bears any resemblance to a cow... Happily there is a potent force at work called will-power which, if properly developed, exerts itself to our bidding when required.

I was once with a man who imagined that he imparted a disease to all and sundry with whom he came into contact. I did not allow myself to imagine the same. Another man of my acquaintance stood on his head for long periods at a time. I was never tempted to follow his example... I once looked after a Vicar who made use of the most disgusting and revolting language I have ever heard. This did not influence me to do likewise. A friend of mine spends eleven months of every twelve, day and night, with a case of shell-shock which takes the form of continuous gibbering, grotesque movements and perpetual masturbation. My friend looks a picture of health. Training, will-power and a determined mind, augmented by good food and healthy exercise, should prevent any male nurse from joining Norman Davey's 'countless legion of madfolk'.

On May 31st he revisited a beautiful area of Surrey that he knew well from happy memories of rare leaves during the War. He found it sadly changed, and fell to reminiscence:

So, after seventeen years... I too have altered greatly, both physically and mentally, partly through forced contact with the world at its worst (I allude to the Great War)... I recall how many years ago I had emerged from here straight into the horrors of war. The guns had sounded their warning signal over the still air. Tonight – how different – I hear bells calling for peace and contentment. Children are passing to the village Church gaily, full of the joy of life. They probably know nothing of the Great War. May they never, never have to undergo a similar experience to mine.

Aug 5th, 1931   The thunder rolled and boomed, and the lightning flashed as if Hell's incarnate Furies had been let loose from 3 to 5 pm. It resembled a two-hour barrage before zero-hour. Happily it was rain that fell in torrents, not lead and shrapnel. All the same, a vivid reminder of the call to War seventeen years ago yesterday.

Did he feel something in the air? Was he tuned-in to the signs that might indicate that some of those very children 'passing to the village Church gaily' would, indeed, have to share his experience?

Jul 14th   There is a great financial crisis in Germany. All Banks are closed.

Jul 16th   The surrounding countryside is alive with troops engaged in summer manoeuvres. Mechanical transport and fast tanks are in action. The soldiers look so youthful and inexperienced. So did I fifteen years ago, yet we won through.

Jul 22nd   I woke to a dull, monotonous whirring coming from the skies. It stilled the soft cooing of the wood pigeon and hushed the cuckoo's greeting. Huge bombers ploughed through the air towards London. Defence schemes are being rehearsed.

Aug 18th   Army manoeuvres mostly with mechanised forces transform the quiet of Frensham and the surrounding county into scenes of activity reminiscent of 'somewhere in France'. A German Graf Zeppelin passed over the Devil's Punch Bowl in the direction of Aldershot. Like a large aluminium cigar it glided smoothly and almost noiselessly through the air at a good height. Twenty-two passengers paid £30 each for the trip. Was there any other motive behind this?

Without explanation, Tim's 1931 diary ends on this note. Either he abandoned the keeping of a diary (albeit temporarily), or the volumes have been lost.

A number of lengthy essays on particular events remain in pencil form, suggesting that he intended to produce an inked 'fair' copy later; but for all practical purposes there is a gap of about three years, until the habit of writing-up each day's events began again towards the end of 1934. Life becomes more tricky for the reader, however, as there is evidence of haste or pressure in that the entries are in pencil and are less neatly articulated.

CHAPTER SEVENTEEN

THE WRITING ON THE WALL

Regrettably around this time some of Tim's entries lack dates, but *one* certainly does not lack significance:

Hindenburg died yesterday. One of the last of the War leaders. Hitler succeeds to the Presidency.

Paul von Hindenburg (born 1847) had been a German Field Marshal, and President of Germany from 1925 to 34. At the election in 1932 he narrowly defeated Adolf Hitler, whom he despised, but was persuaded to make him Chancellor in early 1933. Old and under continual pressure, Hindenburg finally gave Hitler's party some legislative powers; and when the President died in August 1934 Hitler declared himself Führer, effectively becoming President. Tim's tellingly simple entry was almost certainly made on August 3rd '34.

By September, 1934 Tim was living and working in Birchington, north-east East Kent. It was then a seaside resort with several hotels. A number of relatively wealthy people chose to live there, and it was the grown-up son of one such who became Tim's patient. The environment suited TGE perfectly. He loved swimming in the sea; and he was later able to arrange the renting of a semi-detached house only a few hundred yards from the larger house where he worked. Alma and the family (Joan, Royce and Ann) moved there too, and they all enjoyed perhaps the happiest family life Tim ever experienced.

On Sep 7th, 1934, shortly after returning from a stroll on the beach at Walmer, Tim noted that :

At 3.30 a series of heavy reports, probably muffled by distance, brought my mind back to a heavy bombardment prior to our attack.

In the 1930s, when Tim was there, these low chalk cliffs (above) fell straight to the Birchington beach. This photograph was taken some 75 years later, looking towards Margate. The hotels have gone, but Tim's home there remains, as does the larger residence where he worked

York House, Birchington (right), where Tim's patient lived

Windows and doors rattled, and the house shook. I put it down to naval gun-firing practice. The front page of the Daily Express the next morning was headed as follows: 'Riddle of the Roaring guns... Coast Towns Shaken... Deal had the fright of its life... Pandemonium'. Sensationalism at any price is the keynote of the popular press. The people who really know titter contemptibly, while the ignorant reader is gulled. Cheap stunting is not journalism, and it is the journalists themselves who must eventually suffer. The official explanation of the above occurrence was that tests with France's heaviest naval guns were being carried out on land emplacements two miles from Calais. These guns are so powerful that they can be heard from a distance of fifty miles. Some guns, I guess! No wonder windows in Calais were shattered.'

Although Tim's jottings at this time were mainly concerned with family or medical matters, he nonetheless appears to have kept a wary eye on things and events military. He even folded and kept carefully at the back of his diary a review of a book 'The War in the Air, volume 5', by A.H.Jones, published by the Oxford University Press. The statistics relating to the Great War make interesting reading in view of what was to come in the next decade:

In 103 air raids on England, the 8,578 bombs dropped killed 1,414 people, injured 3,416, and caused damage estimated at nearly £3,000,000. We required 6,136 officers and men to man various anti-aircraft stations... and a single raid might mean the firing of 20,000 shells at £2 each..., and so on.

On January 11th, 1935 both Tim and his third child, Ann, had birthdays. She was two, he forty, and he was moved to write a poem which, no doubt, spoke for many a veteran of the Great War:

Reflections at Forty; Alma and I.

As time goes on and life slows down
We'll turn our backs upon the town,
And near a green and pleasant hill
Or stately wood or rippling rill
We'll build ourselves a little cot
With vegetable and flowery plot.

There we will be the first to hear
The cuckoo's message of the year.
The first pale primrose we shall find,
Bluebells and others of their kind.
I'll have a tree with branches low
And watch the blackbirds come and go.

And when the winter days appear
The Radio will be our cheer.
We'll also potter round about
And be so happy, there's no doubt.
And time will pass unknowingly
Together dear – just you and me.

But thoughts of war are to recur during the latter days of 1935:

Thurs Oct 3rd   Italy declares war on Abyssinia (Ethiopia). Reason:- Mussolini states publicly that the Italians 'want a bigger place in the sun' – more room to breathe, expand, develop; and so an up-to-date mechanical army commences a massacre of the innocent for sheer personal lust and gain. The King of Italy and the Pope are apparently powerless against the word of the Dictator. Likewise the League of Nations is ignored and must henceforth be a failure. So once again the bombs are dropping on defenceless women and children.

Can there be any excuse in this the 20th Century for such malicious slaughter? My hope at the moment is that the 'walk-over' victory may be met with many setbacks. All eyes are on Britain and her next move. The position is difficult, but I do not think that we shall be involved. We do not want War, but re-arming will go on apace.

Fri Oct 4th   Adowa heavily bombed. Rumours – dispatches official and unofficial, and the usual contradictions and reports will now be placarded and dished up to a public thirsting for the latest news. Personally I have lost my fever for war. Memories of twenty years ago are still too vivid. I can now look on with great interest it is true, and endeavour to read between the lines of sensational news. When I was just one year old Italy lost 25,000 men in a great defeat at Adowa. Revenge them all, says Mussolini.

Fri Oct 11th   A big majority of the League vote for economic sanctions against Italy. Britain presses for their immediate application. Thousands of Abyssinians are deserting to Italy, according to Press from Rome.

Mon Nov 11th   Seventeenth anniversary of the Armistice. Time does fly. Took Ann for a little walk, and we were in Lyndhurst Avenue [Norbury] *when the maroons, sirens and various signals sounded at 11 am. Ann, very much perplexed, stood beside me whilst Tess* [the dog] *scratched the two minutes' silence away. There is something simple but stupendous in this brief sudden quietude, probably rendered more impressionable this year by the Italian–Abyssinian crisis illustrating only too vividly the nearness and suddenness with which War can be upon us.*

Mon Nov 25th   Arrived at Blackfriars Bridge 10.35 am, and waited in a growing crowd and murky weather to see the passing of the late Earl Jellicoe on his last journey through London to rest beside Nelson at St. Paul's. The little lithesome French sailors formed a striking contrast to the stolid massive Guards, and the white helmets of the Marines struck a ghostly note to a memorable and emotional scene. One by one the old War leaders leave us, to be swallowed up in the past. Those left can now be counted on one hand.

1936

Sun Mar 8th   Germans re-occupy the Rhineland.
Mon Apl 27th   Italians nearing Addis Ababa.

1937

Mon Feb 22nd   Signs of the approaching Coronation are now appearing in the shops. Bunting, flags, all sorts of souvenirs are on sale. The Australian and New Zealand troops have already set sail for England. George VI will never take the place of Edward VIII in my own mind. Still, it is the Crown and not the man. Had my hair cut... [Tim's 1937 diary was clearly printed before details were known of the Abdication Crisis, for Wednesday May 12th is shown as a Bank Holiday and is marked 'Coronation of Edward VIII'. Tim has scored through that printed entry, and writes:]

People wait all night in parks and streets for Coronation of George VI. I walked to Oxford Street and stood outside C&A from around 11, and had a great view of the procession which passed around 2.30. Rain commenced and thousands of people were drenched. The Tubes were unable to cope with the rush.

Thurs June 3rd   Edward VIII, or as as he is now known the Duke of Windsor, married Mrs Simpson in Tours, France; and this completed his plans and realized his hopes which caused such a sensation last November. Good luck to him. His hair is turning grey above the ears; so is mine – one thing at least in common. The rumble like distant thunder of naval gunnery practice in the North Sea rattles and shakes windows, doors and houses. Weather fine. Tide too far out at 3 pm for a swim. Am liking this place [Birchington in north-east Kent] *very much.*

Tim had negotiated a new professional appointment that enabled him to move the family from Norbury to Birchington-on-Sea. This was to prove one of the happiest times of his life. Their Norbury house, a four-in-a-row terraced property, could be let, bringing in a small but relatively reliable extra income which went part way towards the rent of a somewhat more attractive semi in north-east Kent (rather grandly named Norfolk House). His new case was within easy walking distance, so for most of the time he could live at home and enjoy a full family life. He had a good-sized garden, and could therefore provide fresh produce. And, above all, the attractive seafront with its low cliffs and rocky beaches was a permanent delight. Tim was a strong swimmer, as were all the children. Alma enjoyed sitting on the beach. He and the children enjoyed collecting winkles for afternoon tea. Unfortunately, Hitler had him in his sights.

Mon June 7th   All is not quiet on the Northern front. The ' silent navy' are carrying on a noisy cannonade away in the mists.

Wed June 9th   Apart from half a dozen fellows from the Air Force at Manston the foreshore was almost deserted...

Tues Jul 13th   From Minnis Bay we could hear salvos of naval gunfire, with heaps of aeroplanes and searchlights. Memories of 1914!

Tues Jul 27th   Walking towards Manston I realized that this countryside is hedgeless, like Belgium.

Wed Sep 8th   General Nursing Council demand for my annual registration fee arrived today, and with it questions as to my availability in the event of a National Emergency. 'Are you under 45?' I certainly still am. [Two years before the outbreak of war, it seems that the Nursing Council was aware that an 'emergency' might be coming, and were gathering some information which would later prove vital.]

Fri Oct 8th   Newspapers are full of Chinese-Japanese war, and Spanish trouble. International relations everywhere are full of suspicions of each other's actions.

Thurs Nov 11th   Silence at Cenotaph broken by an escaped lunatic from Epsom. [There was a large mental hospital near Epsom.] *Listened in to broadcast of British Legion gathering at Albert Hall. Average age of war veterans now 48. Grey and bald heads are now in the front line.*

Fri Nov 12th   An observation balloon at Manston broke from its moorings and drifted out to sea. I saw it just prior to the mishap. Valuable instruments on board.

Tues Nov 16th   The balloon that broke its moorings on Friday and trailed 10,000 feet of steel cabling with it drifted over 400 miles across France, putting four or five towns in darkness and setting a V.O. [indistinct, possibly P.O. = Post Office] *on fire through cables fouling high tension pylons, came to grief yesterday at Vignacourt.* [Tim was at Vignacourt on the 4th August, 1918.]

1938

Sat Mar 12th   *Hitler coolly takes over Austria. Where is this act going to end ?*

Sun Mar 13th   *Depression over England regarding Austrian annexation.*

Mon Mar 21st   *General National 'wind-up' has abated. Though everyone still apprehensive.*

Thurs Apl 7th   *We must dig our own trenches against Air raids.*

Thurs May 5th   *We spent about £60,000 on the Coronation. Mussolini has spent about £4,000,000 entertaining and impressing Hitler.*

Sat May 28th   *With Alma, Ann and Mrs Raply to Air Force display at Manston. Great thrills, but spoilt by wind and rain. Tea in Hospital, and went over same. Up to date there have been similar displays at about fifty other 'dromes. Have decided that S.M.* [Scoutmaster] *Raply is not a nice person to know- too oily, self-important and egoistic.*

Sun Jun 5th   *Alma and Joan came back from visiting Royce's Camp very much 'alive' and played at 'Hunt the Pigs' Fleas' all evening, till I also felt lousy and back in the trenches.*

At this point, Tim's diaries become confusing. He seems to enter basic facts of domestic life in a tiny, green-leather pocket-book issued by an Italian shipping line (presumably a gift from one of his patients) while recording his thoughts on international affairs in a slightly larger loose-leaf booklet. In the interests of comprehensibility I have omitted all but essential 'family and work' items, and have amalgamated his comments from the two sources where they illuminate his views and experiences both of the 1914 War and of the coming new conflict.

Wed Sep 14th   *Week-end tension akin to 1914. Sudeten Germans and Czechoslovakia at loggerheads. Germany anxious to take over former, with Italy and Japan behind her. Czechs supported by France and Russia, and we, by Pact, must assist France. Hitler is the man of the moment. Will he declare war ? Chamberlain is to fly to Berlin tomorrow.*

Thurs Sep 15th   *Prime Minister flies to Germany to consult Hitler. Aged 69 he is making his first flight. All very significant. Atmosphere friendly.*

Fri Sep 16th   *Chamberlain flies back, 'No statement yet.'*

Sun Sep 18th   *Daladier, French Prime Minister, flies to London for conference. Situation acute.*

Mon Sep 19th   *Noisy London outdoor meetings.*

Sat Sep 24th   *Daily Express has altered its tune from 'there will be no war this year' to 'be prepared'. A man who makes any newspaper his bible is a fool. If any one nation has made up its mind to dominate the world by sheer force, it should be resisted.*

Sun Sep 25th   *Cabinet meeting every day and night. London in a state of restless anxiety Furniture removers inundated.*

Mon Sep 26th   *We discuss shifting to Tilehurst in an emergency.* [Tim's family still owns the house in Tilehurst, near Reading, which is let. Tim evidently realizes that the Kent coast may be a danger-zone in the event of war with Germany, and in this realization is well ahead of the authorities who were later to evacuate areas of London by sending some of the children to north Kent 'for safety'.] *What is the mentality of one man who, against all advice, will wreck the world ?*

Tues Sep 27th   *Chamberlain says, 'I have done as much as any one man can do.' It rests with Hitler. We keep our wireless-sets switched on for news as it comes through. The fleet mobilizes.*

Wed. Sep 28th   *Volunteers enrolling for all wartime services. Trenches dug in Parks. Part of London Tube closed for conversion to wartime* [next word illegible]. *Territorials called up. The family measured for gas-masks.*

Thurs Sep 29th   Chamberlain flies to meet Hitler in last effort to avert World War. Four-power meeting at Munich: Mussolini for Italy; Daladier for France. Alma and I collect gas-masks from New Inn. Royce tests mask in kitchen with gas.

Fri Sep 30th   Everywhere gloom turns to joy at the Prime Minister's 'Peace before midnight'. (But Royce a little disappointed.) Wireless a great asset in emergency. What is Russia thinking ? Air Raid Precautions continue.

Sat Oct 1st   Food hoarders have lots on their hands. Sandbags went up two-and-a half pence to sevenpence. Spades up from 3/- to 7/-.   Thank Goodness the profiteer was nipped. Never has a nation been more thankful to breathe again. [Tim really writes from the heart in his next entry. His words are even more poignant when we contemplate what was to come.]

Sun Oct 2nd   Ground heavy with rain, but hearts light with relief. After twenty years I have discovered that the 1914 sacrifice was not in vain. Our memories of it and its lessons have surely prevented it in 1938.

Thurs Oct 6th   Criticism of Neville continues. But the majority are with him.

Thurs Oct 13th   Alma to A.R.P. class at St Mary's.

Thurs Oct 27th   Alma attended A.R.P. class. Everybody's doing it now.

Fri Nov 11th   Armistice, twenty years after. Most impressive yet. Cenotaph and Albert Hall. Ann giggled in school during silence. Royce at Margate Memorial, Alma and Joan in Birchington.

Sat Nov 12th   Terrible persecution of Jews in Germany.

Mon Nov 14th   Everywhere the topic is the persecution of the Jews by German Nazis.

Tues Nov 29th   Alma is now waiting patiently for War Stock to be cashed so that she can dash to London to buy one, two or perhaps three new suites, but I hope to draw in the reins a bit.

1939

Sun Jan 8th   Sent off for new model aeroplane for Royce: 7s6d. This is a Christmas gift from Alma who thinks it might appease his ideas about the R.A.F., in which he is very interested. He doesn't make many friends here. [Later Royce did join the R.A.F. as a career, rising to the highest non-commissioned rank, Master Aircrew. He then joined Middle East Airlines as a Flight Engineer; and on retiring from there he worked in Holland for Fokker compiling handbooks on weights and loadings. He never lost his interest in flying.]

Wed Jan 11th   I am 44 today.

Thurs Mar 16th   Hitler marches on, and 'takes over' Czechoslovakia, the final proof that he is animated purely and simply by the spirit of conquest. Well, we have been warned enough.

Fri Mar 17th   The largest advertisement in England is to be placed on the centre span of Waterloo Bridge: 143 feet long, 19 feet deep. It will be 'National Service – Have you offered yours ?' Chamberlain broadcasts perhaps the most bitter speech of his career. His policy has broken up – the policy of serious friendship with Hitler, for all that the latter promised in September has been ignored and he tramples on over other nations. Rumania may be next. Prime Minister has done his best for people, and failed. What will he do now ?

Sat Mar 18th   Once again there is only one topic: 'Are we going to Halt Hitler?'

Mon Mar 20th   Government sounding other nations as to their intentions. France will fight if Rumania is invaded, and that will set the box of matches alight.

Tues Mar 21st   President Lebrun arrives in London and is given a tremendous reception. German press is attacking us ferociously.

Thurs Mar 23rd   Will it be Conscription? The Press says Yes. Cabinet is divided.

Wed Mar 29th   Madrid surrenders, and after two-and-a-half years Franco wins war against Red Government of Spain, assisted by Italian and German forces.

Mon Apl 3rd   Prime Minister pledges our aid to Poland in event of attack, and so reveals to the world our new foreign policy of 'We will fight any attempt to dominate the world by force'.

Thurs Apl 6th   Poland and Britain have signed an anti-aggression pact of mutual assistance. How difficult it is to foresee the future of present-day events.

Sat Apl 8th   Mussolini swoops suddenly on the most sacred day of the year, and attacks Albania. 400 bombers against two. 100 warships against four motor-boats. 60,000 troops against 14,000. What bravery! What is the next move?   Visitors are arriving for Easter, but this part of the coast will not be popular while the political situation is as it is.

Easter Monday, April 10th   Cabinet meets to discuss crisis.

Thurs Apl 13th   Chamberlain announces Pact with Poland and Greece against aggression.

Mon Apl 17th   President Roosevelt invites Hitler and Mussolini to sign a 10 or 25 year peace pledge. Rest of world is willing, but what will be the Dictators' replies? Surely we shall now know how we stand.

Tues 25th Apl   Conscription now appears imminent, with 20-21 ages first.

Sat Apl 29th   Hitler made his awaited speech and reply to Roosevelt. No direct answer. Sarcastic. Contradictory, bluffing and egoistic. General inference is that his actions speak louder than his words, so carry on with re-armament and watch closely.

Tues May 2nd   Political front now centred around Poland: Danzig and Corridor. Will Poland take advantage of our pledge to assist them?

Fri May 5th   We cannot reach an agreement with the Soviet at present. She wants a full military alliance. We don't.

Sun May 7th   Family to A.R.P. demonstration and march in Margate. Royce takes part.

Mon May 8th   I hear there are demonstrations by a certain section in London against conscription. But the Bill has passed and is now law.

Tues May 9th   The Budget last week, in an effort to meet the cost of History's biggest re-armament, raised prices of tea, sugar, cars and tobacco. The last affects me personally, so I am seizing the opportunity to cut down on my smoking, not from unpatriotic reasons, but for my health.

Fri May 12th   Military alliance completed with Turkey. Do Hitler and Mussolini realize that they have finished taking over other people's possessions? We shall watch them sit pretty on the fence, chortling loudly.

Sat June 3rd   Signing up of conscripts between 20-21 commences.

Thurs Jun 8th   King crosses to America.

Fri Jun 9th   King and Queen given great reception at Washington D.C.

Thurs Jun 22nd   School sports in high east wind. Royce did well, easily winning the high jump, the hundred yards and the relay. I thought he looked the complete athlete: trim, with no spare flesh. His high jump victory won the most applause. The King returns from Canada.

By August 1939 it is evident that the threat of Britain becoming involved in another major war was real indeed. Tim, nursing a private patient in Birchington-on-Sea (then a resort with four hotels) makes preparations, but does not lose his sense of humour.

Tues Aug 1st   *Provided I am not earning more than £250 per annum I am entitled to an air-raid shelter supplied free by the Government. Alma informs me that a 'doddering old man' called re. the above, and she has signed form for a free shelter. I have wanted one ever since they were first issued, and have an idea that it will be of the greatest assistance in the propagation of mushrooms.*

Fri Aug 18th   *French bombers 'raided' England yesterday to furnish opportunity for practice on both sides.*

Tues Aug 22nd   *A diplomatic bombshell for the world, Germany and Russia sign a non-aggression pact with each other. If Hitler thinks that this move will make the Democratic powers pause in their promise to help Poland should she be attacked he is making the greatest mistake of his career.*

Thurs Aug 24th   *Internatiional tension becomes more acute. Hitler states that he is not going to be interfered with in his intentions. Territorials are all mobilised, and we are prepared for any emergency.*

Thurs Aug 31st   *Situation becomes steadily worse and all reserves report for mobilization. Joan goes to Quex Park* [a small stately home near Birchington] *as Telephone Clerk and has to stay the night for rehearsal. Quex and King Ethelbert's school will become hospitals in event of war. As zero hour approaches everyone displays quiet determination, resolved to face the inevitable with courage. Could not settle down to gardening. The absence of planes about us is noticeable. I suspect they are in France awaiting orders.*

Fri Sep 1st   *Germany attacks Poland all along her frontier and bombs many towns. So War it is, and we now await our entry into what will be a slaughter far worse than ever known - a reversion to savagery and a disgrace to modern civilization. I feel as antagonistic to the enemy as in 1914, but more directly to one man, Hitler, that he should wield such power as to plunge us all into such carnage. Evacuation of children from London proceeds, but here in Birchington quiet prevails, and I pray it may not be disturbed.*

Sat Sep 2nd   *Royce and Jack* [who later became the first of Joan's three husbands] *take Joan up to Quex Park for night duty. Royce is in Scout's uniform with a red 'National Service'*

stitched on his shirt. Great excitement for him as at age 15 he sees only the glamour of war. May much of the other awful side be spared him. Because of the 'black-out' I could not read in bed. Blast Hitler!

2010: Tim's younger daughter, Ann, in the garden of Quex Park, where her elder sister Joan had done 'war-work' in September 1939

153

CHAPTER EIGHTEEN

SO IT'S WAR – AGAIN!

Tim writes about the declaration of war and the siren that, almost immediately, sounded the Alert.

Sun Sep 3rd   It was a genuine alarm, but the 'plane sighted was not an enemy. At least we had a realistic dress rehearsal for what we are in for. I spent the afternoon with Royce hauling mattresses from the loft and converting them into shock-resistors by suspending them from french windows, to be put up and taken down in a few seconds (I hope). This is my own idea, and I have not heard of it being used elsewhere. My celery is drooping for lack of water. Curse this man Hitler for causing me to neglect my garden. The Beach Attendant tells me that at 11.15 he was just about to collect the deckchair fees at the Gap when the siren sounded. Nearly all the occupants dashed for shelter, so instead of collecting about five shillings he took a paltry fourpence.

Tim's diary now has far more space than hitherto, and he writes at length about the carrying of gas-masks, about the night duties of daughter Joan (telephonist at Quex Park, which has become an emergency hospital) and of son Royce (a Scout who has offered his services to the war effort). He also quotes and comments on the reports from various fronts, notably Poland, the strictly-enforced black-out, his attempts to grow vegetables, and so on. Occasionally he contributes a personal insight which is worth reporting:

Sun Sep 10th   Royce takes part in a rehearsal as a 'casualty' – a change from his usual duties as a messenger based at an Ambulance Aid Post.

Tues Sep 12th   British troops are in France with the R.A.F. My mind goes back to 1915 when I arrived at Rouen by boat after a delightful cruise on the Seine. Surely this time our position is stronger and greater.

Sun Sep 17th   Joan, Royce and I went to Beresford Gap at 2.30 pm and went into a sea as rough as the present European situation. Waves repeatedly knocked us down; in fact Joan was in distress at times. Royce stuck it well. The roughest bathe we have had, but to me an immense pleasure and diversion in these apprehensive times.

Mon Sep 18th   I read that we may soon expect an Air-raid shelter from Margate Corporation. I am quite prepared to deal with it with Royce's assistance.

Fri Sep 22nd   Went down dug-out at 'Rossetti' with Dollen and another Chauffeur. Dug during last War. 40 feet deep and holds over 100. Electric light fitted, now being reconditioned. A typical war-zone structure, and as safe as any I have seen in the district – even from a direct hit. ['Rossetti' was a large house in Birchington, named after poet and painter Dante Gabriel Rossetti who was staying in Birchington with the architect Seddon when his dependence on laudanum overcame him. He is buried in the Churchyard, beneath a fine memorial designed by Ford Madox Brown.]

This War, I fancy, is going to be a long job. Is it best to get into something now with a certain amount of choice, or hang on indefinitely until such time as my class of man is called up en masse with no option of choice? A difficult problem at 45 with home and other responsibilities.

Sun Oct 1st   *German/Russian talks and movements cause much speculation. I am firmly convinced that Hitler is not going to benefit in the long run for he has reached his Eastern limits, and Russia as a neighbour is not a happy thought.*

Thurs Oct 5th   *There is a movement afoot to call up old soldiers of the last War, aged round about the 40's, as their experience might blend with the youth of today. Personally I feel as good as ever and just as keen, but I wonder how I should react to conditions now as in 1914-18. Home responsibilities alone keep me back, but later on I may have no choice.*

Mon Oct 9th   *We read today, 'Mud minimized operations on the Western Front.' One brief sentence, but oh! How much it means to any trench-dwellers of the last War.*

Fri Oct 20th   *Four mines, one in Grenham Bay and the others towards the marshes, were washed up with the early morning tide. I hear they were detonated and removed by experts from Chatham.*

Sun Oct 22nd   *We have decided, from our experience of the last three air-raid warnings, that in future after the siren has sounded we will carry on as usual and not immediately take up emergency positions, but wait until anti-aircraft guns give indication of enemy planes' nearness. It is much better to be doing something than just sitting still waiting and wondering.*

Rossetti's grave in Birchington Churchyard

Thurs Nov 2nd   *The Anderson Air Raid Shelter arrived this morning and was deposited under the kitchen window. I hope it will not stay there too long, though much has to be done ere it is installed in its final form. Captain Gough, next door, has elaborate plans to erect an underground shelter under a shed. For me money has a big say in the matter. His idea I reckon will cost £30, mine nothing but honest hard work. Started work this afternoon amid much sarcastic and humorous witticisms from Alma and Joan.*

Thurs Nov 9th   *If my memory is correct it was on this day 25 years ago that I enlisted, and now the cycle of time has brought about a similar, if not worse, state of affairs. So much for our previous 'War to End Wars'.*

Fri Nov 10th   *Took Ann to school, then began digging hole for shelter. Found the work laborious and progress very slow, but with the prospect of Germany over-running Holland any day it would appear that no time is to be lost.*

Sat Nov 11th   *Never did I imagine that I should ever spend the two minutes' silence in respect of the last war entrenching myself against the horrors of another. My mind goes back to the trenches on the Somme and Ypres as I sling out the earth assisted by little spadefuls from Ann's seaside spade on one side and Royce's bigger spade on the other. Can I hope that my children will be spared a repetition of the ghastliness I thought had been permanently banished. Cornflowers are blooming in the garden: they are the French counterpart of our poppy.*

Tues Nov 14th   *Royce stayed home from school and carried on with excavation for the shelter. I joined him at 2pm and during the afternoon managed to complete the digging having*

Norfolk House, Birchington (on the left). Tim's family rented this house during their stay in Birchington-on-Sea. In its garden he and Royce assembled their free Anderson shelter. It was from here that they were forced to move to Tilehurst (near Reading) when that entire Kent coast became a Restricted Area: untenable because of fears the Germans might invade thereabouts. Ironically many long-term residents who risked remaining there had the last laugh, because the invasion never came, and relatively little damage was suffered.

reached a depth of over 4 feet, piercing chalk and sand. Succeeded in laying and bolting iron base and put side sheeting irons in position before darkness set in.

Wed Nov 15th   With much mud clinging to our heels and clothes Royce and I managed to put the shelter together complete in its new home 4'4' down. Ann now possesses a metal case for her gas-mask, and her pleasure is tremendous.

Mon Nov 20th   Spent the afternoon throwing earth on to Anderson shelter with the result that I can now say that this part of the job is almost completed.

Wed Nov 22nd   Spent another afternoon on shelter. Put in step and improved entrance. My idea is to try to disguise its real purpose and prevent it being too much of an eyesore.

Sun Nov 26th   Heavy rain and wind has caused landslide on the shelter.

Sun Dec 3rd   Royce and I take advantage of a cold but sunny day to finish off the Air-raid Shelter. [Tim describes in great detail his attempts to balance the need for a secure shelter against his wish for the whole area to enhance the appearance of the garden.] *We had to pull up two of our garden posts to convert into a ladder which will be our means of entrance and exit.*

1940

Thurs Jan 4th   A strange looking plane flew over the football ground, holding up the match for a few seconds. It was unusual, having the appearance of being encircled in a huge horizontal metal hoop. Most mysterious, and no-one knew anything of it. Royce was not there, and later wanted to know all the details.

Fri Jan 5th   Saw the mysterious hooped plane again, and so did Royce.

Tues Jan 9th   There are now many stories in circulation about the hooped plane, e.g. it may be a gun track, an aerial control centre, a magnetic mine-detector, or a system for using steam rather than petrol. I prefer the third guess. [I recall seeing a photo of this plane in my youth (I was an avid reader of *Flight*), but was unable to find any reference to it. However, while this book was in preparation it came to light that the aircraft was a Type 418 Vickers Wellington DWI. The ring was called a 'degaussing ring' and was fitted under the aircraft to adapt it to be able to detonate naval mines. An electrical generator induced a magnetic field in the loop which was mounted under the fuselage supported by the nose, tail and each wing. DWI stood for 'Directional Wireless Installation' which meant nothing and was intended to be misdirection for the true purpose of the loop. Tim was almost exactly right in his guess.]

Thurs Jan 11th   The children invited to Ann's (and my) birthday party romped and played

156

while enemy planes penetrated into Kent at five points. Ron, our airman friend, was flying unconcernedly about during the afternoon on a practice flight, unconscious of the nearness of the enemy. I asked him what he would have done if contact had been made. 'Rammed one of them and then leapt out in my parachute', said he. He has not yet done a parachute jump, and the manoeuvre is considered too risky to include in his training.

Tim is now using a 6" by 4" notebook rather than a printed diary. This works well because he can write at length on one day, and more briefly on others. His entries are written with greater clarity than hitherto and they cover domestic issues, his job as a private nurse, and (of special interest) his comments on issues relating to the war. Birchington is about three miles west of Margate facing north into the Thames estuary. It has attractive low chalk cliffs and a shoreline which is a mixture of sand and rock. In the thirties it was a 'smart' resort with four hotels. Its two claims to historical interest are (a) the fact that Dante Gabriel Rossetti's grave is in the churchyard, where there is a fine memorial designed by Ford Madox Brown, and (b) the somewhat surprising luxury tower-bungalows designed by Seddon built facing the estuary. In 1940 the Royal Air Force was well-established at Manston, a few miles inland: that 'drome was to come under fierce attack later when the Germans tried to 'take out' the British air defences. Meanwhile, Tim records constant reminders that Birchington is in a somewhat dangerous position should France be overrun:

Sat Jan 13th *I went on duty at 1 pm. There was a big bang at 2.19* [note the accuracy] *followed by a series of others. I may obtain details of the cause later by wireless or newspaper. However, I take little notice of gossip, and this applies in some measure to the press.*

Sun Jan 14th *In the afternoon Alma and I went for a walk to Minnis Bay. We saw a suspicious-looking object about five miles out to sea. Later a deal of machine-gun fire was heard.*

Tues Jan 16th *Royal Army Service Corps troops are billeted in Birchington, and are glad to be under cover for there has been a blizzard and a substantial fall of snow.*

Fri Jan 26th *Soldiers stand in the Square in falling snow and sleet waiting for billets to be allotted them. They are very young and raw and issued with civilian gasmasks. They are attached to the R.A.S.C. We were approached re. taking in some troops, but we have no room.*

Sat Jan 27th *Off duty at 6.30, and despite awful weather we decided to change into evening dress for the dance at the Bungalow Hotel. We struggled through the slush only to find on our arrival that the band had not yet arrived. At 9.15 they put in an appearance, but by then many people had come and gone. There was our own party of nine, seven or eight R.A.S.C. Sergeants, and a dozen or so odd couples left to carry on. Anyway, I had made my first appearance in dinner jacket and wellington boots.*

Mon Feb 5th *Alma and Joan went to a dance at the Bungalow, mainly for billetted troops. Admission sixpence, and the place packed with about 300 troops. The ladies greatly enjoyed the majority against them of ten to one and had the time of their lives: old 'uns, fat 'uns, thin 'uns, young 'uns: all were at a premium. They must have gone home convinced that as far as the War is concerned it is indeed an ill wind that blows no good. Even in these enlightened days a lady loves to be fought for, and so the dance was a whoopee.*

On February 23rd Tim went to London to see the parade and presentations to celebrate what he calls 'The Graf Spee affair'. He writes at length about the day which clearly stirred his patriotic feelings, and remarked:

Afterwards I arrived at Victoria about 3 pm just in time to see the British Expeditionary Force leave- train disgorge its dirty-looking cargo of troops from France. I thought of my own homecomings from the same station a few years ago, and apart from the 'battle-dress' now worn I could see little difference in the kit carried. It is surprising how one gets used to humping it all around.

Sun Mar 17th   This afternoon in a slight drizzle Ann, Royce and I (all suitably clad) set out for an inspection of the Royal Engineer lorries which are parked alongside many roads in the district. They carry pontoon bridges, etc.

Wed Mar 20th   An Army pontoon lorry overturned on the railway bridge embankment. The central lamp-post outside Walkers has been knocked down – it all helps to break the monotony.

Wed Apl 3rd   Churchill appointed War leader in new Cabinet. I filled in the papers for Royce's entrance for Royal Air Force as Mechanical Apprentice.

Fri Apl 5th   Joan and Alma are preparing for Czechs' farewell dance. They must leave this district under new Aliens order.

Mon Apl 29th   The football pitch at the bottom of the garden has been ploughed, and potatoes are now being planted out. As far as the eye can see, and it is a great distance, land has been turned to advantage. May the crops be bumpers.

Whit Sunday, May 12th   Troops everywhere. Pontoon bridges and lorries are drawn up across the Square, and at all approach-points cars are halted for identification purposes. Orders are that all aliens are to be interned. The East and South-east coast are under special supervision. News that enemy parachutists are having great success in Holland has alarmed people here. Sentries about 200 yards apart line the cliffs. Bren guns are being mounted in isolated parts of the marshes. One is being manned by the R.A.S.C. about a mile from our back garden in a field of clover. I have often gazed at this expanse of beautiful scenery, but never did I imagine it would assume this warlike appearance. Even now the Germans are only about ninety miles away (just about the distance from here to Reading). One looks ahead very apprehensively.

Sat May 18th   This part of S.E. England is not now looked on as a safe area. 10,000 evacuated children [ie children who had been moved to supposed safety in Kent from London] *leave tomorrow for south Wales, accompanied by teachers.*

Sun May 19th   Alma and I went to the Allens in the evening to discuss plans for joint evacuation of Mrs Allen and Shirley together with Alma, Joan and Ann as soon as possible. Arrangements left to me.

Mon May 20th   During day our aircraft kept up mass reconnoitering. About 100 new planes have appeared from Manston; nearly all have one wing painted white and the other black. A letter from Mrs Bowley [a resident of Beechwood avenue, Tilehurst, where Tim and Alma owned a house that was let] *told us that Mrs Broome could put us up temporarily. I expect a letter from Hedges* [the letting agent] *tomorrow. Aerial activity has been continuous all day, and the War seems very near.*

Tues May 21st   Spent most of morning getting in touch with Hedges re. a furnished house in Tilehurst [as a temporary measure until Tim's own house is vacated] *but have not settled anything yet.*

Thurs May 23rd   Situation grave. Many people vacating this district. Cannot yet get Alma fixed up with accommodation; trunks all packed and ready to go.

Fri May 24th   Alma very active on phone. The upshot is that they all leave tomorrow and sort themselves out between Marjorie Broome and Doris Bowley [two inhabitants of Beechwood Avenue] *until they can fix up other accommodation. I spent the afternoon feverishly packing and bought single tickets to Reading via Victoria and Paddington. I arranged to*

Right: Joan, Tim, Royce, Ann and Alma in the back garden of 10 Beechwood Avenue ('The Den') about 1943. Both girls wear dresses made by Alma on her trusty treadle Singer Sewing Machine. She made her own red jacket too.

Below: Ann Veronica in the front garden of 'The Den', 10 Beechwood Avenue, Tilehurst in 2010. The garage and burglar alarm are new, but otherwise the house is little changed.

send trunks and other baggage. Fare 15/6 single. Other route too slow and three changes necessary. Audible gunfire now almost incessant and to some people nerve-racking. My chief concern is that the family life as I have known it for over two years is about to be shattered.

Sat May 25th The family are in the final stages of preparations for departure. What shall they take, and what leave? For how long are they going? Will they ever return to this house again? Who can tell what the future holds in store? All baggage is now addressed to Reading Station to be called for as we have as yet no forwarding address. Joan carries a brown suitcase and small bag, Alma a green case and shopping basket, gas-masks are packed, and Ann, who has cut her lip, is looking rather grim and carries her doll. We pick up the Allens who are laden with far too many personal packages for comfortable travelling, and (leaving the trunks outside the respective doors ready to be picked up) we troop off to the station. Many eyes peep from windows, some openly and some surreptitiously. We wave to friends and on to the platform. Why the Southern Railway should choose a time like this to paint the footbridge a bright aluminium colour and the rest of the statiion a brilliant yellow is beyond me. It must stand out as a target for aircraft. The 10.34 arrives on time, they all bundle into a Pullman with luggage anywhere. I manage to say goodbye to Alma, but Ann and Joan are lost in the melée. Royce and I watch the train glide out, give up our platform tickets and stroll slowly home to find that the trunks have been collected during our absence. Traces of their hurried departure are everywhere. We make a pretence of tidying up, but I find I cannot put my mind to it.

Mon May 27th Government has ordered evacuation of all east and south-east coast towns from Yarmouth to Folkestone. This includes Margate and Birchington. I'm waiting to see how this affects Royce, for King Ethelbert's school is on the list. He and I walked to the cliffs to find all entrances to the sea-shore closed with barbed wire and machine-gun posts being erected at key points.

Tues May 28th. The bad news from Belgium [King Leopold has surrendered his army] shocks people generally and speeds their departure from these parts. Women with babies call at the

159

school to see if they can be evacuated with the schoolchildren, but are sent away disappointed.

Wed May 29th   As all my friends prepare to depart, I feel that I cannot escape this War; and I have no urge to try, for having got Alma and the girls away (and Royce probably going soon) I shall feel a certain pride in literally defending my hearth and home if I am not called elsewhere in the meantime.

Thurs May 30th   Alma has written to say she hopes to get into a furnished house in Tilehurst next Monday. She and Ann are sleeping at the Broomes, and Joan with the Bowleys. Meanwhile wounded troops and the first of those able to be withdrawn from Dunkirk arrive at Margate pier. Many people crowd on the railway bridge [in Birchington] to watch them pass by in trains conveying them towards London.

Sat June 1st   This afternoon Royce and I jumped on our cycles and rode to Margate. On the cliffs behind the pier we commanded a good view of a mass of sea craft such as Margate has never witnessed before. Destroyers, launches, tugs, trawlers and all sorts of boats were lying round about like a glorified regatta; even rowing boats answered the Government S.O.S. and played their part manned by local men in rescuing our army from the shell-stricken sands of Dunkirk. On this hot, hazy day, which in ordinary times would have seen holiday crowds lining the pier and beach, we gazed on a scene I had thought never to occur again in my lifetime, as worn-out limping troops badly soiled with Flanders mud and rough fighting discharged themselves in hundreds from the crowded transports and ambled along the pier where waiting buses drove them to the station on their journey to safe spots for rest, recuperation and refitting. I noted that nearly all had retained their rifles and shrapnel helmets; some wore odd garments and sailors' trousers, and many carried souvenirs of battle: one hung on to some dirty bagpipes, another to an old wicker basket. Beaten for the time being these same men will yet teach Hitler the penalty of rousing the British Empire.

Sun June 2nd   Children's day for leaving the south-east coast. In alternate trains troops and kids head westwards, cheering and waving to each other. Troops have lumps in their throats for they have just left bitter scenes, but the kids shout and smile: to them it is a marvellous adventure. Many downcast faces are left behind. At 8.20 pm as Royce and I were coming away from the cliffs we noticed a parachute descending slowly and erratically. One of our pilots had escaped just in time with engine trouble, and the plane ablaze crashed into the shallow water at Westgate.

Mon June 3rd   Agreement has arrived for my signature – a furnished house for three months, 63 Church Road, Tilehurst, two-and-a-half guineas a week payable monthly in advance. I hope Alma and Mrs Allen will soon settle in. I propose giving notice to quit Norfolk House here.

During the 14-18 war Tim had cherished his bicycle as if it were a beloved pet. He continued to find great delight in cycling, and never hesitated to enjoy a pipe of Afrikander Mixture. This picture was probably taken somewhat earlier than his expedition with his son, Royce, to see the troops being brought back from Dunkirk via Margate

Sat June 8th   Reports of machine-gunning of towns round about, but nothing occurred here.

Mon June 10th   With the French fighting for their very existence on the Seine, and Paris under bombardment and evacuation, Mussolini thinks it the ripe moment to stab our Allies in the back. What a cunning rat. We may be on our knees, but I feel as certain as night follows day that this treacherous skunk will bitterly regret his entry into this bath of blood. [Tim was right in his assessment. Italy was ultimately defeated and changed sides, and Mussolini was strung upside-down by his own people.] *Present plans are that Royce will join the rest of the family in Tilehurst on Friday.*

Thurs June 13th   Royce has gone this evening. This breaking of our family life was always inevitable, but it has come about so suddenly and ruthlessly that I cannot keep pace with it or analyze my own feelings. It was a wrench when Alma, Joan and Ann were driven away, for the home at once became silent and cheerless, but while I still had Royce I felt that I had something to look forward to after leaving off duty, and for the last three weeks his companionship has proved a great boon drawing us together as never before. I had given up the garden to spend more time in his company and he never seemed to want for anything better. He was always waiting for me, though we both knew inwardly that only a few days must elapse before the parting must come. After kissing each other goodbye at the station I returned home with a feeling of emptiness and loneliness. I have seen the last of him as a schoolboy, and I can only hope that the experiences he must now face will not be too bitter. I am proud of him, however, and have great hopes.

Mr Horner, who employs Tim to nurse Bob, his severely disabled son, decides to move to Paignton for the duration of the war. He invites Tim to accompany him, and Tim, seeing no other way of covering his outgoings, accepts. There is a frenzy of packing, ensuring that important documents (such as the children's birth certificates) are not overlooked, and within a couple of days Tim travels westwards with his employer, driven by the chauffeur who has somehow obtained sufficient petrol for the journey.

Mon June 24th   The cars arrived at 8 am. Mr and Mrs Horner in one, Bobby, another nurse and I in the other. A lorry follows us carrying fifteen trunks. All the Thanet fields are planted with stakes, sleepers and other obstacles to stop enemy planes landing. We passed through Rochester, Westerham, Dorking, Redhill, Godstone and Guildford and had lunch at a hotel on the Hogs Back. Then on through Farnham, Alton, Salisbury, Sherborne, Shaftesbury and Yeovil. We had long since lost the Horners' car and had tea by the road. Nurse White and I took turns front and behind through Chard, Honiton and Exeter where we were held up for identification. Finally through Newton Abbot arriving at Torquay's Toorah Hotel at 7.15 pm. The Horners had beaten us by an hour and were all fuss and anxiety

Thurs June 27th   Visited Paignton and was struck by its busy attractive shopping centre. The Darewski band are playing on the beach.

Sat July 6th   As I sauntered across the green in front of Torre Abbey just after 11 am, two loud explosions shook the air without the slightest warning. Across the bay to my right a great cloud of reddish smoke rose from the ground at Churston, a village on the coast between Paignton and Brixham about four miles away. At first I thought it was gunfire, but I later discovered that bombs had been dropped involving casualties, one or two fatal. So I have come to Devon to see the first bomb dropped.

Tues July 16th   A letter tells me that Royce has failed in his R.A.F. examination. Hope he will not be too disappointed and that a liking for his present work will be some sort of compensation.

Sat Aug 3rd   Good news from Alma. She has succeeded in finding a house for the Cox's [the occupants of 10 Beechwood Avenue, the house in Tilehurst owned by Tim and Alma] *and so it will be possible for us to move back into 'The Den' at the end of the month.*

Tim was not to 'move back into The Den' at the end of the month, nor, indeed, at any time in 1940. His work kept him permanently in Devon, and (just as in 1914) the 'enemy' had destroyed the life he loved. For four years, as a young man, he had fought in France and Belgium in a murderous struggle between allegedly civilized nations. His 'luck', as he called it, saw him survive; but he was changed. Instead of trying to resume a possible stage career he now carved out a new profession as a mental nurse; and the one really happy meeting that came his way was with Alma, who became his wife and bore him three children. He loved domestic life; and the two years in Birchington were idyllically happy. In 1940, however, Germany once again shattered the idyll, and he was compelled to spend much of the war years separated from the family.

He was to survive the 39-45 war too. Indeed, his most successful professional years were to come considerably later when his reputation brought opportunities to be of service in such venues as Eton College and Kensington Palace. He was to come into contact with royalty, and (since he never abandoned his diary-keeping) there is another story to be told some day. Not, however, under the heading 'Tim's Wars'; and with reluctance I must bring the story of this stage of his life to an end. I leave the last words to Tim, as he wrote them on the very last day of 1940:

Tues Dec 31st   Today is the nineteenth anniversary of my marriage to Alma. I have sent her a letter to remind her that I have not forgotten, and also a few shillings to get herself some chocolates – if any are available. How the years fly by! I am convinced that 1941 is going to be the acid test for us all. But whatever we suffer, victory <u>will</u> be ours. The American novelist Booth Tarkington says: 'Britons are fighting for their life and liberty. The Nazis are fighting to retain other people's property they have stolen. The man fighting for life, other things being equal, will put up a harder battle than the man fighting to keep something he took from somebody else. The British are shrewd and illimitably stubborn, and in the end they will prevail'.

Roadsign in Doullens, photographed in August 2012. The French still maintain such links with the date of the Armistice. But did the War really end on that date? Did the Armistice simply provide an opportunity for the beaten German forces to recover? Was General Pershing correct when he wished to press right on to the gates of Berlin? Did the rise of a certain corporal in the German army to supreme power become inevitable once the outside pressure had been lifted? Or was the so-called World War Two caused by the imposition of impossible terms by the victors of the Great War of 1914-18? Were Tim's efforts on the Somme and elsewhere really wasted? And what has happened to that Anderson shelter? Discuss!

APPENDIX 1

THE WAR ON THE WESTERN FRONT
a potted history

As I compiled the following summary of much reading around the subject, I became amazed at how near Tim had been to much of the main action described below. For that reason I decided to move this potted history (originally intended as an Introduction) from the start of the book to the end, leaving Rifleman Elliott to present his own 'living history' first.

The prelude to war

Most wars have a multiplicity of causes, but it has to be said that the Great War of 1914 to 1918 really started because literate Europeans felt that, at that time, war was on balance a Good Thing. In mid-1914 no-one foresaw four years of blood and mud: a quick settling of accounts seemed sensible.

Bosnia had been formally annexed by the Austrian Empire in 1908. Archduke Franz Ferdinand, in whom was found a strange mix of liberal ideas and reactionary behaviour, took his morganatic wife to Bosnia in June 1914. They were killed at Sarajevo by Gavrilo Princip, a student acting for what he saw as the common good, abetted, some would claim, by the Bosnian government, though this seems highly doubtful.

Germany and Austria-Hungary had been allies since 1879. On July 5th 1914 Kaiser Wilhelm pondered a letter from Vienna about the assassination. His Chancellor, Hollweg, was empowered to give support to any Austrian punitive action against Bosnia, it being argued that support for Austria ensured inaction by the Tsar of Russia, who had long been casting envious eyes on the Balkans. It was reasoned that, given such demonstrated German support of Austria, France might counsel her Russian ally to do nothing. The Kaiser was sure that after a brief period of tension all would subside, leaving him free to enjoy his annual cruise off the Norwegian coast.

Austria, after some procrastination, sent a series of demands to Serbia. Meanwhile the French President Poincaré and his Prime Minister Viviani visited St Petersburg where, contrary to the Kaiser's reading of likely attitudes, the French agreed with the Russians that such Austrian interference in Bosnian internal affairs was intolerable. No doubt at the back of the French minds was the thought that in the event of a show-down with Austria (and hence with Germany) Alsace-Lorraine might be regained.

For twenty years the alliance of Germany, Austria-Hungary and Italy had been balanced by that of France and Russia. But as relations between France and Italy improved, Italian allegiance to the Triple Alliance was becoming unsure. The position of Britain was uncertain. She was engaged in a naval race with Germany, yet her relations with Russia had become strained. Some influential Britons, fearing war, were disinclined to support any Russian action over Serbia. Others wished to deter the Kaiser's ambitions by seeming to support 'a strong line'.

Russia and Germany at war

Serbia's reply to Austrian demands was judged by Kaiser Wilhelm to remove any reason for war, but Austria nonetheless launched a feeble attack on Bosnia by means of some Danube gun-boats. The Tsar telephoned his cousin Wilhelm asking him to restrain his Austrian allies. Meanwhile the Russians began partial mobilization. Diplomatic muscles were flexed; and the Tsar ordered general mobilization on July 30th 1914. Two days later Russia and Germany were at war, Austria joining the German cause five days after that. What was to be the most dreadful war in history had begun over virtually nothing. Inherited pride, added to the availability of weaponry, had triumphed over wiser counsels. The Tsar in particular could scarcely have guessed what all this would lead him to in three years time.

France and Belgium become involved

French reaction was confused. General mobilization was ordered on August 1st, but it was Germany which declared war on the 3rd. Possibly this decision was linked to a strange Plan put forward by Schlieffen, Chief of the German General Staff from 1892 to 1906. His idea was that a pre-emptive strike to destroy France was necessary if ever it seemed likely that Germany would become involved in war against Russia. Only by such means, he reasoned, could the horrors of war on two fronts be avoided. Thus it was that German troops invaded Belgium with the intention of rapidly outflanking the French armies. They reckoned without the determined resistance of King Albert's Belgian army; and it was the violation of Belgian neutrality that convinced sufficient British waverers to intervene. Britain enjoyed closer ties with 'plucky little Belgium' than with any other European state; and the British felt a moral obligation to support the underdog in his hour of need.

Tim's prolonged slog through mud and blood was now inevitable, given that no statesman had sufficient stature to influence events, and that no nation wielded sufficient power to impose its will. War was, on the whole, enthusiastically welcomed in the expectation that it would 'sort things out' in a conflict of short duration.

Mons, Marne and Ypres

The German First Army met stiff Belgian resistance as they attacked Liège, but by August 20th 1914 Brussels had been occupied by fast-moving German troops. Meanwhile a large French army pushed into Lorraine, meeting heavy opposition. The French Fifth Army and the British Expeditionary Force failed to hold the Germans near Mons, largely because poor communications allowed flanking movements to succeed. The alarmed French government left Paris on September 2nd, but their Sixth Army, with British support, counter-attacked. The confused fighting became known as the Battle of the Marne. German forces yielded much ground, partly because they were depleted as troops had been withdrawn to the Eastern Front. The German commander von Kluck declared that it was the British forces which had prevented him from taking Paris.

During September and October each side enjoyed some successes. Antwerp surrendered on October 10th, but among those who managed to escape and join the British troops in Flanders were Winston Churchill, King Albert and most of the Belgian army. The prolonged First Battle of Ypres brought further German advances, but by mid-November the line had virtually stabilized from Dixmude on the Channel coast to the Swiss border.

The Dardanelles; gas and blood-letting in France

Early 1915 saw the ill-fated Dardanelles campaign. The humiliation of this defeat gave support to a growing realization in Britain that victory would not come swiftly. French attacks in Champagne achieved little success; and the British occupation of Neuve Chapelle a month later in March could not be turned to good account. Combined allied casualties were around 100,000. In April the Germans introduced chlorine gas near Ypres, but were unable to capitalize on the advantages inherent in killing men in a yet more hideous fashion. By the end of May the Second Battle of Ypres was over, the only significant change being the altered contortions of the dead.

In early May, the French attacked Vimy Ridge, in Artois, while Haig's British troops were launched against Aubers Ridge, near Festubert. Men died in tens of thousands, but progress on the ground was minimal. After something of a lull in the summer of 1915, a renewed offensive was started in September. The British and the French attacked in Artois, the French also in Champagne. Once again the very limited gains were achieved at enormous cost.

By 1916 the statistics of the war had become immense. On February 21st, for example, in preparation for an attack intended to 'bleed France dry', a million German shells were fired at Verdun. Joffre, the French Commander-in-Chief, had doubts about the wisdom of defending a fortress, especially as he was planning an attack on the Somme and could ill-afford to send Pétain reinforcements at Verdun. Falkenhayn had, however, calculated French reactions accurately: the loss of Verdun would be seen as a blow to French pride, so it was defended in blood long after it would have been expedient to abandon it. So accurate, indeed, was Falkenhayn's assessment, that the memory of French losses at Verdun no doubt influenced Pétain's hasty surrender to German demands in 1940. Ultimately it can be argued that the French secured a victory of sorts at Verdun, inflicting casualties as enormous as those they themselves suffered. But mutiny was near as men contemplated certain death at the end of the long march to the Fortress. France never recovered from Verdun. As a result, the offensive on the Somme became predominantly a British affair, despite the fact that it was technically the French who attacked astride the river: the British and French lines met at Maricourt.

The big push

Haig took his time planning the Big Push. The Germans could watch it in preparation: a fact the British High Command thought unimportant, believing that the intended bombardment, to be followed by an assault by three-quarters of a million men, would be irresistible. It was thought that a gap could certainly be cleared, through which the cavalry would gallop. This was to be the war's turning point!

In the event, nearly two million shells were fired by 1500 guns: almost 200 shells per gun per day between June 24th, 1916 and July 1st. At 7.30 the infantry assault on the chalk Pozières Ridge began. The judgment that the enemy would be incapable of response proved disastrously inaccurate. German machine-gunners killed 21,000 on the first day, and the British gained no ground whatsoever. Ironically only the small contingent of French troops who went over the top at 9.30 achieved its initial objectives. Haig, in a decision which with hindsight must be judged insane, continued to press the attack until halted by snow on November 18th. By then about three million men had been committed on both sides, and a third of these had become casualties. Even if it were argued that the sapping of German strength may have contributed to the ultimate allied victory, it cannot be denied that this battle is unparalleled as an example of a commander's willingness to see his troops slaughtered for so little advantage. No strategic aim was achieved. The British had lost 420,000 dead and wounded, the French 194,000.

1917 saw some attempt by the British and French to launch attacks in concert. Lloyd-George had agreed to the appointment of Nivelle as overall commander, and a joint strike at the Noyon salient was initiated in which the

French came from the south along the Aisne River while the British made a diversionary assault near Arras. The British attack took place in driving snow on April 9th. Some progress was made, notably the capture of Vimy ridge by the Canadians. Nivelle's French troops began their assault on April 16th, clearing little more than the Chemin des Dames ridge at the enormous cost of 150,000 casualties. Mangin was dismissed from his command of the Sixth Army by Nivelle; but on May 15th Nivelle was himself replaced by Pétain. As a virtual mutiny by the French army now became evident, attention was again focussed on the British.

After Vimy Ridge: Flanders; Ypres again

Haig now appeared anxious to attack over flat land in Flanders. He was supported in this aim by the Admiralty who hoped that any territorial gains might remove, or at least diminish, the influence of German submarine bases on the Belgian coast. Haig's confidence was bolstered on June 7th when a million tons of TNT was exploded in tunnels under the German lines, leading to the capture of the Messines ridge.

After lengthy preparation the third Battle of Ypres began on July 31st. Unfortunately August was more than usually rainy. This rain, coupled with the destruction of the dikes and drains by the initial bombardment, gave Flanders mud its historic significance. General Plumer followed his success at Messines by securing part of the Passchendaele ridge in October, but he and General Gough then recommended halting the offensive. Haig, however, continued to press forward until the Canadians captured the village of Passchendael on November 6th. Two and a half weeks later, on November 25th, a true surprise attack across the St. Quentin Canal towards Cambrai brought an advance so swift that it outran supplies and artillery support, allowing the Germans an equal success in their counter-attack. The previous four months had seen another third of a million British troops become casualties.

German successes

As 1918 began, Germany seemed to be gaining the initiative. The Russian Revolution had ended fighting on the Eastern Front; and the virtual collapse of Italian military activity allowed Ludendorff to build up his forces preparatory to an attack at the point where British and French lines met. He calculated that an assault would send the British north-west in retreat in the hope of securing their communications with the Channel ports, while the French would retreat south-west to protect Paris.

The German advance began on March 21st. Within a week General Gough's army had fallen back forty miles. Amiens was threatened, and the French yielded Noyon. Haig, for once admitting that a British rout looked inevitable, conceded the appointment of Foch as overall co-ordinator. Foch switched French troops to assist Haig, and by April the German advance had been halted in front of Amiens. Ludendorff then attacked the British and the Portuguese in Flanders, but his initial advance was stopped before either Hazebrouck or Ypres was captured.

In order to draw Allied reserves from Flanders, where he planned a decisive thrust, Ludendorff then attacked Chemin des Dames on the Aisne front. On May 27th his troops crossed the river and raced on to the Marne near Chateau-Thierry, only forty miles from Paris. He had intended this attack merely to be diversionary, but when it proved so successful Ludendorff continued with it until he was halted by combined American and French troops on the Marne. His next thrust was towards Reims, but this too was held in check, just one German army succeeding in crossing the Marne sufficiently to establish a defensible salient.

The turn of the tide. Armistice

On July 18th Foch counter-attacked using tanks and infantry. Pershing committed the First American Army, and though the Germans were able to retreat across the Marne in order to re-group on the Vesle, their losses had exceeded three quarters of a million men since the start of their Spring offensive.

On August 8th , near Amiens, the Allies launched another successful offensive which became known as the Second Battle of the Somme. As German morale declined, 15,000 prisoners were taken. On the 21st a wider offensive began, eliminating the German gains of the past few months. Towards the end of September Foch and the Americans attacked towards Mezières and Sedan, and three days later combined British, Canadian, Belgian and French armies started a storming operation in the north-west. Though Allied losses were heavy, the gains were significant, causing Ludendorff to recommend the commencement of negotiations for peace.

On November 11th an Armistice was concluded on the basis of President Wilson's Fourteen Points.

Notes: The abbreviations below were sometimes 'official' (e.g. BEF = British Expeditionary Force), sometimes simply derived from usage (e.g. OB = Observation Balloon). It has not been possible to locate explanations of every abbreviation used in Tim's diaries. The entry "Division" is included in order to give some indication of the hierarchy of army nomenclature: platoon, battalion, etc.

ASC	Army Service Corps	KOYLI	King.s Own Yorkshire Light Infantry
Battalion	See Division		
BEF	British Expeditionary Force	LR	Local Reserve
BEFC	B.E.F. Canteen	LRB	London Regiment, B Company
BHQ	Battalion Headquarters	MC	Military Cross
Brigade	See Division	MGC	Machine Gun Corps
CC	Confined to Camp	MO	Medical Officer
CCS	Casualty Clearing Station	OB	Observation Balloon
Company	See Division	OC	Officer Commanding
Corps	A battlefield configuration, usually commanded by a full General, bringing together three, four or even five Divisions	OR	Orderly Room
		OR(s)	Other Rank(s)
		ORS	Orderly Room Sergeant
		Platoon	See Division
CT	Communication Trench	QVR	Queen Victoria's Rifles
CTS	Company Training Squadron, or Central Training Station	QWR	Queen's Westminster Rifles
		RAMC	Royal Army Medical Corps
DAC	Divisional Ammunition Company (possibly)	RASC	Royal Army Service Corps
		RE	Royal Engineers
DCLI	Duke of Cornwall's Light Infantry	RF	Royal Fusiliers
		RFA	Royal Field Artillery
Division	Usually commanded by a Major General, a Division was made up of three Infantry Brigades, each of which had four Battalions. Each Battalion numbered some 1,000 men commanded by a Lieutenant Colonel, and was normally divided into four Companies (A, B, C and D), each under a Captain. Each Company usually consisted of four Platoons, each under a Lieutenant; and sometimes a Platoon was Divided into four Sections.	RFC	Royal Flying Corps
		RGA	Royal Garrison Artillery
		RSM	Regimental Sergeant Major
		RWK	Royal West Kent
		RWR	Royal Warwickshire Regiment
		Section	See Division
		SM	Sergeant Major
		TDS	Training Depot Station (often related to R.F.C.)
		TL	Transport Lines
		VO	possibly Volunteer from Overseas
		WAAC	Women's Auxiliary Army Corps, Some sources give Women's Army Auxiliary Corps, which was in four Units: cookery, mechanical, clerical and miscellaneous
EFC	Expeditionary Force Canteen		
FA	Field Artillery		
HQ	Headquarters		
IBD	Infantry Base Depot	YMCA	Young Men's Christian Association
Km, kM, km, KM	Kilometre		
KOSB	King's Own Scottish Borderers		

Example: Tim mentions Abbeville on 9th June 1915, 15th July 1916 and 10th Nov. 1917.

Note: Where Tim has included varying spellings these may have been treated as separate places below, even though in some cases it seems likely that only one place was intended.

Givenchy-le-Noble	1/5/16	Moulliens- au-Bois	6/5/18
Godewaervelde	31/7/15	Neuve Chapelle	31/10/16
Gommecourt	1/7/17	Neuville Vitasse	24/3/17, 9/6/17
Gouy en Artois	8/3/17, 2/7/17	Neuville-Bray s. Somme	27/8/15
Guémappe	11/6/17	Nomain	25/10/18
Guillemont	30/9/16	Nort-Leulighem	24/7/17, 26/7/17
Gutry	3/4/18	Noyelle-Velle	18/4/16
Guyencourt	8/9/18	Noyon	6/2/18
Hangard	18/4/18, 20/4/18	Orchies	25/10/18
Hazebrouck	6/8/17	Ouderdom	11/8/17, 17/8/17
Hébuterne	24/5/16, 8/6/16	Peizières	22/9/18
Hénencourt	16/5/18	Pernes	3/3/17
Heninel	20/6/17	Péronne	2/9/18, 15/9/18
Hesdin	11/10/17	Péruwelz	8/11/18
Houvain	16/3/16	Picquigny	10/6/18, 12/6/18
Houvin-Houvigny	11/4/16	Pont de Metz	26/4/18
Ivergny	7/3/17	Poperinge	6/8/17
La Garonne	8/11/18	Poulainville	14/2/16
La Houssoye	14/8/18	Praast	2/4/18
La Neuville	1/8/15, 31/1/18	Pressy	3/3/17
Laventie	20/1/17	Querrieu	21/8/18
Laviéville	21/7/18, 26/7/18	Quévaucamps	10/11/18
Le Forest	24/10/18	Regnauville	5/3/17
Le Havre	7/6/15	Reningelst	10/6/15, 22/7/15
Le Mesnil	3/4/18	Reninghelst	11/8/17, 18/8/17
Le Quesnoy	5/3/17	Rheims	5/4/18
Le Souich	3/5/17	Ribemont	3/8/15
Lebucquière	5/9/17, 23/10/17	Riencourt	27/4/18
Lens	28/6/17, 30/9/18	Riez (?Rouez)	7/2/18
Les Boeufs	30/9/16	Roclincourt	17/12/17
Leuze Wood	7/9/16	Roncourt	12/6/17
Liévin	23/10/18	Rongy	7/11/18
Liez	15/2/18	Rouen	7/6/15
Lille	3/11/18	Rougefay	6/3/17
Lillers	3/3/17, 24/7/17	Rouillon	8/11/18
Long	28/4/18	Rumegies	26/10/18, 6/11/18
Longpré	1/4/16, 28/4/18	Sailly au Bois	23/5/16
Longueau	6/2/18, 6/4/18	Sailly- Lorette	11/1/16
Loos-en-Gohelle	27/9/15	Sailly-Lauriette	8/8/18
Lucheux	11/5/17	Saulty	31/3/17
Marest Dampcourt	6/2/18	Serques	25/8/17, 31/8/17
Maricourt	27/9/16	Servais	27/2/18, 5/3/18, 7/3/18
Marroeuil	17/12/17	Servins	22/10/18
Maulde	7/11/18	Sinceny	16/3/18
Maurepas	30/8/18	Soissons	5/4/18
Méaulte	27/9/16, 26/9/18	Sombrin	8/3/17, 3/7/17
Mennessis	9/2/18	Souchez	29/9/15
Merville	7/1/17	St Amand	28/6/16
Miraumont	31/8/17	St Aubin	3/4/18
Moislains	15/9/18	St Catherine	17/12/17
Molliens	5/6/18	St Eloi	16/12/17, 21/10/18
Molliens au Bois	21/8/18	St Eloois	11/6/15, 12/8/17
Moncheaux	25/10/18	St Georges	5/3/17
Monchiet	2/7/17	St Gratien	21/8/18
Monchy	11/6/17, 17/6/17	St Omer	6/8/17, 31/8/17
Morlancourt	12/8/18	St Pol	30/10/16, 24/7/17, 11/10/17

St Venant	3/3/17	Villers-Bretonneux	8/4/18, 11/4/18
Stambruges	11/11/18	Villers-Cotterêts	5/4/18
Steenvorde	23/7/15	Villers-Faucon	24/9/18
Sus St Léger	8/3/17, 3/7/17, 9/7/17	Vimy Ridge	22/12/17
Tangry	4/3/17	Voor Mezele	22/6/15
Telegraph Hill	9/6/17	Wail	5/3/17
Tilloy	12/6/17	Wancourt	10/6/17
Tincques	28/1/18	Warlincourt	1/5/17
Treux	21/8/18	Warluzel	3/7/17
Trones Wood	9/10/16, 24-5/9/18	Watou (?Watteau)	6/8/17, 18/8/17
Trosly	3/4/18	Watten	6/8/17, 25/8/17
Vaux	13/8/18	Wavrans	4/3/17
Vignacourt	4/8/18	Wiers	8/11/18
Villequier	18/2/18	Willeman	4/3/17
Villequier-Aumont	7/2/18	Wizernes	24/7/17, 31/8/17
Villers-Bocage	6/5/18		

TIMOTHY ELLIOTT FAMILY TREE

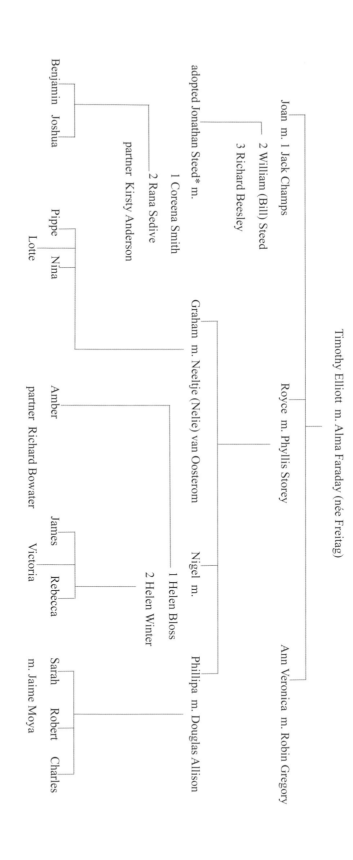

Timothy Elliott m. Alma Faraday (née Freitag)

Joan m. 1 Jack Champs
    2 William (Bill) Steed
    3 Richard Beesley

Royce m. Phyllis Storey

Ann Veronica m. Robin Gregory

adopted Jonathan Steed* m.
    1 Coreena Smith
    2 Rana Sedive
    partner Kirsty Anderson

Benjamin   Joshua

Pippe   Nina
    Lotte

Graham m. Neeltje (Nelie) van Oosterom

Nigel m.
    1 Helen Bloss
    2 Helen Winter

Philipa m. Douglas Allison

Amber
partner Richard Bowater

James   Rebecca
    Victoria

Sarah   Robert   Charles
m. Jaime Moya

*Natural parents = Donald Stanley and Julia May

Tim's survival into his seventies (despite so many occasions when he might have become just one more casualty) has profoundly changed my life. He fathered three children: two daughters and a son. The son (Royce) also fathered three children. The older daughter (Joan) adopted a boy (now a distinguished Professor of Chemistry) who was, in fact, the offspring of a relative of her second husband. All have had (or are still having) successful and fulfilling lives, producing along the way another generation of talented decendants. From my personal point of view, his greatest gift to me was his younger daughter, Ann Veronica, to whom I have been married for more years than I'm willing to reveal. Not only has she been a pearl beyond price, but by marrying her I came to be progressively linked with Tim's children, grand-children and great-grandchildren, all of whom are utterly delightful in every way. For all this, 'Thankyou, Tim'. And, by the way, thankyou not only for the diaries but for dodging all those bullets, shells and bombs. If one had got you, I'd probably now have been a grumpy old bachelor instead of the grumpy old happily married man that I am.

Robin Gregory

ALSO BY ROBIN GREGORY

Unsettledness, Maladjustment and Reading Failure, British Journal of Educational Psychology, 1965

A Shorter Textbook of Human Development, McGraw-Hill, 1969

Lebanese Pictures, Hub Publications Ltd, Bakewell, England

As General Editor: *Ipso Facto*, An International Poetry Society Anthology, Hub Publications Ltd, Bakewell, England

As Editor: *One Man's Road: Twenty-four years of Poetry by J.W. Feather,* Hub Publications Ltd, Bakewell, England, 1977

As Editor: *The Nagars of Runswick Bay,* J.S.Johnson, Hub Publications Ltd.

Plays:

When the Wind Blows, Hub Publications Ltd, Bakewell, 1970

Long Live the King, Hub Publications Ltd, Bakewell, 1971

The Passing of Leena, suggested by Soviet short story of Menshikov, Hub Publications Ltd, Bakewell

And most importantly: Published letters to the Times, one referring to the stage acting of Elizabeth Taylor, in response to her Obituary; and another comparing the recording careers of Marta Eggerth and Petula Clark.